Joan of Arc

Joan of Arc
The Legend and the Reality

FRANCES GIES

1817

HARPER & ROW, PUBLISHERS, New York

Cambridge, Hagerstown, Philadelphia, San Francisco,
London, Mexico City, São Paulo, Sydney

To my Jenny

DC
103
.G47
1981

Grateful acknowledgment is made for permission to reprint excerpt from *Memoirs of a Renaissance Pope* abridged and translated by Florence A. Gragg and Leona C. Gabel. Copyright © 1959 by Florence A. Gragg and Leona C. Gabel. Reprinted by permission of G. P. Putnam's Sons.

FIRST EDITION

Designer: Ruth Markiewicz

Library of Congress Cataloging in Publication Data

Gies, Frances.
   Joan of Arc: the legend and the reality.
   Bibliography: p.
   Includes index.
   1. Jeanne d'Arc, Saint 1412–1431. 2. Christian saints—France—Biography.
DC103.G47 1981   944′.026′0924 [B]   80–7900
ISBN 0–690–01942–4

81 82 83 84 85 10 9 8 7 6 5 4 3 2 1

Contents

Illustrations

Maps

Acknowledgments

This book was researched at the Library of Congress, the McKeldin Library of the University of Maryland, the graduate library of the University of Michigan, and on a tour of Joan of Arc country.

Special thanks are due to the following people for their help with the book:

RaGena De Aragon of the Department of History of the University of California at Santa Barbara, who read the manuscript and gave me valuable suggestions;

The Count of Maleissye-Melun, a descendant of Joan of Arc's family, who not only gave me permission to reproduce photographs of Joan's letters in his collection, but supplied me with a copy of his grandfather's book containing facsimiles;

My brother and sister-in-law, Doctors John and Ruth Carney, who furnished medical information;

And last but certainly not least, my husband, Joseph Gies, who lent me his considerable editorial skills and served as military expert and photographer, as well as giving indispensable aid and encouragement (he did not, however, do the typing).

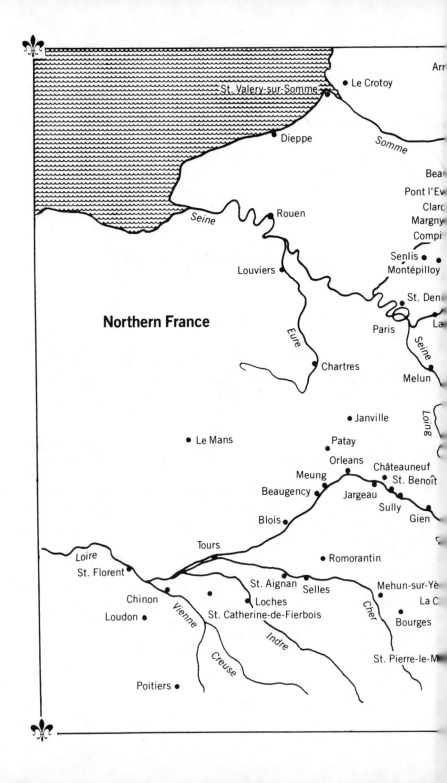

Arr

Le Crotoy

St. Valery-sur-Somme

Dieppe

Somme

Bea

Pont l'Ev

Clar

Margny

Compi

Senlis

Montépilloy

Rouen

Seine

St. Deni

Louviers

Paris

La

Seine

Northern France

Eure

Chartres

Melun

Janville

Loing

Le Mans

Patay

Orleans

Châteauneuf

Meung

St. Benoît

Beaugency

Jargeau

Sully

Blois

Gien

Tours

Loire

Romorantin

St. Florent

St. Aignan

Selles

Mehun-sur-Yè

Chinon

Vienne

Loches

La C

Loudon

St. Catherine-de-Fierbois

Cher

Bourges

Indre

Creuse

St. Pierre-le-M

Poitiers

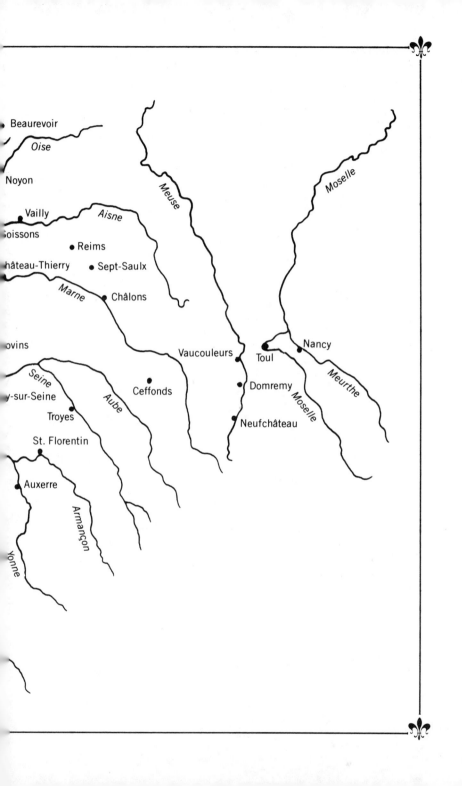

1. Joan of Arc: The Story and Its Sources

JOAN OF ARC was born in Domremy, in northeastern France, into a prosperous peasant family, probably in the year 1412, at the moment of the resumption of the devastating Hundred Years War. Suspended by a truce in 1395, the fighting recommenced in 1411 in the form of a civil war between two factions, Burgundians and Orleanists (later called Armagnacs), rivals for control of the government of mentally ill King Charles VI.

English king Henry V took advantage of the civil strife to renew his dynasty's claim to the French throne, invading France in 1415 and winning the battle of Agincourt. In 1418 the Burgundians seized Paris, and in 1419 the assassination of the duke of Burgundy drove his son Philip the Good into alliance with the English. The following year Charles VI signed the treaty of Troyes disinheriting his son, the dauphin Charles, and making Henry V heir to the French throne. When both kings died in 1422, Henry's infant son Henry VI was proclaimed king of England and France, while the dauphin, assuming the title of Charles VII, became leader of the Armagnacs, now the national party. In the early 1420s Anglo-Burgundian forces conquered and occupied most of northern France.

In 1425, when she was thirteen, Joan began to hear voices, which she identified as those of Saints Michael, Margaret, and Catherine. They told her about the "great misery in the kingdom of France" and that she must go to the aid of Charles VII. After the English began the siege of strategically crucial Orleans, on the Loire, in the fall of 1428, Joan went to the nearby royal stronghold of Vaucouleurs and persuaded Robert de Baudricourt, captain of the royal garrison, to give her an escort to the king. Arriving at the royal castle of Chinon at the end of February 1429, Joan revealed her mission: to relieve Orleans, have the king crowned at Reims, and drive the English out of France. She persuaded the king, his council, and a commission of prelates and theologians to give her a chance to fulfill it.

Led by Joan, French forces drove the English from Orleans and the Loire, won the battle of Patay, and triumphantly escorted the king to his coronation at Reims. After the coronation, the royal army liberated several more towns and assaulted but did not capture Paris, where Joan was wounded.

In April 1430 Joan undertook her last campaign and in May was captured by Burgundians in a sally from the besieged town of Compiègne. For seven months she was moved from prison to prison before finally being turned over to the English, who brought her to Rouen, in English-occupied Normandy. There she was tried as a heretic by a Church court on the grounds that her visions were diabolical and her deeds evil. The trial began February 21, 1431, and lasted three months. On May 24, taken to the cemetery of the abbey of St. Ouen, in Rouen, to be sentenced, Joan signed a last-minute abjuration, agreeing to submit to the judgment of the Church. Four days later she withdrew her abjuration and on May 30, 1431, was burned at the stake as a heretic.

The primary sources for the story of Joan of Arc are abundant and diverse, unique for a medieval personage and rare for a historical figure of any pre-modern period. They include the records of her trial and Rehabilitation, chronicles, fiscal accounts, letters, and legal and political documents.

At Joan's trial in Rouen in 1431, her testimony was taken down in French by notaries who collated their notes at the close of each day's sitting. Four years after her death, the resulting record was translated into Latin and put into official form by Thomas de Courcelles, a University of Paris master who took part in the trial, with the aid of the chief notary, Guillaume Manchon. Copies were sent to the English king Henry VI, to presiding judge Pierre Cauchon, bishop of Beauvais, and to the Inquisitor General of France. Manchon retained his original French record among his personal papers. Three of the five copies of the official Latin record are still in existence, two in the Bibliothèque Nationale in Paris, the other in the library of the French National Assembly. The original manuscript of Manchon's French minutes has disappeared, but two manuscripts believed to be copies survive, one in the Bibliothèque Nationale, the other, included in a compilation made for Louis XII around 1500, in the Bibliothèque Municipale of Orleans.[1]

Twenty-five years after Joan's death, more than a hundred witnesses testified at a second Church proceeding convened to judge the work of the first. Among them were neighbors and childhood friends from her native village, companions in battle, nobles and prelates who had known her at court, the grateful citizens of Orleans, the churchmen who had assisted at her trial, the notaries who recorded it, the physicians and clerics who had visited her in prison. Three copies of the record of this "Rehabilitation" process have been preserved, two in the Bibliothèque Nationale, a third in the British Library.[2]

Both records, rich as they are, have shortcomings. The trial report is written in the third person: "Interrogated whether she did this, she responded that she did that." Only occasionally are Joan's answers recorded directly, whether because they were particularly dramatic or because the exact wording was especially important. The only complete text is in Latin; the existing copies of the French minutes which supply more of the flavor of the interrogation are incomplete. Occasionally even the Latin record is elliptical, indicating that some connective discussion or question has been omitted.

The material that the trial record supplies about Joan's life is fragmentary. The record is, however, the only source of information about the nature of her visions, since she never described them to any of the Rehabilitation witnesses. Even more important, the authenticity of the trial record, attested by the notaries, affords a unique opportunity to observe Joan and to hear her speak, for all the distance that the form imposes.

The Rehabilitation document is also written in the third person and, except for the testimony of a preliminary inquiry and a single deposition made in absentia, in Latin. (If the testimony was originally taken down in French, as with the trial, the minutes have disappeared.) The document poses additional problems: the witnesses whose statements it records were testifying to events that had happened a quarter of a century before, and their memories are sometimes confused and often conflicting. Furthermore, the testimony was limited to a fixed list of topics designed for the specific purpose of clearing Joan's name. The Rehabilitation record gives ample if sometimes contradictory information about Joan's career from childhood through the Loire campaign, but for the important year between the battle of Patay and her capture, almost none.

Gaps in the information supplied by the records of both the trial and Rehabilitation can be filled in part from three other kinds of sources: contemporary chronicles, letters, and documents such as accounts and municipal records.

Several French and Burgundian chronicles present eyewitness or close-secondhand information about Joan. No contemporary English chronicle of the war exists.

Each chronicle has its viewpoint and often its prejudice. The most nearly contemporary of the accounts is a chronicle of the family of Joan's comrade-in-arms the duke of Alençon, written five years after her death. Its author, Perceval de Cagny, a member of Alençon's household, provides information about the march to the coronation at Reims, Joan's assault on Paris in September 1429, and her last campaign; but his bias toward his master and consequently in favor of Joan and against Charles VII distorts his account.[3] Guillaume Gruel, squire and biographer of Arthur de Richemont, constable of France, who reports firsthand on the Loire campaign and the battle of Patay, shows a similar bias in favor of his patron, but not particularly in favor of Joan.[4] The anonymous *Journal du Siège d'Orléans,* written a generation later, draws on a number of chronicles and the Rehabilitation record to enrich a day-to-day account made during the siege in 1429, and constitutes one of the best sources on the relief of Orleans.[5] A chronicler known as the "Herald of Berry" gives valuable information about the period from the coronation to Joan's capture at Compiègne.[6]

Several other French chronicles were written at a further remove from Joan's story, among them that of Charles VII's official historian, Jean Chartier, derived from secondary sources;[7] Charles's official biography, by his councillor Thomas Basin, bishop of Lisieux;[8] and the *Chronique de la Pucelle,* written in the 1460s or 1470s, drawing on Chartier's chronicle, the *Journal du Siège,* the Rehabilitation record, and other sources.[9]

A number of Burgundian chroniclers were eyewitnesses to parts of Joan's story. Enguerrand de Monstrelet, a noble in the service of the Burgundian lord whose men took Joan prisoner in 1430, observed the post-coronation campaign and Joan's final campaign of April–May 1430 from the Burgundian side and was present at her capture.[10] Jean Le Fèvre de St.-Rémi, councillor and chronicler of the duke of Burgundy, witnessed the same battles as Monstrelet.[11] Jean Wavrin du Forestal, leader of a mercenary band, fought at Patay under the English captain Sir John Fastolf and left a firsthand account of the battle.[12] Another contemporary source on the Burgundian side was the *Journal d'un Bourgeois de Paris,* now believed to have been written not by a "bourgeois" but by a cleric of Burgundian sympathy connected with Notre-Dame cathedral. His gossipy narrative of events in Paris is full of relevant if not wholly reliable material.[13]

At a farther remove was a contemporary chronicle from a neutral source, written by Eberhard de Windecken, treasurer of the German emperor Sigismund, evidently from information gathered by ambassadors.[14]

A number of fiscal accounts survive, such as those of Orleans recording the expenses of provisioning the relieving army during the siege, French royal accounts reporting the ordering of Joan's armor and standard, and English accounts detailing the payment of fees and expenses to Pierre Cauchon and his assistants at the trial.[15] Contemporary letters include Joan's challenges to the English and her communications to the inhabitants of various cities; a few letters of courtiers and associates;[16] and a series of newsletters written from Bruges by Venetian merchants and assembled in the *Chronicle of Antonio Morosini.*[17] Finally, there are government records, like the register of the Parlement of Paris, the reports of deliberations of town councils, and accounts of diplomatic negotiations; and legal documents, such as the exemption of Domremy and the neighboring village of Greux from taxation and the ennobling of Joan's family.[18]

From this array of evidence the biographer must choose the most authentic, weigh the questionable, and discard the untrustworthy, in searching for the truth about Joan of Arc.

2. Domremy

RISING IN NORTHEASTERN FRANCE and flowing six hundred miles to the North Sea, the Meuse in its early stages is a gentle stream, making its wandering course between green water meadows, on the floor of a valley bordered by low wooded hills. The region remains today, as it was in the Middle Ages, almost exclusively agricultural.

In an earlier era, the upper Meuse was the scene of a busier civilization, the crossroads of trade routes from Lyons, from Cologne, and from Italy and Switzerland via the St. Gothard pass. Sizable Gallo-Roman towns that occupied the valley in the fourth century had vanished by the fifteenth, to be replaced by scattered villages. The ruins of Grand, dedicated to the cult of Apollo Grannus, preserved the site of one of the largest amphitheaters of the Roman world. The medieval church still honored the memory of a young Christian martyr of the reign of Julian the Apostate who, on being beheaded, picked up his head and delivered a sermon before expiring.

In the early Middle Ages, the upper Meuse formed the boundary between rival kingdoms of Franks and Burgundians. By the treaty of Verdun (843) that partitioned Charlemagne's empire, it remained the frontier between France and Lorraine, a duchy owing allegiance to the

The Meuse at Domremy

Holy Roman Empire that soon fragmented into a mosaic of small political entities. Inevitably, the upper Meuse was the scene of perpetual conflict.

On the west bank of the river along the main north-south highway that followed the valley lay the village of Domremy. Though the first documentary mention of it dates only from the eleventh century, its Latin name, Domnus Remigius, indicates an origin in an earlier era when it may have been a dependency of the abbey of St. Rémi at Reims, named for the archbishop who baptized Clovis.

Domremy in the early 1400s was what modern historians call a "nucleated" village (concentrated in one place), essentially a single street bordered by houses, with gardens in the rear. Between the village and the forested hills lay the cultivated fields, divided into narrow strips and planted in rotation. The slopes above the fields were crowned with vine-

Joan's birthplace, Domremy

yards. Sheep and cattle grazed on the wet meadows bordering the stream.[1] The presence of both vineyards and animals reflected changes that had recently taken place in European farming. A rise in aristocratic and urban living standards had created a demand for garden products and wine, and for wool, beef, and milk. At the same time, shortage of labor and lowered land values associated with the Black Death had favored a shift from labor-intensive cultivation, such as wheat farming, to land-intensive agriculture, such as herding.[2]

Serfdom had largely vanished from western Europe. Most peasants owned the soil they cultivated. Although they owed money rents to a lord, they did not owe labor services and could lease, sell, or divide their lands. Like all medieval villages, Domremy had its social and economic distinctions, rendered sharper by the calamities of the fourteenth century, particularly the Black Death. Better-off and more enterprising peasants took advantage of lower land values, higher wages, and the substitution of money payments for labor services to increase their hold-

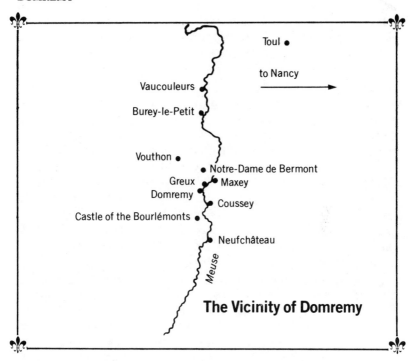

The Vicinity of Domremy

ings. Such prosperous peasants were the natural leaders of the village community.

One of these was Jacques d'Arc (written variously in contemporary records as Darc, or Tart, or Day). It is generally agreed that he was born in Champagne, in a village called Ceffonds, northeast of Troyes. His surname may derive from a family connection with the village of Arc-en-Barrois, fifty kilometers from Ceffonds. Jacques's wife was Isabelle Romée, whose name may indicate that she or a forebear had made a pilgrimage to Rome. Isabelle was born in the village of Vouthon, west of Domremy.[3] Joan did not use her father's surname. She testified at her trial that in Domremy "she was called Jeanette, and in France [the royal domain] Jeanne; of a surname she knew nothing."[4] She later elaborated: girls in the region where she lived often took their mothers' maiden names and she was sometimes known by the surname of Romée.[5] During her military career and for a century afterward, however, she was known

6

Pucelle, Joan the Maid, or simply as the Maid.* (The first
⸱ Joan by the surname "d'Arc" came only in 1576.)
⸱⸱nily lived in a house which has survived to the present, thanks
⸱⸱one construction, a rare sign of prosperity in a day when nearly
all ⸱⸱uses, rural and urban, were timber. The house comprised two
stories, the upper covered by a sharply sloping roof. During the course
of later centuries, other farm buildings were erected around the original
structure, which at various times was used to house a winepress, as a
stable, and as a wine cellar. In the early nineteenth century the added
buildings were razed and the house restored.

Jacques and Isabelle had five children—Jacques, Catherine, Jean,
Jeanne (Joan), and Pierre—though in exactly what order is uncertain. The
best information about the date of Joan's birth is her own statement
during her trial in 1431 that she was "about nineteen" *(quasi XIX),*"
which would place her birth in 1411 or 1412.[6] In the absence of parish
registers and birth records, such vagueness about birth dates was universal; at the Rehabilitation, the witnesses, even the learned theologians, gave
their ages as "sixty years or thereabouts *(vel circa),*" "fifty-two years or
thereabouts." Joan's birth date is sometimes given as January 6, 1412.
This date is derived from a letter of June 1429 from one of Charles VII's
councillors, Perceval de Boulainvilliers, to the duke of Milan, Filippo
Maria Visconti. De Boulainvilliers described Joan's birth on the night of
Epiphany (January 6) when "the cocks, like heralds of the new joy, broke
out in unheard-of songs, flapping their wings, and for some two hours
seemed to prognosticate the event.'"[7] The writer's description is accompanied by other fables long on color but short on credibility, and although
as a royal councillor he knew Joan personally, he could hardly have
known her precise birth date when she herself did not.

In the large geographical sense, Domremy was situated in Lorraine,
but politically it was one of the bits of the mosaic that had broken off
from the duke of Lorraine's rule. Most of the western bank of the upper
Meuse belonged to the dukes of Bar (with their capital in Bar-le-Duc,
south of Verdun); but a long finger of land, extending from Vaucouleurs
on the north to the southern part of the village of Domremy, comprised
the castellany of Vaucouleurs, part of Champagne, and belonging to the

*Whether the word *pucelle* necessarily connotes virginity has been a subject of controversy. From the Latin *puella* (girl), it was evidently sometimes used in the sense of "serving
maid." In Joan's time *pucelle* seems to have had an implication of virginity. Her squire
wrote that she was examined to see whether she was *"une vraie pucelle,"* a true maiden.

French royal domain, that is, land held directly by the king. A group of houses at the south of the village, beyond the church, separated from the others by a brook that flowed into the Meuse, belonged to the lords of Bourlémont, whose castle dominated a wooded hill to the south, and who held the village in fief (as payment for regular military services) from the dukes of Bar, who in turn owed similar services to the king of France for this part of their own fief.[8] (The brook has changed course several times, leading to disputes over whether Joan was actually from Barrois or Champagne.) To the east, across the Meuse, lay Lorraine.

Domremy's situation in a frontier area loyal to the king of France was of critical importance in Joan's story. Equally so was the moment of her birth. What history would call the Hundred Years War had after a half-century of intermittent conflict been suspended in 1396 by a truce now sixteen years old. But in the meantime France had become embroiled in a civil war that left the country vulnerable to its foreign enemy —placed it, in fact, in the worst jeopardy of the whole war.

The Hundred Years War[9] had begun in 1337 with a feudal quarrel superimposed on a dynastic dispute. Though these quarrels were new, the rivalry between French and English kings went all the way back to 1066, when the French duke of Normandy conquered England and so became ruler of a dual domain, straddling the Channel, in which he was independent sovereign of England while still owing feudal homage to the king of France for Normandy. Another French prince, the count of Anjou, inherited the kingdom of England as Henry II, and through a brilliant marriage added most of southwest France (Aquitaine) to his realm. In the reigns of Henry's sons (Richard the Lion-Hearted and John) and grandson (Henry III) English possession of these French territories was contested by the kings of France, who in the course of the thirteenth century conquered and annexed most of them. The last remaining English provinces (Guienne and Gascony) became the focus of a legal-constitutional war in which the French kings' feudal jurisdiction clashed with the jurisdiction of the English kings.

The dynastic issue arose with the English kings' claim to the throne of France. The claim had substance. Edward III of England was the nearest male relative (nephew) to Charles IV of France, who died in 1328. But a rival, Philip of Valois, first cousin of Charles, assumed the throne as Philip VI, on the pretext that in France succession could not pass through the female line (via Edward's mother). Actually, in fourteenth-century France, succession through the female line, and even female succession in default of a male heir, had considerable legal precedent. Edward protested, and in 1340 began using the title of king of France.

By that time a breach of the feudal code had already triggered war. In 1337 Philip VI's brother-in-law Robert of Artois, banished from France, sought refuge in England. When Edward welcomed him, Philip ordered the confiscation of Edward's French lands. Making use of an alliance with Flanders, Edward invaded France from the Low Countries in 1339, setting a pattern for the war with a *chevauchée,* a massive raid that devastated the countryside. The following year the French fleet was destroyed at Sluys by Edward and his Flemish allies, but for the time being shortage of money halted operations.

Except for its long duration, the Hundred Years War was characteristically medieval in its military aspect, dominated by sieges and raids. Pitched battles were extreme rarities; in the thousand years of the Middle Ages scarcely a dozen battles of memorable importance are recorded. When they occurred, however, battles were typically bloody and tactically decisive, with the defeated army more or less wiped out. Crécy, the first large battle of the Hundred Years War, in 1346, was marked by the striking success of English archers on foot, armed with powerful longbows, against French mounted knights. In the second, Poitiers, in 1356, the French tried to correct their tactics by dismounting to attack, with equally disastrous results. Yet despite the slaughter of numbers of French knights and lords, the two battles had only limited strategic effect. Crécy merely permitted the English king Edward III to continue his siege of Calais, which he finally captured after a year's effort. The battle of Poitiers, fought by Edward's son the Black Prince to protect the booty collected in a large *chevauchée,* had the fortuitous result of making the French king John II (the Good) a prisoner, but even this did not bring peace. Despite a treaty (1360) that confirmed English possession of southwest France, the war resumed in 1369 with incessant though small-scale fighting.

The new French king, Charles V (the Wise—reigned 1364–1380), was wise enough not to rely on the feudal levy of knights and lords that had lost Crécy and Poitiers, but to entrust the war to professional captains, at the head of bands of crossbowmen and men-at-arms. The new-style combatants, though militarily much more effective, had a serious drawback. In the frequent periods of truce, or when financial exigency interrupted their pay, they turned brigand. So severe were the depredations of the "free companies" employed by both sides that Bertrand du Guesclin, the French hero of this stage of the war, won almost equal fame by combatting the English and by ridding France of the free companies, which he led into a civil war in Spain.

Much worse than the free companies was the Black Death, which first reached Marseilles in 1348 from Genoa and spread north, killing perhaps a quarter of the population of western Europe and the British Isles. In the following century it recurred six times, growing progressively less virulent.

Amid these disasters, the military pendulum swung to the French, whose new-style guerrilla warfare of ambuscades, skirmishes, raids, and sieges slowly pressed the English back to the sea, until when a general truce was made in 1396, they held only Calais in the north and a reduced Guienne-Gascony in the south.

The war might never have seriously resumed but for a bizarre non-military disaster to the French monarchy. In 1392 Charles VI, who had succeeded his father ten years earlier, was riding through the forest near Le Mans when he was startled by a clash of arms, the accidental blow of a lance against a helmet. To the bewilderment of his followers, the king drew his sword and began laying about himself violently, killing four people before he could be disarmed. His madness proved intermittent but incurable. Over the remaining thirty years of his life he had forty-three seizures, usually of several months' duration. Disoriented, violent, he forgot who he was, attacked his attendants, broke dishes and furniture, tore his clothes, danced and ran frantically about the palace, or sank for hours into a melancholy trance. As time went on the intervals of remission grew shorter. In 1405 he experienced a five-month depression during which he refused to bathe or change his clothes, causing a skin ailment that provoked imaginative therapy—ten servants with blackened faces frightened the poor king into allowing them to bathe him. In his lucid intervals, he learned to anticipate his attacks and warned his courtiers to hide weapons. When he recovered he wept at the havoc he had wrought.[10]

The worst aspect of the king's illness was that its intermittent nature, with repeated recoveries, prevented the appointment of a regent. Between attacks, Charles took part in the royal council, received ambassadors and heads of state, and performed all the functions of king. But during the periods of royal incompetence, two personalities dominated

the council and the kingdom: Charles's younger brother, Louis, duke of
Orleans, and his uncle, Philip the Bold, duke of Burgundy.[11]

Apart from his blood relationship to the king, the duke of Burgundy
possessed enormous material power. French kings customarily endowed
younger sons with large gifts of land called appanages—donations *ad
panem* (for bread)—to support them. Appanages were transmissible to
male heirs, but returned to the crown in default of such. The old dukes
of Burgundy, whose line became extinct in 1361, had been a collateral
branch of the royal Capetian family, but had ruled Burgundy so long
(nearly four hundred years) that the Burgundians felt themselves to be
virtually a separate nationality. King John II inherited the duchy in
1361, not as king of France but as the nearest male relative. He was
therefore free not to unite it with the royal domain, but his decision was
at least influenced by the separatist sentiments of the Burgundians. The
recipient of the appanage, King John's youngest son, Philip the Bold,
married the heiress of the count of Flanders, making him a wealthy and
practically independent sovereign, at the same time that he contested
power in the disabled French royal government with his nephew Louis
of Orleans.

The two dukes differed sharply on policy. Louis wanted to revive the
war and drive the English completely out of France. Philip, whose
Flemish subjects depended on England for the raw material of their rich
wool cloth industry, favored peace. When Philip died in 1404, his son
John the Fearless took over both role and policy, and added something
of his own—leadership of a reform party centered in Paris that was
clamoring for more government efficiency and less corruption and waste.
John's embrace of reform did not inhibit him from accepting liberal
grants from the royal treasury in addition to the large pension paid him
"to maintain his estate."

Thus in the court of the mad king two parties aligned themselves
behind two contrasting chiefs: Louis of Orleans, handsome, openhanded,
pleasure-loving, admired by knights and ladies, but regarded by the Paris
merchants and shopkeepers as a spendthrift and a tyrant; and John the
Fearless of Burgundy, who posed as a plain man, defender of liberal
ideas, friend of the middle class, enjoying the adulation of the wealthy
citizens and of the intellectuals of the University of Paris. A contemporary verse chronicle celebrated John's popularity with the common people, describing a welcome given him by the citizens of Paris:

There was neither mason, nor roofer, nor carpenter,
Weaver, nor fuller, nor hose-maker, nor draper,
Armorer, nor goldsmith, innkeeper, baker,
Neither woman nor child who to rejoice
Did not shout "Noel" in a loud voice.[12]

Added to their conflicting interests and policies, the cousins felt a mutual and violent personal antipathy. Tension grew, through charges and countercharges, until one dark night in November 1407 Louis of Orleans was ambushed on a Paris street by a party of assassins. Everyone knew who had commissioned the killers, and John himself, confessing that "led on by the devil, he had had the murder committed," departed for Flanders to allow public indignation to cool. His partisans set to work to excuse him by claims that he had merely struck first, and their propaganda was so successful that in a few months John was able to re-enter Paris to cheering crowds, a justification by the University, and a pardon from the king. Hardly a year later he succeeded in persuading Isabelle of Bavaria, Charles's queen, to make him a kind of unofficial regent. At the same moment the Orleanist party was provided with a new leader, a Gascon noble named Bernard of Armagnac, whose daughter married the son of the slain Louis of Orleans. Henceforth members of the anti-Burgundian party were known as "Armagnacs." In 1411 open civil war broke out, and John the Fearless, profiting from his support in Paris, seized control of the city and the national government.

Thus at the moment of Joan of Arc's birth in 1412, the war with England had been replaced by French civil war. From the first, the possibility threatened of the two wars merging, as both Armagnacs and Burgundians turned to the English for help. John the Fearless succeeded in making an alliance that brought 1,200 English men-at-arms to Paris. A few months later the Armagnacs enlisted English king Henry V's brother, the duke of Clarence, and had trouble getting rid of his army when a truce was concluded. Each faction accused the other of making terms with "the enemies of the kingdom." The accusation reflects the growing sense of patriotism and national identity that was gradually supplanting the old personal loyalties of feudalism, and in whose flowering Joan of Arc played so great a role. The uneasy sense of both Armagnacs and Burgundians that in courting the English they were behaving treasonously was soon to be intensified.

In 1413, the Paris Parlement promulgated the Burgundian faction's

reform ordinances, streamlining the government. But the reform movement got out of hand, and as riots broke out, Paris fell into the hands
of the radical element, in the "Cabochin revolution" (named for Simon
Caboche, a leader of the powerful guild of merchant butchers). Unable
to control his followers, John the Fearless gave up the city to the Armagnacs, whose bloody reprisals against the radicals were accompanied by
the annulment of reform.

At this moment, with the country afflicted by a mad king, civil war,
and an unpopular faction ruling Paris, Henry V landed in Normandy to
resume the Hundred Years War.

As duke of Burgundy and premier magnate of France, John the Fearless was the obvious leader to take charge of the defense of the kingdom.
But when the Armagnacs refused terms that would restore his control
of the government, he declined to take part in the fighting. Military
leadership devolved on Charles of Orleans, Louis's son and a gifted poet
but a bad general. In October 1415, at Agincourt, the English won
another bloody and tactically decisive victory, this time equipping their
archers with pointed iron-tipped stakes which they drove into the ground
in front of their position. The French feudal levy, attacking this strong
defensive position on foot, as at Poitiers, was cut to pieces.

John the Fearless's two younger brothers and many Burgundian vassals were killed, along with Armagnac knights and lords. Charles of
Orleans was taken prisoner. But Agincourt, like Crécy and Poitiers,
settled nothing. Henry had actually been on his way home from a *chevauchée* when the battle occurred, and simply continued on to Calais. For
his projected conquest of Normandy, the first step toward making good
his claim to the French crown, he needed money, and he spent the year
of 1416 in England collecting it.

But in May 1417 Henry struck a blow more decisive than Agincourt.
He concluded a secret pact with John the Fearless at Calais by which
the Burgundian duke recognized Henry and his descendants as heirs to
the French throne and agreed to give him "all the help he could by secret
ways and means." Thus the greatest French vassal, most influential
magnate of the French court, and hero of Paris public opinion gave his
support to the English cause, and the Hundred Years War first impinged
on, then fused with and absorbed, the French civil war.

While Bernard of Armagnac continued to make himself unpopular in
Paris, exiling members of the University and curtailing the privileges of

the guilds, John first occupied the province of Champagne, east of the capital, and then took the important city of Chartres, threatening Paris's supply routes, while the English besieged and took Caen and other fortified towns in Normandy. In 1418 John successfully executed two coups. First he abducted Queen Isabelle and installed her at Troyes, in Champagne, as head of a new national government. Next, through his partisans, he recovered Paris from within, killing his rival Bernard of Armagnac.

John now had two options. He might openly acknowledge his secret alliance with the English, or he might come to terms with the discomfited and leaderless Armagnacs. The second course derived its attraction from the fact that the recent deaths (from illness) of two older brothers had unexpectedly created a new dauphin, Charles, only fifteen years old. John arranged a meeting with Charles at which the middle-aged man and the boy swore an oath of friendship and agreed to meet again.

Their second meeting, on September 10, 1419, brought a disaster with fateful consequences. Held in the middle of a bridge over the Yonne at Montereau, it broke up in a scuffle in which John the Fearless was killed. Though Charles, who had just left the bridge, protested his innocence, he was inevitably blamed by the outraged Burgundians. The truth was never ascertained, but the assassination was the Armagnacs' most catastrophic blunder. John had a fully grown son, Philip the Good, whose response was immediately to transform the secret Anglo-Burgundian pact into an open alliance. As historian Henri Pirenne says, "The Montereau murder marked the opening of a new phase. From then on the Burgundian dynasty sought to accomplish its purpose, not in France or by means of France, but outside France and against France."[13]

In Paris, the University, Parlement, and public opinion added their weight to the Anglo-Burgundian alliance and peace project, which bore fruit in May 1420 in the treaty of Troyes. Acting under Philip's direction, seconded by Queen Isabelle, the unfortunate Charles VI disinherited and banished his son Charles, "the so-called dauphin," and named Henry V of England "his only true son . . . heir and regent of France." He signed a letter to the citizens of Paris explaining that the treaty was punishment "for the evil deed [the dauphin] did to the duke John of Burgundy," and, asserting that "one should not take account of the youth of the said Charles [in extenuation] because he is quite old enough to tell good from evil."[14] On December 23, 1420, a *lit-de-justice* (a royal convocation) was held in Paris, and Charles VI, with his "heir and regent" Henry V at his side, declared the dauphin guilty of the murder of John the Fearless. A month later the marriage of the dauphin's sister Catherine to Henry V sealed the union of England and France.

The realms were to remain separate and distinct. The sense of the treaty of Troyes was not an annexation of France by England but the creation of a dual monarchy, two kingdoms each retaining its own laws, customs, and institutions, united in the person of a monarch. The royal marriage assured that Henry's successor, who was born within the year, would be half French, half English.

But while the peace treaty was greeted in Paris with cheers, processions, and celebrations, much of France refused to join in. During the Burgundian seizure of the capital in 1418, the dauphin had fled the city to Bourges, in central France. There he received news of the treaty of Troyes, and at once established his own court as a rival to that of his father in Paris. The discredited, reactionary Armagnac party rallied around him, and thus by an ironic turn became the party of national resistance.

Fighting resumed. Despite the defection of king, queen, duke of Burgundy, and Paris, and despite the military skill and resources of Henry V, no quick English victory resulted. French and Scottish troops in the dauphin's service even won a battle, at Baugé, near Angers, in west-central France (March 22, 1421), and two years after the treaty of Troyes the strategic position remained essentially unchanged. Instead of being driven from France, the dauphin remained in his stronghold at Bourges, protected by his castles in the Loire region, commanding enough resources to sustain himself against his enemies.

As long as Henry V and Charles VI lived, the question of who was to be the future king of France remained in suspension. But suddenly in the summer-fall of 1422, both kings died, thirty-five-year-old Henry V of the common military affliction, dysentery, Charles VI worn out by age and illness. At once two kings were proclaimed: Henry's infant son, Henry VI of England, as Henry II of France; and the dauphin as Charles VII of France. But neither the infant Henry nor youthful Charles (now eighteen) was anointed in the cathedral of Reims, the ancient legitimizing ritual of French kings. Reims lay in Champagne, deep in Anglo-Burgundian territory, inaccessible to Charles, while Henry was in England and under age.

On his deathbed at the castle of Vincennes, east of Paris, Henry V had named his brother, the duke of Bedford, regent for France. An able leader on and off the battlefield, Bedford undertook to end the two-king political anomaly by a military offensive. In 1424 he inflicted a "second Agincourt" on the French and their Scots allies at Verneuil, north of Chartres. Yet there was a difference between Verneuil and Agincourt. Though the French-Scottish army of professional companies was decimated at Verneuil, the English army also took heavy casualties. The war resumed its form of small-scale raiding, counter-raiding, plunder, pillage, and burning.

It was this aspect of the war that brought Joan of Arc onto the stage. The devastation was not accidental but deliberate. English captain Sir John Fastolf summarized fifteenth-century military doctrine vividly by prescribing that English soldiers should march through enemy territory "burning and destroying all the lands as they pass, both house, grain, vine, and all trees that bear fruit for man's sustenance, and all cattle that may not be driven, to be destroyed; and those that may be . . . spared in addition to the sustenance and provisioning of the army, to be driven into Normandy, to Paris, and to other places in the king's obedience. . . . And it seems verily that by these ways and governance, the king shall conquer his realm of France, and harm and destroy his enemies and save his people and his soldiers. . . ."[15]

The scale of havoc, it is true, hardly compared with that of modern wars. Armies were small, and though gunpowder had arrived on the scene, it served only as a propellant for missiles (usually stone cannon-balls), not as an explosive charge. The chief agent of destruction was fire, applied deliberately to houses, farm buildings, crops, and orchards. Such damage was not long-lasting. Crops could be replanted, provided seed grain was available. Livestock, barns, stables, mills, houses, and tools, though costly, were replaceable. Even razed vineyards and orchards recovered in time. Nevertheless, in a society with very limited capital resources the destruction had serious effect.[16] Fastolf hoped it would demoralize the population into submission, and it undoubtedly produced widespread longing for peace. At the same time, however, it stimulated hatred for the foreign invader. Amid the political complexities, dynastic legalisms, and princely intrigues, it was the burning of villages and destruction of the countryside that created the spirit of national resistance embodied in Joan of Arc.

Through the early stages of the war, Domremy lay outside the combat zones of the north and west, though it may have been visited by occasional raiding bands (and probably suffered from the Black Death). The Armagnac-Burgundian civil war spread to this peaceful corner in 1419 by way of a local nobleman-turned-brigand, the damoiseau (squire) de Commercy, who at various times allied himself with each side. Jacques d'Arc and an associate, Jean Biget, led a delegation that leased an abandoned fortress on an island in the Meuse opposite Domremy from its absentee owner, the lady d'Ogéviller, heiress to the Bourlémonts, lords of Domremy; and the villagers took refuge there with their animals.[17]

The following year (1420) the English and Burgundians moved into Champagne, to the west of Domremy. When the duke of Burgundy sent diplomatic emissaries to the bishop of Verdun, they were arrested on their return by the damoiseau de Commercy, at that moment on the Armagnac side, and Robert de Baudricourt, a captain who commanded the garrison of the fortified town of Vaucouleurs for the dauphin Charles. Subsequently, a band of Burgundians and English invaded the district and may have raided as far south as Domremy.

In 1423 a Gascon *routier* (brigand) named Étienne de Vignolles, who fought for the dauphin and for himself under the name of La Hire, was besieged by the Burgundians in the fortified town of Sermaize. In the course of the siege the husband of one of Joan's cousins was killed by a stone cannonball. In that same year, the damoiseau de Commercy extorted a protection arrangement from Domremy, with Jacques d'Arc signing for the village an agreement to pay an annual fee levied on each household in return for immunity from pillage.

The value of the protection proved slight. In 1424 and 1425 bands of soldier-brigands roamed the district, while La Hire and Robert de Baudricourt warred with Burgundian captains, including the damoiseau de Commercy, who had switched sides. A *routier* named Henri d'Orly carried off to his castle the cattle of Domremy and Greux, together with furniture and goods. An appeal to the lady d'Ogéviller brought recovery of the property when the lady's cousin, the count of Vaudemont, pursued the raiders, fought off an ambush, and returned cattle and belongings to the villagers.

That year Joan was thirteen. Practically nothing is known about her life up to this point, except that she had been baptized in the church whose graveyard touched on Jacques d'Arc's property. Dedicated to St. Rémi, the small stone building stands today, though much restored; the tower and some of the walls survive. One statue, that of the fourth-century martyr St. Margaret of Antioch, dates to Joan's time. We know the names of her godparents—one godmother was the mayor's wife—and that she was baptized by a priest named Jean Minet.[18] She was illiterate, as were all peasant women and nearly all peasant men (a few peasant boys were educated for the priesthood).[19]

Joan's religious instruction, she testified at her trial, was administered by her mother, who "taught her the Pater Noster, Ave Maria, and Credo."[20] Her parents were "very strict with her."[21] Her mother taught her to sew and spin, and Joan took pride in her skill.[22] Her childhood acquaintances recalled that she did "woman's work, spinning and such," and "household chores."[23] Like other peasant women, she also helped her father in the fields, probably following the plow to break up clods with a stick, and joining in the harvesting.[24] Her childhood friend Hauviette said that Joan sometimes watched her father's animals, although Joan said that she did not do this much after "she was grown up and reached the age of understanding."[25]

The village children worked, but they also had amusements. They played in the fields, and they took part in the celebration of festivals. Three in particular centered around a place in the oak forest (the Bois Chenu) on the hill above the village where there were two springs—the Frogs' Spring and the Fairies' Spring—and a magnificent old beech, the Ladies' Tree, "beautiful as the lilies," according to one villager, and believed to be over two hundred years old.[26] Legends clung to the tree, evidently once the site of pagan celebrations. One of Joan's godmothers had heard that in the olden days "ladies that cast spells, who are called fées [fairies], used to go under that tree, but because of their sins, it is said, they do not go there any more."[27] Joan herself had heard another godmother say that she had actually seen a fairy, and there was a story that in ancient times a lord of Bourlémont named Pierre Granier had met a fairy under the tree and fallen in love with her.[28]

As it had many other pagan rites and customs, the Christian Church had absorbed the mystic power of the springs and the Ladies' Tree. On the fourth Sunday in Lent, known as Laetare, Jerusalem, from the epistle for the day, "Rejoice, Jerusalem," the young people of Domremy visited the tree to "spread a cloth," dance, play games, drink the water from the springs, eat little loaves of bread, and pick flowers to make garlands which they hung on the tree, in accordance with ancient custom, but with the blessing of the Church. On May Day the children came to cut boughs from the tree to decorate their houses.[29] Not only the village children, but the local lords and ladies frequented the spot. The sexton of the church at Domremy had seen two of the Bourlémont ladies picnicking under the tree with their attendants and the village girls.[30]

Later in May, the Monday, Tuesday, and Wednesday before Ascension (Rogation Days) were celebrated, as they were all over Christendom, by priests carrying the cross at the head of a procession, with banners, bells, and torches, "beating the bounds of the village," that is, following its boundaries, and pausing at certain points to bless the growing crops. Most villages had a "Gospel Tree" as one such point; in Domremy, this was the Ladies' Tree, where the curate "recited the Gospel, and then went to the Frogs' Spring and the other springs, reciting the Gospel."[31]

The war entered the lives of the children in many ways. They shared the partisanship of their elders. Joan said that the village children did not play war games in which they pretended to be French and English, but that fights broke out between the children of Domremy and those of Burgundian Maxey, across the Meuse, and she sometimes saw her friends come back "wounded and bleeding." At Domremy, she knew only one Burgundian—"whose head she would like to have seen chopped off, that is, if it pleased God."[32] When the Burgundians raided the area, Joan helped drive her father's animals to the fortress on the island in the Meuse.[33] In all probability, she had never seen an Englishman.

Thus Joan's early life had resembled that of other girls in all the villages of France. She had worked with her mother and father, played in the fields with her friends, hung garlands on the Ladies' Tree, and picked flowers to make wreaths. Except that she may have been a little more pious than most, there was little to distinguish her from all the others.

3. Voices

In 1425, the year that *routier* Henri d'Orly carried off the villagers' cattle and goods, Joan had her first vision. It was summer, "at about the hour of noon," and she was in her father's garden when she heard a voice, "on the right side, toward the church." With it was a light coming from the same direction as the voice. The first time she was "much afraid." But she knew at once that it was "a worthy voice . . . sent by God," and when she had heard it three times, she knew that it was "the voice of an angel." When the voice returned, it was almost always with an accompanying light, "usually a great light."

At first the voice simply advised her how to behave, and told her to be good and go to church. But later it began to tell her that she must "go to France."[1] Although Domremy was part of the kingdom of France, its geographic isolation was such that to Joan going to France meant going to the central part of the realm, where the king was.

Joan soon identified the voice as that of St. Michael; he spoke "the speech and language of angels."[2] She saw him before her own eyes, "the eyes of my body," she emphasized.[3] He was accompanied by other angels. He told her that St. Catherine and St. Margaret would come to her, and that she should follow their counsel, and he told her about the

great misery *(grand pitié)* that was in the kingdom of France.[4] After St.
Michael and his accompanying angels had left, she "kissed the ground
on which they had stood, doing them reverence."[5]

As St. Michael had promised, St. Catherine and St. Margaret soon
appeared. Their heads were "crowned with beautiful crowns, very rich
and precious." At her trial Joan refused to describe the saints further,
saying only that they spoke "most excellently and beautifully, and that
she understood them perfectly."[6]

The first time Joan heard the voice of St. Michael, she vowed her
virginity "as long as it should be pleasing to God."[7]

Few religious experiences have been subjected to as extensive examination and analysis as has the phenomenon of Joan's voices. At her trial
at Rouen in 1431 the judges questioned her shrewdly about her mystical
experiences, almost like modern psychologists diagnosing a crisis of
adolescence. Was she fasting when she first heard the voices? No.[8] Did
she ever kiss or embrace St. Catherine or St. Margaret? Yes, she had
embraced them both. What part did she embrace, the upper or lower?
It was more fitting to embrace them below than above.[9]* Was St. Michael
naked or was he clothed?—which provoked Joan's famous answer, "Do
you think that our Lord has not wherewithal to clothe him?"[10]

Yet Joan's judges made no serious attempt to prove that her voices and
visions were hallucinations. They themselves believed in the possibility
of supernatural revelation, as did most of Joan's contemporaries. The
crucial question was not so much the genuineness of the experience but
the origin of the revelations. People who communicated with the supernatural outside normal Church channels were necessarily suspect. Mystics were often critical of the Church, and almost every saint who was
a mystic came at some time into conflict with Church authority. But the
difficulty was not merely that mystics undermined authority. On the face
of it, such irregular communications seemed far likelier to originate with
demonic than with divine sources, which might reasonably be expected
to transmit their messages through the Church rather than through
eccentrics and neurotic women.

The century preceding Joan's has been called the "flowering time

---

*This reading is given by both the Latin record and the d'Urfé MS (one version of the
French minutes). The Orleans MS (the other version) says the opposite: "It was more
fitting to embrace them above than below." The implication in the Latin and d'Urfé version
is that Joan embraced them around the knees, as a supplicant (as she did the king), rather
than above, as a friend or lover.

of Mysticism,"[11] but every previous age had its mystics, and a large proportion had always been women—sibyls, prophetesses, priestesses. In the Middle Ages women mystics had remarkable careers, exerting influence over princes as well as peasants. Four in particular have significance in relation to Joan. Hildegarde of Bingen (1098–1179), whose visions, like Joan's, were accompanied by light—"a great flash from heaven"[12]—was consulted by popes, emperors, and kings, whom in her correspondence she addressed as equals. Elizabeth of Schonau (1128–1164), who was visited by angels and saints, was inspired to write books freely admonishing her social betters, both clergy and lay, to mend their ways.[13] Another visionary, Mechthild of Magdeburg (1210–1297), criticized the laxity and materialism of the contemporary Church.[14] Still another, Catherine of Siena (1347–1380), played a role in ending the Great Schism.[15]

Of these four, Hildegarde had the least conflict with the Church. In 1147 she submitted the first chapters of her book *Scivias* to the archbishop of Mainz, who referred them to Pope Eugenius III and to St. Bernard for approval, which was readily given. Elizabeth of Schonau had more difficulty in gaining acceptance; she wrote Hildegarde that she could bear the criticism of lay people but not "of those who wear clerical garb; they bitterly oppress my spirit. . . . They ridicule the grace of God that is within me, and do not hesitate rashly to condemn what they do not understand."[16] Mechthild was criticized for the unorthodox theology that lay beneath the romantic poetry she wrote, and she was even threatened with excommunication. As for Catherine, when she visited Avignon as an unofficial mediator in the Great Schism, she was subjected to an Inquisition-like examination in doctrine, but ended by convincing the pope that he should restore the papacy to Rome.

Thus Joan of Arc had illustrious predecessors in women who claimed direct inspiration from God. In one interesting respect, however, Joan was strikingly different from the other mystics. Hildegarde suffered protracted bouts of illness and may have had a functional nervous disorder. Elizabeth was delicate and often fell into trances in which she lost consciousness of her surroundings. Mechthild lived a long life, but in constant ill-health, while Catherine, a severe ascetic, died exhausted at the age of thirty-three. Many other mystics were subject to physical or nervous maladies. In marked contrast, Joan was strong and healthy, readily bearing hardship, recuperating quickly from wounds, and impressing soldiers with her endurance.

One physical defect has been attributed to her, but with scanty evidence: her page Jean d'Aulon said that he "had heard it said by a number of women who had seen the Maid naked several times, and knew her secrets, that she had never had the secret malady of women"—had never menstruated.[17] But his testimony is hearsay, and none of the many women who testified in the Rehabilitation, some of whom had shared bed and bath with Joan, reported it. D'Aulon thought he was gilding Joan's reputation, and that her supposed freedom from this distasteful feminine weakness was a sign of her purity.*

"Primary amenorrhea" or failure to begin menstruation is today not diagnosed before the age of eighteen (the normal age of menarche in the Middle Ages is a matter of controversy, but it is generally agreed that even as recently as the past century it was higher than today). Joan was probably barely eighteen at the time when she parted from d'Aulon after her capture. Beyond that age, modern medicine considers primary amenorrhea a sign of illness, mental or physical, that is, resulting from psychosis or emotional shock, tuberculosis, thyroid or pituitary disorder, diabetes, or glandular dysfunction accompanied by abnormal development of secondary sexual characteristics.[19] Joan's competence and cheerful common sense belied psychosis. Her physical development was normal. Her companion-in-arms, the duke of Alençon, said that he had seen her when she was dressing and that "her breasts were beautiful."[20]

Three interpretations are logically possible for Joan's revelations: that they were supernatural manifestations; that they were illusions—"hallucinations"; or that she saw and heard real (as opposed to supernatural) people. The last conclusion, advanced by anthropologist Margaret Murray in 1921 in arguing that Joan was a member of a witch cult, can be dismissed in the light of the number of Joan's experiences and the variety of places in which they occurred—in her father's garden, in battle, in prison. The conflict between the other two interpretations, psychological and supernatural, was neatly illustrated in the 1930s French film *The Baker's Wife,* in which the village schoolmaster argues with the parish

*D'Aulon's view was echoed in the nineteenth century by Michelet, who pictured Joan as a kind of spiritual Peter Pan: "In her the life of the spirit dominated, absorbed the lower life, and held in check its vulgar infirmities. Body and soul, she was granted the heavenly grace of remaining a child. She grew up to be robust and handsome; but the physical curse of women never affected her. This was spared her, to the benefit of religious thought and inspiration."[18]

priest. The priest's view is that Joan "heard voices," but the schoolmaster concedes only that "she *thought* she heard voices—as for me I'm not so sure."

Modern Catholic biographers accept the voices as revelations from God; skeptics attribute them to neurosis, adolescent hysteria, or physical illness.* Modern psychiatry interprets hallucination as a response, often generated by anxiety, to such psychological situations and needs as wish-fulfillment, enhancement of self-esteem, feelings of guilt, satisfaction of repressed impulses, or dissatisfaction with reality. Auditory hallucinations are most common, and are usually "unpleasant, derogatory, obscene, or in the nature of accusations . . . the projection of disowned personality aspects or desires which may not be allowed into the consciousness in undisguised form." Auditory hallucinations are often associated with the movement of the muscles of the larynx, suggesting that the patient is saying the words silently to himself.[22] This description is suggestive in accounting for the fact that Joan's voices told her to do things which she believed were beyond her powers and which she resisted doing, but it does not satisfy Joan's description of the ecstasy which she felt during her mystical experiences, an emotion shared by many other visionaries. Hildegarde's "living light" erased "every sadness and pain . . . from my memory," Mechthild said that her soul was "in high delight," and the English mystic Margery Kempe experienced "a flame of fire, wondrous hot and delectable."

Psychological explanations of Joan's revelations fail to take adequate account of the difference between the context of the fifteenth century and that of the twentieth. In Joan's time, for people to hear voices and see visions was unusual but by no means inconceivable. Where today a person who claimed communication with the supernatural is at once diagnosed as either abnormal or a fraud, in the fifteenth century (and indeed throughout the pre-industrial era) such claims met with only a

---

*A recent work on the diagnosis of illness in historic personages attributed Joan's voices and visions to Ménière's disease, an infection of the inner ear that causes ringing in the ears, minor visual disturbances, and dizzy spells (accounting for Joan's frequently falling on her knees to pray!). To take this theory seriously, one would need to believe that the symptoms lasted seven years during which an otherwise intelligent woman persistently interpreted a ringing in her ears as voices with explicit messages, mistook dancing specks for angels, and experienced dizzy spells that made it impossible to stand but did not interfere with riding a horse.[21]

degree of skepticism, a demand for a sign of the genuineness of the experience.

In a word, no really convincing scientific interpretation of Joan's voices has been advanced. For that matter, some modern theologians, such as Paul Tillich, might raise the question of what exactly one means by a psychological as opposed to a religious experience. What is certain is that Joan's revelations were a tremendously powerful force that enabled her to maintain her composure in the face of skepticism, to argue aggressively with her social betters, to brave danger and wounds, and finally to outface a crowd of male persecutors threatening her with death by burning. Whatever the source of Joan's voices and her belief in them, it conferred on her a strength of resolution possessed by few, women or men.

The hypothesis advanced by several proponents, including humanist pope Pius II, Voltaire, and Anatole France, that political or ecclesiastical powers learned of Joan's visions and exploited them to advance their cause, suffers from two fatal defects. First, Joan insisted that she never told anyone about her visions, not even the parish priest, a fact which was used against her by the judges at Rouen, and again by the devil's advocate in her canonization proceedings. Second, the success of her mission was so improbable that it is beyond belief that anyone would base a calculation on it.

The identity of Joan's saints is not surprising. All three were prominent in medieval iconography. The archangel Michael appeared on the dauphin Charles's standard, slaying a dragon with a drawn sword. St. Margaret of Antioch, an early Christian martyr, patron of women in labor, was represented in a statue that still survives in Joan's church at Domremy. St. Catherine of Alexandria, another virgin martyr, was the patron saint of the church of Maxey, across the Meuse from Domremy.

Joan's childhood associates at Domremy were unanimous about her character. She was simple, chaste, truthful, obedient to her parents, hard-working, charitable. A neighbor boy who was "brought up with her" said that when he was sick in childhood Joan comforted him.[23] She sometimes gave up her bed to the poor.[24] She had a number of friends. Her closest, Hauviette, "wept bitterly" when Joan left Domremy, because she "loved her very much for her goodness, and because she was her friend."[25]

Everyone agreed that she was unusually pious. Her godfather, Jean

Joan as a shepherdess, initial from a fifteenth-century
manuscript of the Rehabilitation record

Moreau, of the neighboring village of Greux, recalled that she regularly
confessed to Guillaume Front, curate of the church at Domremy.[26] Her
confessor had been heard to say that there was no one like her in the
village and no better Catholic in his parish.[27]

In the woods to the north of Greux was a hermitage whose tiny chapel,
Notre-Dame de Bermont, with its painted wooden Virgin, still survives.
On Saturdays Joan visited it to light candles with her sister Catherine
and other women of the village.[28] Jean Moreau said that she sometimes
went there when her parents believed that she was working in the fields.[29]

On occasion, when Joan was playing with the other girls, she drew
apart from them to pray. Colin, a peasant of Greux, remembered that
he and his friends laughed at her excessive piety.[30] When the bells rang,
she crossed herself and genuflected.[31] Joan's friend Mengette, who lived
near her and often sat spinning with her, told her she was too devout.[32]
When the sexton forgot to ring the bells for compline in the evening Joan

scolded him and cajoled him with a promised gift of wool if he would
be less derelict.*[33]

After the voices began to talk to Joan about her mission, her life
changed; the trial record reported that she said "she played very little,
the least that she could."[34]

Exactly when the voices began to tell her that she must "go to
France," we do not know. She testified at Rouen that after they made
the first announcement it was repeated "two or three times a week."[35]
She said nothing to her parents or to the parish priest. Apparently her
father had some inkling of what was in her mind. Her mother told her
that he had dreamed that Joan would "go off with the soldiers," and that
he had said to her brothers, "If I thought that such a thing could happen
as I have dreamed, I should want you to drown her; and if you did not,
I would drown her myself."[36]

At about this time, in the spring of 1427, Jacques d'Arc journeyed to
Vaucouleurs to represent the people of Domremy and Greux in a legal
case. The villagers had failed to keep up with the yearly payments of
protection money they had pledged to the damoiseau de Commercy, in
the agreement Jacques d'Arc had signed in 1423, and the damoiseau had
impounded wood, grain, and horses belonging to a wealthy villager who
had agreed to stand security for the payment. His fellow townsmen had
scraped together the money, but the damoiseau refused to deal. Joan's
father argued the village's case before the king's captain and provost,
Robert de Baudricourt (the outcome is unknown).

Probably it was soon after her father's return that the voices began to
tell Joan that she should go to Robert de Baudricourt, and that he would
give her men to accompany her to "France." She pleaded that she was
"only a poor girl, who knew nothing of riding or of leading in war," but
the voices insisted.[37] Finally, the following spring (1428), she began to
lay plans.† She kept them secret, afraid that her parents would "lose their
minds" when she left, and that her father might "hinder her journey."
She also feared the Burgundians might prevent her.[38] She could not resist

*In supplementary testimony in Joan's trial which the notaries refused to authenticate
and which therefore is considered dubious ("Postmortem Information"), Joan is supposed
to have said that she heard her voices best at compline, when the bells were ringing.

†There is controversy over whether Joan made two trips to Vaucouleurs, or went there
for the first time in January 1429. The evidence, though confusing, seems to support a first,
abortive journey in May 1428.

giving a hint, however, to one of the young men of the village; Gerardin of Épinal reported that she said to him, "Friend, if you were not a Burgundian, there is something I would tell you." Gerardin concluded that "it was something about a man she wanted to marry."[39]

Joan's cousin, daughter of her mother's sister, had married a man named Durand Laxart or Lassois. Durand was about thirty-five, enough older than Joan that she called him "uncle." She took Durand into her confidence and told him that she wanted "to go to France, to the dauphin, to have him crowned." She begged him to take her to Robert de Baudricourt, "to ask him to lead her to the place where my dauphin was." Joan asked Durand if he had not heard a current prophecy: "Was it not said that France would be ruined through a woman, and afterward restored by a virgin?"[40] The woman was Queen Isabelle, mother of the dauphin, who had given her adherence to the Burgundians and the English.

This was one of several prophecies circulating in France that seemed to have reference to Joan. Another supposedly originated with a mystic named Marie Robine, known as Marie of Avignon, who had told Charles VI of her vision of "pieces of armor" that made her "afraid that she would be forced to put this armor on. But she was told to fear nothing, and that it was not she who would have to wear this armor, but that a Maid who would come after her would wear it and deliver the kingdom of France from its enemies."*[41] Still another prophecy was supposed to date all the way back to King Arthur's Merlin: that from the oak forest in the marches of Lorraine a virgin would come who would perform marvelous acts and save France. Prophecies attributed to historical or mythical personages were a popular propaganda device; ambiguous and flexible, they left scope for interpretation while affixing the validating seal of the past to new enterprises and giving them a sense of predestined success.

In May 1428 it was arranged that Joan should ask her father if she could go to Burey-le-Petit (today Burey-en-Vaux), near Vaucouleurs, to help her cousin, Durand's wife, who was expecting a baby. According to Joan's own testimony, she stayed there a week before Durand took her to Vaucouleurs.[42]

*From the Rehabilitation testimony of a lawyer named Jean Barbin. Barbin cited as his source Jean Erault, a member of the commission that examined Joan at Poitiers. The surviving written record of the revelations of Marie Robine does not contain the prophecy.

The walled town of Vaucouleurs lay along the western bank of the Meuse, its royal castle looming protectively above. Joan must have entered town by the southern gate and climbed the steep streets to the fortress. Durand Laxart seems to have gained access to Robert de Baudricourt without difficulty. Joan said that she recognized the captain, "although she had never seen him before . . . by her voices, which told her that it was he."[43]

The interview did not go smoothly. Baudricourt was a veteran professional soldier about forty years old, who had succeeded relatives as bailiff of Chaumont and captain of Vaucouleurs. A knight named Bertrand de Poulengy, present at the first interview, "at the time of the Ascension of Our Lord" (May 13, 1428) reported their conversation: "She said that she had come to him, Robert, on behalf of her Lord, to ask him to send word to the dauphin that he should hold still and not make war on his enemies, because the Lord would give him help before mid-Lent; and Joan also said that the kingdom did not belong to the dauphin, but to her Lord; and that her Lord wanted the dauphin to be made king, and that he would hold the kingdom in trust, saying that despite the dauphin's enemies he would be made king, and that she would lead him to be consecrated. Robert asked her who was her Lord, and she answered: 'The King of Heaven.' "[44]

Baudricourt's reaction was unsympathetic. He told Durand Laxart "to take her home to her father and box her ears." Joan did not insist. "When she saw that Robert did not want to have her taken to the dauphin, she handed [Durand] his cloak, and said that she wanted to go back," reports the Rehabilitation record.[45]

A month later (June 1428) Domremy suffered a calamity. Antoine de Vergy, Burgundian governor of Champagne, had been subsidized by the English regent, the duke of Bedford, to equip a thousand men-at-arms to capture Vaucouleurs. Early in July de Vergy's troop set out, burning the villages in its path. The castle on the island offered insufficient protection; the people of Domremy and Greux, carrying their possessions and driving their animals, fled to the fortified town of Neufchâteau, nine kilometers to the south.

There Joan's family lodged with the widow of one Jean Waldaires, nicknamed "la Rousse (the Redhead)," who kept an inn where soldiers, monks, merchants, and pilgrims lodged. Here they stayed, according to Joan a fortnight, according to the other villagers four or five days.[46] Joan said that she performed household tasks, the other villagers that she also occupied her time in taking her father's cattle to pasture.[47] Several times she went to the Franciscan monastery for confession. One of her friends from Domremy reported later that Joan was unhappy in Neufchâteau and wanted to go home.[48]

During the stay in Neufchâteau Joan was sued for breach of promise by "a certain man in the city of Toul." Evidently Joan's parents had arranged a marriage for her which she would not accept. Nothing further is known—the identity of the man, or his connection with Joan's family. Joan journeyed to Toul and argued her case before a judge, who dismissed the charge.[49]

The villagers returned to find Domremy burned to the ground by the Burgundians. Even the stone church was damaged, and on saints' days Joan went to Greux to hear mass.[50] About a month after her return, her friend Michel Lebuin recalled, she made a cryptic remark: "There was a maid between Coussey [south of Domremy] and Vaucouleurs who within a year would have the king of France anointed."[51]

The Burgundian raid, which evidently failed to achieve its chief purpose, the capture of Vaucouleurs, was part of a general Anglo-Burgundian offensive of the summer of 1428. The main thrust was planned (after much debate) as a move south from Paris aimed at the heart of the "kingdom of Bourges," the part of France loyal to Charles VII. Bourges itself, Charles's capital, was in the province of Berry, south of the Loire. To invade Berry and seize Bourges, a crossing of the Loire had to be secured. The principal crossing was at Orleans, an important commercial center about halfway between Paris and Bourges. An attack on Orleans would be a breach of the feudal code, because the city's lord, Charles of Orleans, was a prisoner in England, but the strategic value of the city easily outweighed knightly scruple, and in mid-August a mainly English, partly Burgundian force moved south, establishing a base at Janville, north of Orleans, and isolating the city by capturing towns on the river above and below it, Meung and Beaugency on the west, Jargeau and Châteauneuf on the east. Moving by the south bank of the Loire, the attackers converged on Orleans, arriving on October 12 across the river from the city, cutting it off from the south. There they settled in for the winter.

Thus at the beginning of the momentous year 1429 the English and Burgundians occupied France north of the Loire except for beleaguered Orleans, on the river, and a few scattered pockets of resistance such as

Vaucouleurs. Remaining in French hands was a large, compact territory south of the Loire, comprising the ancient provinces of Berry, Touraine, Poitou, Auvergne, Languedoc, Dauphiné, and parts of other principalities. The fall of Orleans could open the way for a final offensive against Charles, whose military situation was not desperate but serious. The political situation paralleled the military. Though his father had been dead six years, Charles was still commonly called the "dauphin," or crown prince, implying an unrealized claim to the throne.

Such were the circumstances when in January of 1429 Joan returned once more to Vaucouleurs, again with Durand Laxart. For the second time she left without seeking her parents' permission or explaining her intentions, for fear that they would try to stop her. She told several other people, however. She bade farewell to her friend Mengette and commended her to God, and to Gerard Guillemette, a farmer of Greux, she said plainly, "Farewell, I am going to Vaucouleurs."[52]

At Vaucouleurs, she lodged for three weeks with acquaintances of the Laxarts, Henri and Catherine le Royer. Once more she called on Robert de Baudricourt; once more he refused her request.

One of Baudricourt's knights, Jean de Metz, described Joan's visit. She was wearing "poor woman's clothing, red," probably the reddish-brown homespun material known as russet. Jean de Metz began by addressing her playfully. "*M'amie* [sweetheart], what are you doing here? Is it not necessary that the king should be driven from the kingdom and that we should become English?" Joan answered: "I have come here to the royal chamber to speak to Robert de Baudricourt, so that he may take me or have me taken to the king; but he does not care about me or my words; nonetheless, before mid-Lent, I must go to the king, even if I have to walk my feet off to my knees. No one in the world, neither king nor duke nor the king of Scotland's daughter [a reference to a royal marriage project] nor anyone else can restore the kingdom of France, nor will [the king] have any help except from me, although I would rather stay with my poor mother, for this is not my station in life. But I must go, and I must do this, because my Lord wants me to do it." Jean de Metz asked who her lord was, and she said that it was God.

Joan's impassioned simplicity won over the knight—her first convert. He "promised the Maid, placing his hand in hers as a sign of faith [actually, the sign of homage between lord and vassal] that, God willing, he would take her to the king." He asked her when she wanted to go.

She said, "Rather now than tomorrow, and rather tomorrow than later."[53]

She still had to convince Baudricourt, to whom she now laid tenacious siege. Amid her appeals, she frequently visited the castle chapel, where a ten-year-old altar boy named Jean le Fumeux often "saw her at morning mass, and she remained afterward to pray . . . sometimes with her head bowed, sometimes lifted."[54]

One day Robert de Baudricourt and the priest, who by now knew Joan well, presented themselves at the house of Joan's hosts, the le Royers. The priest had brought his stole, and in front of the captain he pronounced the formulas of exorcism, saying that if there was any evil in Joan, it should go away, and if good, it should come forth. Joan at once approached the priest and fell on her knees, but rebuked him— he had heard her confession and knew that there was no evil spirit in her.

To Catherine le Royer, Joan repeated Merlin's prophecy "that France would be lost by a woman and restored by a virgin from the marches of Lorraine." Catherine remembered that she had heard it before and was "stupefied." "Joan wanted [to go] so much, and the time was as heavy to her as if she were a pregnant woman, until she could be taken to the dauphin."

Still Baudricourt remained firm. Joan's impatience at one moment drove her to set off with only Durand Laxart and a man named Jacques Alain, of Vaucouleurs, but at the shrine of St.-Nicolas-de-Septfonds, not far from town, they prudently decided to turn back.[55]

Jean de Metz broached the question of Joan's manner of dress. According to his own Rehabilitation testimony, he "asked her if she wanted to travel in her own clothing; she answered that she would prefer a man's dress." Whereupon he gave her "clothes and hose to wear belonging to his servants; and later the people of Vaucouleurs ordered a man's clothing made for her, hose, leggings, and everything necessary, and they gave her a horse worth sixteen francs."*[57] Bertrand de Poulengy explained that they "had her get rid of her woman's clothes, red in color, and put on a man's tunic and clothes, hose, leggings, sword, and the like."[58]

Though Joan's male clothing became a major issue at her trial, at

---

*Durand Laxart also said that he and Jacques Alain bought Joan a horse for twelve francs "out of our own pockets," and that Baudricourt afterward reimbursed them.[56]

Vaucouleurs no one seems to have thought it anything but a matter of convenience.

By this time, word had spread beyond the town that there had come to Vaucouleurs a girl with supernatural powers. Duke Charles II of Lorraine, ill at his court in Nancy, sent a safe-conduct for Joan to come to cure him.

Joan perceived the opportunity to enlist the support of a powerful magnate. Jean de Metz rode with her as far as Toul; Durand Laxart may also have accompanied her. Presented to the duke, Joan "told him that she wanted to be sent to France." The duke, who was politically in the camp of the duke of Burgundy, was more concerned about his illness. To his disappointment Joan gave him no promise of a cure, offering merely to pray for his health if he helped her get to the dauphin. She asked him to "lend her his son" as an escort (his son-in-law René of Anjou, at that time also in the Burgundian camp).[59] Beyond that, she advised him to mend his ways, to stop living with his mistress (by whom he had five children), and take back his wife.[60] The duke, exasperated but impressed, gave her a small sum of money and another horse "with a black coat," and sent her back to Vaucouleurs.[61]

She returned to find a small miracle awaiting her. Robert de Baudricourt was prepared to give her an escort to the king. Joan's persistence, backed by the weight of public opinion, had finally persuaded him.*

If Jean de Metz is correct in his recollection, Joan left Vaucouleurs on February 13, with an escort of six: Jean de Metz, Bertrand de Poulengy, two of Bertrand's servants, a soldier called Richard the Archer, and a royal messenger named Colet de Vienne.[62] Joan herself remembered that Robert de Baudricourt made the escort swear to conduct her well and safely, and as they departed, he spoke words that indicate his mixed feelings: "Go, and let come what may."[63]

Henri le Royer, Joan's host in Vaucouleurs, said that a number of people asked her how she would fare with so many soldiers and brigands about. "She answered that she was not afraid because the path was open to her, and if there were soldiers on the way, she had God, her Lord, who would clear the road for her to go to the dauphin, and that she was born for this."[64]

*An anecdote in the *Journal du siège d'Orléans* attributing Baudricourt's change of heart to a clairvoyant revelation by Joan of the French defeat in the Battle of the Herrings (February 12, 1429) is almost surely apocryphal.

All the same the party took the precaution of traveling by night "for fear of the Burgundian and English soldiers who then commanded the roads," and circled around most of the towns.[65] The trip took only eleven days, according to both Bertrand de Poulengy and Jean de Metz, swift for a journey of five hundred kilometers in late winter. Joan longed to hear mass, but Bertrand resisted until they came to the Burgundian city of Auxerre, across the river Yonne. There Joan took the risk of going to pray in "the great church," the cathedral.[66]

At night she slept beside Jean de Metz and Bertrand, "keeping on her surcoat and her hose laced and tied."[67] A Rehabilitation witness (Marguerite La Touroulde, of Bourges) who had talked to Joan's traveling companions reported that they had initially been tempted to make sexual advances to her, but when about to speak were so overcome by shame that they dared not utter a word.[68] Jean de Metz declared that on his oath he had no desire or "carnal motion" for her, and Bertrand echoed his words, adding that he would not have dared to approach Joan, because of the goodness that he saw in her.[69] All of the men first thought Joan not quite right in the head, but "once they were on the road, escorting her, they were ready to do whatever pleased her, and they wanted to bring her to the king as much as she was eager to get there, and they could not resist her wishes."[70]

On the road Jean de Metz asked Joan several times whether she would really do what she said. Joan replied that they "should not be afraid, and that she had been sent to do this, because her brothers in paradise told her what she had to do, and that four or five years before, her brothers in paradise and her Lord—that is, God—had told her that she must go to war to restore the kingdom of France." Jean de Metz was thoroughly convinced by her; he was, he said at the Rehabilitation, "on fire with her words and with a divine love for her, as he believed. And he believes that she was sent by God. . . .

"And so they led her to the king, to the place of Chinon, as secretly as they could."[71]

4. Chinon

THE KING whom Joan went to meet at "the place of Chinon" has traditionally been portrayed as a pleasure-loving weakling, at the mercy of his favorites. The Renaissance historian du Haillan wrote that Charles VII "did nothing but amuse himself making love to his fair Agnes [Sorel] and creating parterres and gardens, while the English . . . marched through his kingdom."[1] Charles's nineteenth-century biographer Vallet de Viriville pictured him enslaved by his mistresses, feeble, indolent, indulging in "immorality and remarkable sensuality."[2]

Modern historians have generally followed their predecessors. Carl Stephenson's standard *Medieval History* (1935) typically described Charles as a valetudinarian "with a weak, shambling body and a mind that also seemed likely to give way at any time." Conceding that Charles later demonstrated "that he was by no means unintelligent," Stephenson asserted that "his trouble was rather the burden of doubt and despair that bore him down. From earliest childhood his life had been spent under a shadow of chronic fear and suspicion, and more recently the legitimacy of his birth had been denied by his own mother. It was no wonder that he now remained sunk in apathy, utterly hopeless and quite indifferent to affairs of state . . . leading a miserable existence in the

Charles VII: the famous but unflattering portrait by Fouquet

gloomy castle of Chinon and hardly earning the title, King of Bourges, that was ironically allowed him by his foes."[3]

Another leading modern historian, Albert Guerard, says of Charles in *France, a Modern History* (1959): "His chief weakness was within. He had no self-confidence and no ambition. . . . Life was not unpleasant in the castles of his little kingdom—Mehun-sur-Yèvre, Chinon—but state affairs were exceedingly annoying. No sooner had he become attached to a favorite . . . but someone had him murdered 'for the good of the state.' "[4]

General J. F. C. Fuller, the British military historian, in his *Military History of the Western World* (1954) dismissed Charles as "a weak king and a degenerate" (implying homosexuality).[5]

Recently, however, a more favorable evaluation has been put forward, notably by historian M. G. A. Vale in his *Charles VII* (1974), and by French archivist and historian Yvonne Lanhers, who wrote: "Together with Joan of Arc, [Charles] became a symbol of resistance to the enemy and of the hope of liberation. By war and diplomacy, Charles succeeded in making peace with Burgundy and eventually in expelling the English from almost all of France. Aided by able and energetic counsellors, he renovated the administrative structure of the French monarchy. . . . Charles VII's reign was one of the most important in the history of the French monarchy. . . . He always preferred peace to war, and his conciliatory policy . . . contributed much toward restoring unity to his country."[6]

The new, more believable interpretation better explains his role in Joan of Arc's story than did the older version.

Charles was twenty-six when Joan came to Chinon. His famous portrait by Jean Fouquet, now in the Louvre, was painted perhaps twenty years later. Bernard Shaw's detailed stage directions for *Saint Joan* are drawn from this painting: "He is a poor creature physically, and the current fashion of shaving closely and hiding every scrap of hair under the head covering . . . makes the worst of his appearance. He has little narrow eyes, near together, a long pendulous nose that droops over his thick short upper lip."[7] A bust from Charles's tomb bears a family resemblance to the portrait, but is more prepossessing, lacking the curious skinned look that Fouquet, a disciple of the new Flemish realism, gave all his subjects, even beautiful Agnes Sorel.

Artistic realism notwithstanding, Fouquet may not have done Charles justice. Contemporary writers described him quite differently. Burgundian chronicler Georges Chastellain, who had no interest in flattering his master's rival, described him as "pale of face, but good-looking enough."[8] To chronicler Pierre de Fénin, he was "a very handsome prince."[9] "A handsome person who carries himself well," wrote the inhabitants of Châlons to those of Reims in July 1429.[10] Chastellain referred to his "penetrating glance." The chroniclers all agreed that he was thin and under medium height, but personable, with a voice "very agreeable and subtle," according to Chastellain;[11] "a fine talker to all men," wrote Fénin, "and charitable to the poor."[12] He was unusually literate for a prince of his day, knowledgeable about books and fluent in Latin. Almost as pious as Joan, he customarily heard two or three masses a day, which did not prevent him from consulting astrologers.

He had a number of phobias. He "did not dare to lodge on a floor, nor cross a wooden bridge on horseback, unless it was sound." He avoided strangers and large gatherings.[13] Such apprehensions were not without rational foundations: medieval timber bridges often failed; the floor of a room where Charles was holding court at La Rochelle in 1422 collapsed, killing several people; danger of assassination was most acute amid crowds and strangers. He was fond of luxury, but the mistresses with whom Vallet de Viriville reproached him came later in his life. Agnes Sorel first appeared at court in 1444; if he had earlier ones, he was discreet about them.

Born in 1403, when the conflict that led to the civil war was already on the horizon, Charles grew up as the French monarchy plunged to its nadir with Charles VI's madness. Contrary to the popular view, there is no concrete evidence to suggest that Charles was illegitimate, or that he believed that he was. Gossip, fostered and encouraged by the Burgundians and the English, made Louis of Orleans Charles's father. Henry V proclaimed that Charles was the "son of incestuous adultery,"[14] but did not question the legitimacy of the dauphin's sister Catherine, whose marriage to Henry cemented the treaty of Troyes. The alleged liaison between Louis of Orleans and Isabelle of Bavaria is possible but unlikely. In 1402 Isabelle was thirty-one, had borne ten children, and was growing fat, while Louis was in love with the wife of a royal councillor who in 1405 bore him the son who as the "Bastard of Orleans" (later count of Dunois) became Joan of Arc's companion-in-arms. The story that at the time of the treaty of Troyes Isabelle confessed that Charles was illegitimate seems to have been a Burgundian invention. Louis's relationship with Isabelle is more likely to have been political than romantic.[15]

Legitimate or not, a matter impossible to prove, Charles was raised as third in succession to the throne and treated like other royal children. In 1413, at the age of ten, he was betrothed to his nine-year-old second cousin, Marie of Anjou, daughter of Duke Louis II of Anjou and Yolande of Aragon, king and queen of Naples and Sicily. His mother-in-law, Yolande, a woman of strong character, became an important influence in his early life and at his court.

Beginning in 1417, when through the death of his brothers he became dauphin, Charles shared in his father's government, presiding over councils and signing edicts. In June 1418, at fifteen, he assumed the title of lieutenant general of the kingdom. The struggle for survival began immediately after: the flight from Paris in August 1418, the assassination of the duke of Burgundy at Montereau in 1419, the treaty of Troyes, disinheritance and banishment in 1420. In April 1422 Charles and Marie of Anjou were married at Bourges, and on the death of his father that October he assumed the title of king.

His government was established at Bourges and Poitiers—the *chambre des comptes* (treasury department) at Bourges, court of justice at Poitiers, great council sometimes at Bourges, sometimes at Poitiers, the Parlement at Poitiers. Refugee Armagnac magnates and prelates thronged to both cities. The king divided his time among his castles—Chinon, Loches, Mehun, Tours.[16]

The reign began inauspiciously with military defeats, especially Verneuil (1424), on the border between English-held Normandy and Charles's territory, but for the time being the enemy came no closer. Charles eschewed the example of his knightly great-grandfather John the Good, who rode off to battle and capture at Poitiers, in favor of that of his sensible grandfather Charles V, who stayed home and entrusted his armies to professionals. Charles VII "preferred negotiation to shedding blood," one contemporary commented.[17] "He never willingly donned armor or made war if he could avoid it," said another.[18]

His talents, in fact, lay in manipulating men. "Willingly," wrote his Burgundian contemporary Chastellain, "would he surround himself with wise and bold men, and let himself be led by them. But unbeknown to them, he would all the while be planning something new."[19]

The main source of the court intrigues with which Charles was surrounded was his financial problem. Unable to maintain his government on the taxes and other revenues from the shrunken royal domain, he borrowed from financiers and from nobles. In time his creditors usually fell from favor. Jean Louvet contributed funds from his personal fortune, and was exiled and disgraced in 1425, to be replaced as favorite by Arthur de Richemont,* brother of the duke of Brittany, who became

---

*"Richemont" is actually a French rendition of "Richmond." This famous Breton lord, a younger son of the quasi-independent duke of Brittany, received the title of earl of Richmond from his stepfather Henry IV of England. He fought on the French side at Agincourt, but gave his support to the treaty of Troyes and Henry V in 1420. Denied an

constable of France and caused two court rivals to be assassinated. In 1427 Richemont was unseated by Georges de la Tremoille.

Chastellain saw these palace revolutions as deliberate policy on Charles's part: "Leagues and factions formed between the courtiers [to] . . . get into power. . . . The master . . . let them clash and reaped the profit from it. For he had a disposition such that after a time, when someone had been raised up high beside him, to the very top of the wheel, he began to tire of him; then at the first opportunity he could find, he deliberately knocked him down from high to low. . . . Thus others, having struggled for a long time outside the door, achieved new favor and arrived at an exalted position, which they had long coveted, where . . . they worked to deserve their position more fully . . . but they, having ruled for a time as well, when he had drained from them what was there, suddenly found themselves thrown out like the others and paid the same wages."[20] Thus Charles is credited with a Machiavellian strategy of survival worthy of his crafty son, Louis XI. Not the sort of man to be a hero in the age of chivalry, nor perhaps in any age, he was nonetheless no witless weakling.

The unwavering main thrust of Charles's policy was to sever the alliance of Burgundy and England. In 1425 Richemont, who was married to a sister of Philip the Good, made an attempt to negotiate a separate peace between France and Burgundy, but after two years the talks ended in failure and the Anglo-Burgundian offensive against Orleans.

Our only information on how Charles viewed his situation in February 1429 is from chroniclers writing either much later or from a distance. A contemporary Scots chronicler claimed that Charles meditated escape to Scotland.[21] Thomas Basin, writing almost half a century later, said that Charles planned to flee to Spain.[22] In 1516 Pierre Sala, who had lived at the courts of Louis XI and Charles VIII, reported that he had heard from Charles VII's former chamberlain that Charles felt himself threatened with "death or prison," and thought of retreating to Spain or Scotland.[23] An official from Dauphiné wrote in 1456 that Charles had planned to "withdraw . . . into this land of Dauphiné."[24] No reliable contemporary evidence exists. Charles's circumstances do not, however,

---

important military command, he returned to the French side, where, despite Charles VII's prudent distrust, he performed valuable services.

seem desperate enough to force him to contemplate flight. As long as Orleans held, the Loire was secure, and although the city was under siege, its fall was not regarded as imminent; in fact, preparations seem to have been already underway to provision and possibly relieve it.

Just before the end of February Joan and her little party arrived at the village of St.-Catherine-de-Fierbois, thirty-five kilometers east of Chinon. In spite of the secrecy with which they had traveled, rumors had preceded them. Just as Duke Charles of Lorraine had heard about Joan when she was in Vaucouleurs, reports about her had been carried into the king's territories. Merchants, peddlers, friars, soldiers, pilgrims, all the inveterate travelers of the Middle Ages, bore news that was eagerly received and swiftly diffused. Word of the peasant girl and her dramatic mission had even penetrated besieged Orleans. The garrison commander, the Bastard of Orleans or, to give him the name by which he is known to history, Dunois, was so intrigued that he sent two emissaries to the court at Chinon to inquire about her.[25]

From St.-Catherine-de-Fierbois, Joan sent messengers to Chinon bearing a letter to the king requesting an interview, explaining that she had "traveled one hundred and fifty leagues to come to him and bring him aid," and that she knew "many good things touching him."[26]

St.-Catherine-de-Fierbois was a place of pilgrimage with special significance to French soldiers. A ruined chapel where Charles Martel was said to have left his sword had been rebuilt in 1375 by a blind and paralyzed knight whom St. Catherine had rewarded with a cure. Subsequently Catherine had become the patroness of French prisoners of war, who prayed to her for deliverance from the English and Burgundians and afterward visited the chapel to present their ropes, chains, and armor in gratitude. (Many of them seem to have followed Joan's own principle when she later attempted to escape from captivity—"Help yourself and God will help you.")

Joan waited two days, spending much of her time at mass in the chapel. On the third day a reply came from the king's council inviting her to court, and she started at once for Chinon.

The town of Chinon lay along the north bank of the river Vienne, dominated by the huge castle-fortress that crowned the ridge above. Built on the foundations of a Roman stronghold, the castle remained a massive monument to the centuries-long struggle between the English and French kings. A favorite residence of English king Henry II, who died there in 1189, it had been captured by French king Philip Augustus in

The castle of Chinon. Extreme right, Fort St. Georges, gate by which Joan entered; left center, royal residential buildings; to their immediate left, cylindrical Tour du Coudray where she lodged.

Joan of Arc's arrival at Chinon, from a fifteenth-century German tapestry in the Musée Historique, Orleans

1205 after a long siege and had changed hands several times since. Charles had acquired the castle in 1416 when he became dauphin, as part of the appanage of the duchy of Touraine. It was here that he had taken refuge after the Burgundians seized Paris in 1418, and from here he had launched his first appeal to the kingdom for support of his cause.

Joan testified at her trial that she arrived at Chinon about noon, found a room in an inn, and "after dinner went to see the king, who was in the castle."[27] She was accompanied by Jean de Metz and Bertrand de Poulengy. They presumably climbed the road that circles the castle, to enter it on the north, by the easternmost of its three main structures, Fort St. Georges. Crossing the drawbridge, Joan's party passed into the Château du Milieu, where the king had his residence in a cluster of buildings against the northern curtain wall.

According to a story told by the priest who became Joan's confessor, as she crossed the bridge, a mounted soldier among the crowd called out, "Isn't that the Maid?" and with an oath declared that if he had her for a night she would no longer be a maid. Joan replied, "Ah, you take God's name in vain, and you are so close to death!" Within the hour the man fell into the moat and drowned. The confessor was not present, but claimed to have heard the story from Joan and others who were.[28] True or not, the incident became part of Joan's legend.

She was taken to the king's residence, but not immediately to the king. First the council interviewed her to decide whether she should be allowed to see him.

Aside from the detail of her masculine dress, we can only guess at the visual impression Joan made on the council. Although statues, murals, and stained-glass windows of Joan abound today, all were made long after her death. Not one contemporary portrait exists. The sole contemporary representation that has survived is a caricature in the margin of the Paris Parlement's official record of the siege of Orleans, sketched by a scribe who never saw her. Joan testified at Rouen that during her captivity at Arras she had seen a painting done by a Scot showing her armed and kneeling to present a letter to the king, and other portraits are mentioned by chroniclers, but all have vanished.

Of the witnesses at the Rehabilitation, only Joan's squire Jean d'Aulon provided any information about Joan's appearance; in his eyes and memory she was "beautiful and well-formed." He was not, however, sexually aroused by the sight of "her breasts and sometimes her bare legs, when he dressed her wounds . . . although he was then strong, young, and in

Sketch of Joan done by a clerk who never saw her, in the margin of the Paris Parlement's report of the relief of Orleans

his full powers . . . and neither were any of her other men-at-arms and squires, as he had heard them say many times."[29] Some writers* have concluded from this absence of sexual response that Joan was not attractive. Not only does d'Aulon positively affirm the contrary, but he makes clear that he and his companions regarded their restraint toward her as truly miraculous. Several men on the Anglo-Burgundian side, in whom she did not inspire the same sentiments of awe and respect, later made sexual advances to her.

A scribe of La Rochelle, not himself present at Chinon, but apparently recording (the following September) an eyewitness description, confirms

*Notably Henri Guillemin, in *Joan, Maid of Orleans,* translated by Harold J. Salemson, New York, 1970.

that Joan "wore male dress: that is to say that she had a black doublet with hose attached, a short tunic of coarse black material, black hair, cut round, and a black cap on her head. . . ."[30] An eyewitness, Perceval de Boulainvilliers, adds an impression in a letter written three months later to Filippo Maria Visconti: Joan was "rather elegant; she bears herself vigorously, speaks little, shows an admirable prudence in her words. She has a light, feminine voice, eats little, drinks little wine; she enjoys fine horses and arms, likes the company of noble knights, hates large gatherings and meetings, weeps readily, wears a cheerful countenance, and is incredibly strong in the wearing of armor and bearing of arms, sometimes remaining armed for as much as six days and nights."[31]

Was she tall, medium, or short? Contradictory evidence has been deduced from the amount of material ordered for her court robes, the size of a suit of armor which she may never have worn, the hearsay testimony of an Italian writer. The fact that Joan was able to wear the clothes of Bertrand de Poulengy's servant suggests that she was slightly above average height for a woman, and the absence of comment implies that her stature and size were not strikingly unusual.

What the council sought to find out was why Joan had come and what she wanted. Joan was not the first or the last person during the Hundred Years War to be inspired with a mission to the king. One who impressed the chroniclers was a well-to-do peasant in Champagne who, working in his fields in 1356, heard, according to the *Chronique des quatre premiers Valois* (Chronicle of the Four First Valois [Kings]), a "horrible and frightful" voice warning him that the king must on no account fight a battle. His parish priest twice advised him to fast for three days and then return to the place where he had heard the voice; each time the voice spoke again, accompanied by "a great brightness . . . wonderfully terrifying," and threatening him with death if he did not comply. The peasant obeyed, but unable to gain access to the king, he told his story to two priests, the royal almoner and the confessor. King John II told the priests to give the man money and send him away (that he refused the money seemed to the priests more of a marvel than his prophecy). John then set out for the disastrous battle of Poitiers.[32] Joan in the peasant's place would surely have persisted better.

John II's two successors had similar visitations. Charles V invited a woman visionary named Guillemette de la Rochelle to Paris and built chapels where she could pray for him, and Charles VI communicated with several mystics, including Marie Robine, the woman from Avignon whose visions seemed to predict Joan's mission.

To the questions of Charles VII's council, Joan at first protested that she wanted to speak directly to the king, but under persuasion she informed them that she had come on behalf of the King of Heaven to raise the siege of Orleans and to take the king to Reims for his coronation and consecration. Simon Charles, a royal official then on embassy to Venice who learned about the discussions on his return in March, reported that some of the councillors felt that the king should place no trust in her, while others believed that he ought to give her a hearing. The king himself asked to have her questioned by "clerics and ecclesiastics," Simon Charles said, "and this was done."[33]

In the end, as at Vaucouleurs, Joan's sincerity and invincible confidence in her mission overcame the opposition. Some of her hearers noted that she "spoke well," an expression repeated by observers throughout her career.

Promised an audience with the king, Joan apparently returned to her inn, and two days later, according to one source,* again returned to the castle. The king and council temporized. Then a letter arrived from Robert de Baudricourt confirming her story. The successful journey "through territory of enemies of the king," including the "almost miraculous crossing of many rivers,"[34] impressed the councillors enough to tip the scales, and Joan at last was admitted into the king's presence.

The great hall where he received her was dark, thronged with "more than three hundred knights." Besides the flicker of fifty torches, Joan said at her trial, there was the "spiritual light" that accompanied her revelations.[35] In her letter from St.-Catherine-de-Fierbois she had promised the king that she "should know him well from among all the others." She made good her boast, recognizing Charles as she had recognized Baudricourt, "by the counsel of her voices."[36]

A story repeated by two Rehabilitation witnesses who were not present at the meeting at Chinon, Simon Charles and a merchant named Jean Moreau, found its way into literature: that the king deliberately hid himself among the courtiers but Joan singled him out from the crowd.[37] Jean Chartier's mid-fifteenth-century chronicle embroidered further, asserting that the king had a courtier pose in his place,[38] a detail that proved

*The two emissaries sent by Dunois to Chinon.

irresistible to later writers about Joan, including Shakespeare, Chapelain, Southey, Schiller, Mark Twain, and Shaw.

Eyewitness Raoul de Gaucourt, grand master of the king's household, said that "the poor little shepherdess" greeted the king "in great humility and utter simplicity," saying, "Most noble Lord Dauphin, I have come and am sent by God to bring aid to you and your kingdom."[39] Simon Charles's informant told him that after the initial greeting, Joan talked to the king for a long time, and when he had listened to her the king "was seen to be joyous."[40] Poet Alain Chartier, who was present, confirmed this statement in a letter: Joan talked to the king, who listened attentively —what she said, no one knew.[41] Other witnesses to the momentous interview—Dunois's two emissaries (Jamet du Tillay and the lord de Villars) and a knight named Regnault Thierry—did not mention such a private conversation, the emissaries reporting to Dunois only that Joan had promised publicly that she would deliver Orleans and take the king to Reims for his consecration, for which purpose she asked him for troops, arms, and horses.[42]

Joan's confessor, Jean Pasquerel, said that Joan later told him she had first explained her mission to the king—"the King of Heaven has sent me to see that you are consecrated and crowned in the city of Reims, and you shall be lieutenant of the King of Heaven, who is king of France" —and assured him, "I tell you on behalf of *Messire* [my Lord] that you are the true heir of France and the king's son." (If Pasquerel is to be believed, in this latter speech she addressed the king by the familiar *tu* —which Shaw imitated in English by having her call him "Charlie.") Then, Pasquerel said, the king told those present that Joan had told him "a certain secret that nobody knew or could know but God. That is why he had great confidence in her."[43]

Whether at the first meeting or later in Joan's stay at Chinon, a number of people say that she told the king a secret, or showed him a sign, that persuaded him that he should accept the aid she offered. Her squire Jean d'Aulon said that he was told that Joan talked to the king in private and told him "certain secrets which I do not know." Shortly afterward the king sent for d'Aulon and some people of his council and told them that Joan had been sent them by God "to help him recover his kingdom, which was mostly occupied by the English, his ancient enemies."[44] Charles's biographer Thomas Basin, writing thirty-five years later, stated that Dunois had told him (evidently from other information than that of his emissaries) that Joan "had revealed, in proof of her words, matters so secret and hidden that no mortal except himself could have known about them, except by divine revelation."[45] Other contemporary sources echo the story. The scribe of La Rochelle wrote, "It is said that she told him certain things in secret, which the king marveled at."[46] A nobleman in Lyons who had connections in Chinon wrote a letter to Brussels in April describing Joan's determination to relieve Orleans and to take the king to Reims, adding that she had told him "many other secret things."[47] Later chronicles repeated the assertion.

Many a fragile hypothesis has been built on the "king's secret" or the "king's sign." According to the "bastardy theory" propounded by a number of French writers in the 1950s, '60s, and '70s, the secret was Joan's revelation to Charles that she was his illegitimate sister; but it is hard to see how such news would make him "joyous," or why he would place any special confidence in his sister to lead his armies. A more credible interpretation was that Joan told the king that he was the legitimate son of Charles VI. According to Pasquerel, however, she told him that he was the "true heir of France and the king's son" and *also* told him "a certain secret." The second secret has been conjectured to be a proof of his legitimacy, which raises the question of what such a proof could be. Pierre Sala, in his chronicle of 1516, claimed that Joan had been able to tell the king the substance of a prayer which he had made "in his heart, without utterance of words," that if he was the true heir, God should keep and defend him, "or, at worst, to grant him the mercy of escaping death or prison, and that he might fly to Spain or Scotland."[48] Apart from its dubious source, this "secret" seems tame and unconvincing.

The judges at Rouen were among those persuaded that Joan had given the king a sign. In their eyes, it was something magical and diabolical, and by means of a merciless interrogation they harassed her into telling them a tale about an angel who carried a crown, which signified that the king should "hold the realm of France."[49] The circumstances in which Joan told this story rob it of all authenticity.*

The truth about the "king's secret" can never be known, but the

*Historian Jules Michelet offered an ingenious suggestion: that Joan's "very obscure answers to her judges" on the subject of the king's sign were the result of a charade enacted by the "astute court," who, "to confirm her in her visions played a sort of mystery before her in which an angel carried a crown." That the court, which had put up strong resistance to allowing Joan access to the king, should resort to an elaborate stratagem to "confirm her in her visions" defies logic.[50]

likelihood, as indicated by the sequel to Joan's interview at court, is that her sign was nothing more—or less—than the promise to fulfill her mission, conveyed with the self-confidence that never deserted her.

The king ordered lodgings prepared for her in the Tour du Coudray, in the Château du Coudray, the westernmost section of the castle.

That Charles proved easier to win over than either his councillors or Robert de Baudricourt is less surprising than it seems at first glance. Unlike them he had no higher authority to answer to for a rash action. Yet Joan's capacity to impress persons far above her on the social scale seems to testify not only to her personality but to the fact that the class distinctions of the Middle Ages imposed less distance than is sometimes thought. Charles was not the only royal or princely personage to be taken with Joan. The very next day he was joined by his kinsman Jean, the duke of Alençon. About twenty-five years old, a prince of the royal blood* and married to Jeanne, daughter of Charles of Orleans, Alençon had been quail hunting near Saumur when a messenger brought news that "a certain maid had come to the king asserting that she had been sent by God to drive out the English and to raise the siege the English had laid against Orleans." Alençon was so intrigued that the following day he rode the thirty-two kilometers to Chinon, where he found Joan in conversation with the king. Joan captivated him from her first greeting: "You are very welcome. The more of the royal blood of France that are gathered together the better."[51]

The next day, according to Alençon, Joan attended mass in the king's chapel, and afterward the king held a private conference with Joan, Alençon, and Georges de la Tremoille. Joan urged Charles to give his realm to the King of Heaven, who would then do to him as he had done to his predecessors, and restore him to their prior status. After dinner the king went for a stroll in the fields, while Joan amused herself by taking a lance and running at a tilt. Alençon, watching and admiring, resolved to make her the gift of a charger.

Joan also acquired a page: Louis de Coutes, the orphaned fourteen-year-old son of an old knightly family attached to the house of Orleans, who later testified at the Rehabilitation. Louis waited on her throughout

*Great-grandson of King Philip III of France. His wife, Jeanne, was the product of Charles of Orleans's first marriage, to Isabelle, Charles VII's older sister, and was thus herself of royal blood on both sides of the family (Charles of Orleans was Charles V's grandson).

the day, and at night "she had women with her." He often saw her go off to talk to the king, and observed other men of high rank coming to see her. What they talked about he did not know, because, like a good page, when they approached, he withdrew.[52]

Impressed though he was with Joan, Charles wanted more assurance about her. Finally, at the council's suggestion, it was decided to take her to Poitiers, where a number of Armagnac prelates and masters of the University of Paris had taken refuge. From them a commission could be selected to subject her to rigorous examination. Chosen to preside over the inquiry was the king's chancellor, Regnault of Chartres, the archbishop of Reims. About March 1 the whole court—the king, Queen Marie of Anjou, her mother Yolande of Aragon, the council, and Joan —moved to Poitiers.[53]

The examination lasted three weeks. Joan lodged with Jean Rabateau, advocate general to the Parlement at Poitiers, one of the Armagnac refugees from Paris, who had a house on the Rue Notre-Dame-la-Petite* near the Palais de Justice. The inquiry was conducted at Rabateau's house, the theologians arriving in relays to interrogate. A number of civilians were present—lawyers, members of the council, and people drawn simply by curiosity or sympathy. Foremost of these latter was Alençon, but there was also a young Gascon, Jean d'Aulon, who volunteered to be Joan's squire.

The commission numbered some eighteen clerics, several of whom had already questioned Joan at Chinon, and included the bishops of Poitiers and Maguelonne, the confessors of the king and queen, two prominent theologians (Pierre de Versailles and Jourdain Morin), several less famous masters of the Universities of Paris and Orleans, a Carmelite, and four Dominicans. One of the Dominicans, Guillaume Seguin (also known as Seguin Seguin), was the only member of the commission who survived to testify at the Rehabilitation.

A record was kept of the proceedings. Several times in her trial Joan appealed to "the book of Poitiers": "It was written down at Poitiers." "If you do not believe me, go to Poitiers." Whether the record still existed at the time of the trial is not known; by the time of the Rehabilitation in 1456 it had disappeared.

According to one witness, when Pierre Versailles opened the questioning by explaining that he and the others had been sent by the king, Joan

*Today Rue de la Cathédrale.

replied, "Then I suppose you have come to question me. But I do not know A from B."[54]

The prelates asked her why she had come to the king. She told them about her voices and described her journey from Vaucouleurs and how it had occurred "without any hindrance." Guillaume Aymeri, a Dominican, posed a difficult question: "You have said that the voice told you that God wishes to deliver the people of France from their present calamity. If he wants to deliver them, it is not necessary to send soldiers." Joan's answer carried conviction: "In the name of God, the soldiers will fight and God will give victory." The Dominican was satisfied.[55]

Joan's remarks about the inquiry at her trial in Rouen indicate that the commission questioned her at length about her visions, but only one exchange has come down to us. Seguin asked what dialect her voice spoke. Impatiently Joan replied, "A better one than yours." Seguin, whose French had a Limousin accent, apparently took the tart rejoinder without offense, as he did several responses that followed. He told Joan that God could not wish them to believe her without giving them some sign, and that they could not advise the king to entrust soldiers to her on her simple assertion, without more assurance. Joan answered, "In the name of God, I did not come to Poitiers to give signs; but take me to Orleans, and I will show you the signs for which I was sent." First she must be given the soldiers she needed, and then they must let her go to Orleans. She then prophesied four events: first, the English would be destroyed, the siege of Orleans would be raised, and the city freed; second, the king would be consecrated at Reims; third, the city of Paris would return to the king's obedience; and fourth, the duke of Orleans would return from captivity in England. "And I have seen all these prophecies fulfilled," Seguin testified at the Rehabilitation.[56] Joan had a parting shot for her learned interrogators, as she later recalled for a woman at Bourges: "There is more in the books of our Lord than in yours."[57]

Fifteen-year-old François Garivel, later a royal official, present at the interrogations, reported that the commission had asked Joan why she called Charles "dauphin" rather than "king," to which Joan replied that she would not call him king until he had been crowned and anointed at Reims, where she herself intended to take him.[58]

As did the judges at Rouen later, the prelates at Poitiers questioned Joan about her assumption of male dress. The Bible (Deuteronomy

22 : 5) prohibited wearing the clothing of the opposite sex: "The woman shall not wear that which pertaineth unto a man, neither shall a man put on a woman's garment: for all that do so are abomination unto the Lord, thy God," an injunction designed to combat sexual aberration—transvestism and homosexuality. Joan had put on male clothing at Vaucouleurs at the suggestion of her traveling companions, as a matter of convenience. As time went on, her new mode of dress became increasingly important to her, until during her trial it became a symbol of her resistance to her judges. To relate it, however, to "uncertainty about her sexual identity," as some "psycho-biographers" have done, is going far afield.* There is no evidence of sexual abnormality about Joan. The man's tunic and hose signaled her identity not as a man but as a soldier. The Poitiers commission evidently agreed that it was appropriate.

The first part of the inquiry concluded, the commission reported that Joan was "a good Christian and a true Catholic," and, in the words of her squire Jean d'Aulon, "a very good person."[59]

Next a committee of ladies under the direction of Yolande of Aragon examined Joan physically to discover, as Joan's confessor Jean Pasquerel phrased it, "whether she was man or woman, wanton or virgin."[60] They found her, according to d'Aulon, who was present when their report was made, "a true and complete virgin *(une vraye et entière pucelle)*."[61]

The examination, which seemed so curious to post-medieval minds that Voltaire turned it to comic account in his mock-epic poem, *La Pucelle* (1755), derived part of its significance from fifteenth-century superstition. Medieval Christianity, like pagan antiquity, attributed special powers to virginity. That France would be saved by a virgin was the burden of the "prophecy of Merlin" and also that of Marie Robine, which was cited by one of the commissioners.[62] A second reason for the physical examination was to disarm suspicions that Joan was a witch. A witch could not be a virgin, because her pact with Satan involved sexual intercourse with a demon. Superstition aside, there was also the natural suspicion that Joan was a man and, beyond that, that she was not what

*Rehabilitation witnesses who testified that Joan "always had women with her," "always had another woman sleeping with her at night," or "always slept in the company of young girls and did not like to lie with old women" (Joan was only eighteen, and preferring the company of other girls seems normal) would be appalled and astonished to find that their statements, intended to show Joan's chastity, were used by modern writers to infer "latent homosexuality."

she said she was. The integrity of her mission was involved in the truth
of her claim to virginity.

Still not content with the exhaustive investigation, Charles dispatched
two Franciscan monks to Domremy and Vaucouleurs to inquire into
Joan's background.[63] Of their report, probably delivered the first week
of April, nothing is known except that it must have confirmed her story.

During her stay in Poitiers, according to Seguin, Joan was an object
of close observation by the noble ladies and merchants' wives of the
town.[64] A Venetian merchant, Pancrazio Giustiniani, wrote his father
later from Bruges: "Many barons hold her in esteem, and many of the
people of [Poitiers]. . . . To many knights, hearing her speak of so many
marvelous things, and new ones every day, it seems a great wonder."[65]
One knight who encountered her at Poitiers, Gobert Thibault, said that
Joan tapped him on the shoulder, saying that she would like to have a
few men of good will like him with her in battle.[66]

At the end of the first week of April, the conclusion of the theologians
was finally made public: Joan's faith, way of life, and past were irre-
proachable, there was nothing in her but good, humility, simplicity,
virginity, honesty. The ready wisdom of her responses and the sanctity
of her life weighed in favor of her mission's being a divine one. Therefore
the king's duty was to put the presumption to the proof; if Joan was sent
by divine grace and the Holy Spirit, he must not risk rejecting the gift.
The sign Joan had promised the commissioners was the relief of Orleans.
For that it was necessary to give her soldiers.[67]

The report was submitted to the king's council, which unanimously
adopted it.

Two distinguished authorities not present at Poitiers were also consulted by the king. In March or early April he wrote Jean Gerson, former
chancellor of Notre-Dame and of the University of Paris, and Jacques
Gelu, archbishop of Embrun. Both Armagnacs, devoted to the king's
cause, the two churchmen replied with cautious endorsements. Gelu
began by proving that God had good reason to help the king: Charles's
cause was just, his predecessors had been praiseworthy, his people were
oppressed, his enemies unjust, and the English insatiably cruel. God
might well have chosen a peasant girl to save France in order to "humble
the proud" who had failed. The king must not turn his back on God's
inspiration. At the same time, he must observe the rules of prudence in
war: "It is written, 'Thou must not try the Lord thy God.'" Thus in

Gelu's view, every bit as common-sense as Joan's, the king must "prepare
for battle, employ machines, furnish supplies, do everything human
foresight could devise"; on the other, "when divine wisdom demands
special action, human prudence must bow before it."[68]

Gerson's reply warned against following false prophets, but concluded
that Joan did not belong in that category; she was good, divinely inspired, and worthy of leading the king's armies. On the question of Joan's
male clothing, he felt that the Biblical prohibition applied only to inde-
cent dress and did not forbid women to wear men's clothing for military
purposes, citing Esther and Judith.[69]

As a result of the commission's report and the council's decision, Joan
was given, in Simon Charles's words, "the direction of the war."[70] She
was accorded the title of *chef de guerre,* or war chief, a deliberately
ambiguous designation, but one that carried an astonishing prestige for
a woman, and a peasant at that.

Joan lost no time in asserting her new status. On March 22, even
before the final decision, she had dictated a challenge to the English,
written down by a member of the Poitiers commission, Jean Erault.
Headed "JESUS MARIA," the letter (as presented at the trial in Rouen)
challenged the king of England, the regent Bedford, and the English
generals Suffolk, Talbot, and Scales to surrender and "yield up to the
Maid sent by God, the King of Heaven, the keys of all the good towns
which you have taken and violated in France." She was ready to make
peace if the English would leave France and pay an indemnity for the
damage they had done. Addressing the "archers, companions-of-war,
soldiers, and others who are before the town of Orleans," she advised
them to go back to their own country; and if they did not do so, they
would soon hear from the Maid, who would in a short time come to see
them, "to your very great harm."

To the king of England, she said that wherever she met his people in
France, she would drive them out, willy nilly, and if they would not go,
she would have them all killed. "I have been sent by God, the King of
Heaven, to drive you, body for body [*corps pour corps*], out of all of
France." The king of England did not hold France from God; Charles
was the true heir, for God had revealed it to the Maid, and Charles would
enter Paris with his army. "If you will not believe the news sent you by
God and the Maid, wherever we find you, we will strike you and make
such a great *hahay* [harrying] that France has not had in a thousand

years." The King of Heaven would give her and her good men-at-arms more strength than the king of England could bring in all his assaults, and he would show who had the better right. In conclusion, she urged the duke of Bedford not to allow himself to be destroyed, and she invited the English to join the French in a crusade against the Turks. "And answer if you want to make peace in the city of Orleans; and if you do not, you may shortly be reminded of it, to your very great harm."[71]

The letter was not dispatched immediately, but was held until Joan started for Orleans. First, she returned with the court to Chinon, then rode on to Tours, on the Loire, fifty kilometers northeast, where she lodged at the house of a prominent citizen whose wife was one of Marie of Anjou's ladies-in-waiting. Meanwhile Alençon, delegated by the king to organize troops and provisions, went to Blois to enlist the help of Charles's mother-in-law, Yolande of Aragon. He found that provisions had already been assembled. What was needed was the money to pay for them and to pay the soldiers.[72]

This was no trifling detail. The fifteenth-century company combined crossbowmen and men-at-arms (making it a self-sufficient combat unit) at seven pounds, ten shillings Tournois per month and fifteen pounds Tournois per month respectively, and captains liked to receive much or all of their men's wages in advance.[73] The relief army for Orleans meant a staggering financial burden on Charles's government.* Marguerite La Touroulde, wife of the king's receiver general, said of the winter of 1428–1429: "At that time there was such misery and such shortage of money in this kingdom and in the parts obedient to the king that things were in a pitiable state. And even those who were loyal to the king were all in despair. I know this because my husband . . . had not four crowns all told, of the king's money or his own."[75] The fact that Charles was able to furnish the necessary cash implies that he had begun preparations for the revictualing if not the relief of Orleans long before Joan's arrival. The sources focus so closely on Joan that other activities are obscured, but a large army and extensive provisions could hardly have been raised in a space of three weeks. Some form of expedition was evidently planned before Joan's arrival; she gave it leadership and motivation.

*A similar burden weighed on the English, whose army at Orleans has been estimated to have cost 50,000 pounds a month (the English paid their archers five pounds a month, their men-at-arms fifteen). Among other measures, a forced loan had been exacted from all officials of the English governments in Normandy and Paris.[74]

Joan herself required an extraordinary expenditure: one hundred pounds Tournois "to the master armorer" of Tours for a suit of plate armor made especially for her.[76] A late fifteenth-century Flemish manuscript contains a miniature of Joan in armor which probably closely resembled what she actually wore: a neck piece of five overlapping curved steel plates ended in a point, below which a steel corselet was clasped in front. Three overlapping plates covered the hips. The thighs were protected by a skirt of steel, divided for riding. Shoulder plates, steel sleeves hinged at the elbows, and steel gauntlets protected her upper limbs; thigh pieces, knee joints, leg coverings, and shoes the lower. Her helmet had a steel cup-shaped band to protect the chin and a visor that could be drawn down over the face. Over her armor Joan wore a *hucque,* a cloak of velvet or cloth of gold.

The treasurer's accounts also recorded the payment of twenty-five pounds to "Hauves Poulnoir" (actually a French rendering of the Scottish name Hamish Power), a painter of Tours, to make "a large and a small standard for the Maid." The large pennon, Joan's personal standard, probably fork-tailed, and mounted on an ash staff topped with an iron lance, was described by Joan at her trial: on white linen with a silken fringe sown with heraldic fleurs-de-lis, it represented Jesus seated in majesty, holding the world in his hand, with an angel kneeling on either side; to the right of the scene were the words JHESUS MARIA. Several chronicle sources suggested a design on the reverse, but more probably it was decorated only with fleurs-de-lis.[77]

Joan explained at Rouen the particular importance of the standard; she was "fonder of it than of her sword," and she herself carried it in the attack, "in order to avoid killing anyone."[78]

The smaller standard seems to have borne an Annunciation scene, with a dove carrying a scroll in his beak on which was written, *"De par le Roy du Ciel* (on behalf of the King of Heaven)," and was apparently the standard of Joan's company. Joan evidently had a special affection for the painter who made the two standards; in February 1430 she wrote to the town council of Tours asking them to supply a hundred crowns for the *corbeille* (wedding gift) of Hamish Power's daughter Heliote. The council deliberated and decided that all the money in the municipal treasury was needed for "repairs to the town" (probably the walls), but that in honor of Joan they would attend the wedding and provide bread and wine to the value of four livres ten sous.[79]

A final item of Joan's equipment, added at Tours, created another mystery. Joan had already been given a sword at Vaucouleurs, but from Tours she sent "an armorer" to the village of St.-Catherine-de-Fierbois to look for "a rusty sword with five crosses on it" that her voices had told her was buried in the ground in the chapel behind the altar. At the same time she wrote the chapel clergy asking "that it might please them to let her have the sword." When the sword was found, she told the court at Rouen, the clergy rubbed it "and the rust fell off without any effort." Both the clergy of St.-Catherine and the people of Tours gave her sheaths for it, one of crimson velvet, the other of cloth of gold. She herself had a more practical sheath made of "very strong leather."[80]

At Tours Joan assembled her entourage—her "household"—a band of mostly young enthusiasts. To her page Louis de Coutes and her squire Jean d'Aulon was added a second page, Raymond; while her two traveling companions from Vaucouleurs, Jean de Metz and Bertrand de Poulengy, became respectively her treasurer and a second squire. Two more young men arrived from the east to join the party, Joan's brothers Pierre and Jean, who remained with her during most of her military career, although their names seldom appear in the chronicles or court testimony. Two heralds who functioned as messengers, one of whom carried Joan's letter to the English, were also recruited.

Finally, she acquired a chaplain, Jean Pasquerel. A mendicant of the order of Hermit Friars of St. Augustine, from a monastery in Bayeux, Pasquerel a few weeks previously had been on pilgrimage to the cathedral of Notre-Dame in Le Puy-en-Velay, in the Auvergne (south central France), where a celebrated statue of a black Virgin, brought from Egypt by Louis IX in 1254, attracted crowds of pilgrims. There he had met Joan's mother Isabelle Romée and "some of those who had brought Joan to the king"—probably the two servants of Jean de Metz and Bertrand de Poulengy—who "would not let him go until they had brought him to Joan." Pasquerel accompanied them to Chinon and thence to Tours, where his escorts introduced him: "Joan, we have brought you this good Father. If you knew him well, you would like him very much." Joan answered that she had already heard of him, and that she would confess to him on the following day. The next day he heard her confession and "sang the mass before her, and from that hour he always followed her...."[81]

Escorted by her little band, Joan moved on to Blois, on the north bank of the Loire, about half the distance to Orleans. The stone-arch bridge at Blois was the last crossing west of Orleans remaining in French hands. There men and supplies were assembling and leaders converging. Joan arrived at the same time as Raoul de Gaucourt and chancellor Regnault of Chartres. Shortly after, two veteran professional soldiers came out from Orleans to help direct the revictualing operation. One was Poton de Xaintrailles, who became one of the outstanding French leaders of the war, the other La Hire, the famous captain who in 1423 had defended Sermaize, where Joan's kinsman was killed.* Gilles de Rais, a young Breton nobleman whose later crimes inspired Charles Perrault to write "Bluebeard," brought a company from Anjou and Maine.

Alençon did not accompany Joan, but apparently remained at Blois. He testified only, "I was not present [at Orleans] and did not accompany the army. . . . I did not see Joan again from the time she left the king until after the raising of the siege of Orleans."[82]

Joan directed Pasquerel to have still another standard made, representing the crucifixion, to be carried by the priests and monks who would accompany the army. Twice a day, morning and evening, at Joan's instruction, Pasquerel assembled the priests to sing anthems and hymns under the banner. "And she would not allow the soldiers to mix with the priests unless they had confessed," Pasquerel testified at the Rehabilitation, "and she exhorted all the soldiers to confess in order to come to this gathering."[83]

From Blois, Joan dispatched her letter to the English. What the duke of Bedford and the English captains Suffolk, Talbot, and Scales made of it, we do not know. They sent no answer.

On April 27, the army, some 4,000 strong, crossed the bridge and marched east headed by the company of priests carrying their standard, singing the "Veni Creator Spiritus."

*La Hire is remembered for the prayer attributed to him (and others): "God, I pray You that You will today do for La Hire what You would wish La Hire to do for You, if La Hire were God and You were a man-at-arms."

5. Orleans

WHEN JOAN SET OUT FROM BLOIS on April 27, 1429, Orleans had been under siege for seven months. The English leadership had been divided over the question of whether to attack the easier objective of Angers, close to Normandy, or the more difficult but more valuable Orleans.[1] The decision to try for Orleans was largely owing to Thomas Montague, earl of Salisbury, who brought an expeditionary force of 2,700 men from England in the summer of 1428. Detachments drawn from garrisons, including some French and Burgundians, raised the total to about 5,000.[2] Dividing his force, Salisbury had sent part under the earl of Suffolk to capture Jargeau, east of Orleans, while with the remainder he secured Meung and Beaugency, to the west. The two detachments met on the southern bank of the Loire opposite Orleans on October 12. The river was more than 350 meters wide, shallow, rapid, but navigable, with many sandbanks and islands, and spanned by a twelfth-century stone bridge of nineteen arches. On the second arch from the southern shore stood a twin-towered stone fortress called "Les Tourelles (the little towers)"; leading to it, the last span was a drawbridge.[3] A short distance south of the bridge stood a monastery, Les Augustins, which had been fortified to protect the bridgehead. At the moment when the English

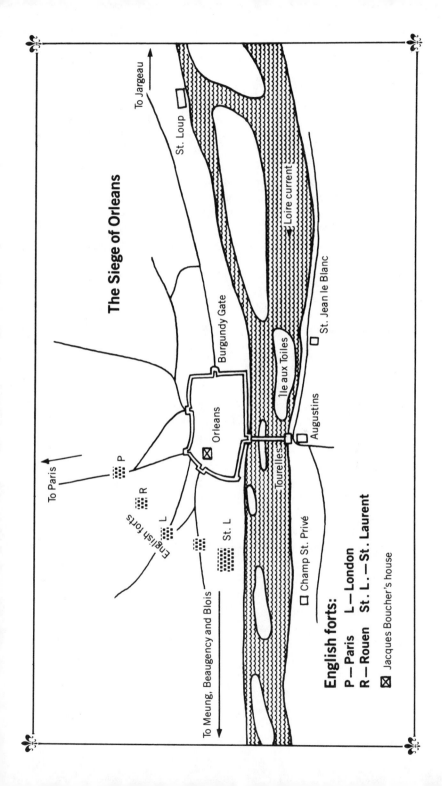

The Siege of Orleans

To Paris

To Jargeau

Burgundy Gate

Orleans

St. Loup

Loire current

St. Jean le Blanc

Île aux Toiles

Augustins

English forts

P

R

L

St. L

Tourelles

Champ St. Privé

To Meung, Beaugency and Blois

English forts:

P — Paris   L — London

R — Rouen   St. L. — St. Laurent

☐ Jacques Boucher's house

arrived, the defenders of the city were hastily building a timber and earthwork rampart parallel to the bridge roadway to connect the bridge-head with the monastery, but at once abandoned the monastery and next day blew up the bridge span immediately north of the Tourelles, isolating the fort, in which only a small garrison was left. On October 24 the Tourelles was stormed by the English.[4]

Despite these enemy successes on its periphery, the city itself remained formidable behind its walls. Its population was perhaps 20,000, probably swelled by refugees from the countryside and the suburbs. At the outset of the siege, the city had a small royal garrison of professional soldiers backed by its own communal militia, able-bodied citizens who furnished their own arms.[5]

That Orleans would be no easy prey was indicated by an incident the very evening of the fall of the Tourelles. A cannon mounted on the city wall fired a round that smashed into one of the towers of the fortress on the bridge and dislodged an iron bar that mortally wounded the earl of Salisbury.

Both attackers and defenders had cannon. But though artillery, first used effectively in the late fourteenth century, was slowly tilting the advantage in siege warfare in favor of the attackers, the shift was not apparent at Orleans. The seventy-one guns of many calibers mounted on the city walls were more than a match in numbers for the artillery of the besiegers. In addition to the heavy guns, which fired stone cannonballs, the garrison possessed a number of culverins, small cannon firing lead balls that could be carried outside the ramparts almost as easily as modern mortars, and were effective against enemy personnel.[6]

Salisbury's place was taken by two veteran generals, Sir John Talbot and Sir Thomas Scales, who arrived from the English base at Chartres on December 1. Orleans meantime acquired an illustrious defender when on October 25 Dunois, the "Bastard of Orleans," entered the city, assuming command in the name of his half-brother, the captive Charles of Orleans. Dunois ordered the suburbs outside the walls razed, to deprive the besiegers of cover that might be used either to prepare an assault or to mine, a favorite medieval siege technique. A standard warning system was installed in the shape of jars of water at intervals on the walls, the disturbance of whose surface would signal digging underneath. But the English lines throughout the siege remained at a distance from the city walls (500 to 600 meters) that precluded mining. For the time being the

Dunois, Bastard of Orleans, Joan's most illustrious companion-in-arms, statue at Chateaudun

English withdrew some or most of their troops to the captured river towns of Meung, Beaugency, and Jargeau. Those remaining garrisoned the Tourelles.

In December, Talbot and Scales brought some of their troops back from the river towns and began to construct a ring of small fortresses blocking the roads on the Orleans side of the river, still at a distance of about 500 meters from the walls. Thus the English did not undertake a close investment of Orleans, but sought rather to blockade the town and starve it into surrender. The church of St. Laurent, directly west of the city and close to the river, was converted into a fortress, and three new forts, christened "London," "Rouen," and "Paris," were built facing the western and northwestern gates. Another fort was built on the Île Charlemagne, in the river downstream from the bridge, and two more were constructed on the southern bank flanking the Tourelles and Augustins, at Champ St. Privé and at St.-Jean-le-Blanc. Finally, the English fortified the church of St. Loup, two kilometers outside the eastern Burgundy gate, threatening the only remaining road out of Orleans.

Yet the city was never completely cut off. At intervals reinforcements and supplies were brought in, by the river and by the Burgundy gate. Early in January Admiral Louis de Culan entered with 200 men, and a month later a force of over 1,000 arrived, under a number of captains, including La Hire. The English also received reinforcements, including some 1,500 Burgundians, along with victuals convoyed from Paris.

Skirmishing was intermittent, as was bombardment. The English artillery had a range of up to 800 meters for its expensive stone cannonballs, which descended almost vertically into the center of Orleans, damaging roofs but usually little else. On December 1 the *Journal du Siège d'Orléans* recorded a bombardment that caused "much harm and damage to several houses and handsome edifices," but did not kill anyone. A cannonball plunged through the roof of an inn in the Rue aux Petits Souliers and crashed onto a table where five men sat at dinner, but all escaped.[7]

On Christmas Day a truce was agreed to from 9 A.M. to 3 P.M. "During this time," the *Journal du Siège* reported, "[Sir William] Glasdale and others of the English lords besought the Bastard of Orleans and the Marshal of Sainte-Sevère that they should have the French minstrels sound the trumpets and clarions: which was granted; and they played the instruments for quite a long time, making much melody. But as soon as the truce was over, everyone was on his guard again."[8]

On the last day of the year, two French knights challenged two Eng-

Siege of Orleans, from the late fifteenth-century Vigiles de Charles VII

lishmen to a joust outside the walls of the city. While French and English lords watched, a Gascon of La Hire's company named Jean le Gasquet unseated his English opponent with a single thrust of the lance, while the other two contenders fought to a draw.[9]

Despite such courtly exchanges, both sides suffered casualties in skirmishes near the various town gates, as the defenders sallied out, or the besiegers attempted surprises.

With the approach of spring, the tension mounted. By hanging on grimly, though they could not storm or even closely invest the city, the English hoped to force a capitulation, while the Orleans defenders hoped for decisive aid from outside. On February 12 an attempt to capture a large wagon train bringing supplies to the English from Paris miscarried in the "Battle of the Herrings," in which Sir John Fastolf skillfully deployed his men and wagons and repelled the attack with heavy casualties. Dunois was wounded, and Sir John Stewart, constable of Scotland, one of the many Scots enlisted on the French side, was killed. The count of Clermont, the king's cousin, escaped but left Orleans, along with several other captains, including La Hire, and a number of troops of the garrison.[10] Other notables, evidently anticipating the fall of the city, departed: Admiral de Culan, chancellor Regnault of Chartres, and the bishop of Orleans. "The people of Orleans were by no means pleased to see them go," commented the *Journal du Siège,* "but they who were leaving, to appease them, promised to send men and supplies."[11]

La Hire and the troops had in fact departed for this purpose, but the citizens of Orleans had a sense of being forsaken. They dispatched an embassy headed by Poton de Xaintrailles to the duke of Burgundy, to ask him to take the city under his personal protection, in behalf of Charles of Orleans.[12] The delegation left Orleans on February 19 and located the duke, probably in one of his Flemish cities. Philip welcomed the opportunity of establishing himself at Orleans, and took the envoys to Paris to offer the proposition to the English regent, the duke of Bedford, who had recently sealed England's alliance with Burgundy by marrying Philip's sister Anne. But Bedford was convinced that Orleans was about to fall into his hands and, in the words of a chronicler, did not wish to "chew meat so that the duke of Burgundy could swallow it." He turned down the idea of a Burgundian Orleans, and the delegation returned on April 17 to report the failure of their mission.[13]

Yet in an unforeseen way the mission was a success. Philip, furious at Bedford's rebuff, withdrew from Orleans his own contingent of troops. Their number, not known though estimated at 1,500, was sufficient for their withdrawal to have "greatly weakened the power of the English," according to the *Chronique de la Pucelle.*[14]

Thus on the eve of Joan's entry into Orleans the Battle of the Herrings had directly weakened the garrison but had indirectly reduced the besieging forces, while a sizable relieving army was assembling at Blois.

The total forces engaged were large by medieval standards. Historians generally agree that the French force at Blois numbered about 4,000. The town's garrison by now numbered perhaps 2,000, and the town militia may have added another 2,000. The strength of the English after the Burgundians had left has been estimated at about 5,000. Thus altogether the French inside and outside Orleans probably outnumbered the English army.[15]

Joan mistakenly believed that the force she was accompanying to Orleans was a relieving army, that is, one intended to drive off the besiegers. In actual fact, it had as its immediate aim the revictualing of

Orleans, from across the Loire just above the site of the old bridge; the cathedral in left foreground

the city. This is shown unmistakably in the route the army took, which surprised and displeased Joan.

Orleans stood on the northern bank of the Loire, its bridge blockaded by the English garrison in the Tourelles, backed by the subsidiary forts on the southern bank. All the bridges between Blois and Orleans were in English hands, as was the bridge at Jargeau, east of Orleans. On the northern bank, the city gates were all blocked by English forts except for the Burgundy (eastern) gate. On this side the English held the fortified church of St. Loup, but St. Loup was situated at such a distance—two kilometers—that land access to the city was quite possible. Access by water from here was even easier, since boats and barges, loaded west of English-held Jargeau, could move downstream. This approach, while practicable for supplies, was not feasible for large numbers of troops.

A relieving army from Blois would have had to march to Orleans on the northern bank of the Loire, through an enemy zone, avoid the forts around the city, and make its entrance at the Burgundy gate, at the risk of attack from St. Loup. The captains who led the army which escorted Joan (Gilles de Rais, Ambroise de Loré, Raoul de Gaucourt, and Poton

Jacques Boucher's house, Orleans, where Joan lodged

de Xaintrailles) instead approached by the southern bank. The *Journal du Siège* explained that the leaders feared for Joan's safety, since the English "hated her and made fun of her letters," and had imprisoned the herald that brought them.[16] Whatever weight Joan's safety carried, a more compelling reason was that the southern approach was more secure for the supply train, since it put the river between the wagons and the bulk of the enemy forces.

Without explaining to Joan what they were doing, they set out from Blois through the Sologne, the flat wooded, marshy area filling the loop of the river south of Orleans. The army slept in the fields. According to her page, Joan had put on her armor and did not take it off to sleep. On Friday, April 29, the army made a wide detour around the English forts guarding the southern end of the Orleans bridge and arrived at a point about two kilometers to the east, across the river from the English-held fort of St. Loup. Dunois and La Hire (who had returned to the city) took "a number of soldiers" of the Orleans garrison, boarded boats, and rowed upriver to meet the army.[17]*

When Joan and Dunois met, a spirited colloquy took place, reported by Dunois. Evidently Joan had expected to confront the main body of the English and force a path through their lines; no one had explained the geography to her, and that Orleans was inaccessible to the army from the southern bank. She was exasperated by Dunois's prudent plan to sail boats and barges eastward (upstream) from the city, load them with the provisions brought by the army, and float them back downstream with the current. Furthermore, a contrary wind balked the operation. Joan addressed Dunois with scant ceremony: "Was it you who advised me to come here, on this side of the river, instead of going straight to where Talbot and the English are?" Dunois explained that he and others wiser than he had made the decision, believing it to be better and safer. Joan answered: "In the name of God, the counsel of God is safer and wiser than yours. You thought you had deceived me, and you deceived yourselves more, for I bring you better help than any knight or city, the help of the King of Heaven. It does not come for love of me, but from God Himself, who, at the plea of St. Louis and St. Charlemagne, has pity on the town of Orleans and will not suffer that enemies hold both the lord of Orleans [Dunois's half-brother] and his city."[19]

At that moment, according to Dunois and Raoul de Gaucourt, the wind changed,† and the boats which had been unable to put out from Orleans hoisted sail and headed upriver. While a party of the garrison created a diversion by skirmishing against the English at St. Loup, the ships loaded the supplies and returned to Orleans.[21]

The army that had escorted the supply train now prepared to return to Blois. Dunois, impressed like others before him by Joan (as well as by the "miracle" of the change of wind), now "had great hopes of her." He wanted to take her at once to Orleans where "they were most eager for her." Joan was reluctant to leave the soldiers "since they were all well confessed and repentant and of good will," and without her they would

---

*According to the testimony of Joan's squire Jean d'Aulon. The *Journal du Siège* says that Joan crossed the river to the northern bank and spent the night at Chécy, east of St. Loup, before Dunois came, but does not explain how she crossed, or what happened to the army that was with her; this version is also contradicted by Dunois's testimony.[18]

†Pasquerel gives a different account: the water, which had been too low to float the ships, suddenly rose.[20]

backslide. Reassured that Pasquerel and his contingent of priests would accompany the soldiers back to Blois, she consented to cross the river with Dunois, La Hire, and her two brothers. On the northern shore, the party delayed until dusk "to avoid the tumult of the people."[22]

At last at eight o'clock an extraordinary real-life historical tableau was enacted as Joan rode through the Burgundy gate, fully armed, on a white horse, her standard carried before her, Dunois at her side, followed by "many other noble and valiant lords, squires, captains, and soldiers, some of the garrison, and citizens of Orleans." The cavalcade was surrounded on all sides by a crowd of soldiers and citizens carrying torches, "as joyful as if they had seen God descending among them," commented the *Journal du Siège,* or "as if she had been an angel of God," said Jean Luillier, one of the citizens. The whole city had taken Joan to its heart in advance, and all "regarded her very affectionately, men, women, even little children." Pressing close, they sought to touch her, or even her horse. A torch coming in contact with Joan's standard set it ablaze. She spurred her horse, turned him, and deftly extinguished the fire, to the marvel of the crowds, "as if she had long fought in wars," commented the *Journal du Siège.* Closely escorted, Joan rode all the way through the city to the Rue du Tabour, where she was to lodge, with her two brothers and her household, at the house of Jacques Boucher, treasurer of the duke of Orleans.[23]

That she did not perceive her role as that of a mere mascot became clear at once. The following day, Saturday, April 30, she called on Dunois to ask about his plans. When she discovered that he intended to return to Blois himself to bring back the relieving army, she was disappointed and frustrated, for she had expected to attack the English that very day. Her page Louis de Coutes reported that she came back from the interview very angry.[24]

She occupied herself by dictating a letter to the English commander Talbot "in her mother tongue, in very simple language" (according to Dunois), advising him to give up the siege and go home, or she would drive him out.[25] She also demanded that the English free her herald Guyenne by whom she had dispatched her letter from Blois. By holding him, in violation of military courtesy, the English made clear that they did not regard her as a military commander. Dunois backed up her demand with a threat to kill English prisoners and emissaries in Orleans. The English replied rudely that "they would burn her, that she was nothing but a whore, and that she should go back to watching her cows."[26]

The gibe indicates that the English too had heard about her and were aware of her peasant origin. The "whore" may have related partly to her dress; camp followers often wore pages' costumes.[27] That a woman could live with soldiers without having sexual relations with them was beyond their belief, just as Joan's comrades-in-arms had regarded their continence in respect to her as nothing short of miraculous. The attitude was not limited to medieval military circles. St. Bernard of Clairvaux bluntly warned against two-sex religious orders because "to be always with a woman and not to have intercourse with her is more difficult than to raise the dead."[28]

To the English retort, Joan delivered a reply in person. Riding out on the bridge that evening, she called across to the English in the Tourelles to surrender in the name of God, on pain of their lives. The English captain Sir William Glasdale and his men retorted with curses and derision, calling her a cow wench and repeating the threat to burn her. One Englishman demanded sarcastically if Joan expected them to surrender to a woman, and called her French escorts "faithless pimps."[29]

Meanwhile Dunois, preparing to leave for Blois, borrowed 600 pounds Tournois from the people of Orleans to pay the garrison and captains "to serve until the army that came with the Maid, and has gone back to Blois, returns to this city to raise the siege," and 500 pounds for crossbow bolts ordered from Blois, "to give to the crossbowmen in this town to raise the siege of the English."[30]

On Sunday, May 1, Joan heard that Dunois and Jean d'Aulon were about to depart. Mounting her horse, she took La Hire and some soldiers and escorted Dunois, interposing herself and her little company between the English and Dunois's party. Once Dunois was on his way, she rode back into the city.[31]

Joan spent the next few days acquainting herself with Orleans, an activity that was enthusiastically reciprocated. The people were so eager to see her, according to the *Journal du Siège,* that they almost broke down the door of Jacques Boucher's house. When she rode out on Sunday, the streets were thronged, "for the people could not get enough of seeing her." They admired her horsemanship, for which she showed a natural ability. She again rode out to an English post to call on its garrison to surrender, this time at the Croix Morin, west of town, but again received only insults in reply.[32]

On Monday, May 2, Joan carried out an extensive reconnaissance of the English forts and army, followed by "a great crowd of people, who had much joy in her sight and nearness." Afterward she returned to town and heard vespers in the cathedral.[33]

On the morning of Wednesday, May 4, Dunois returned with the relieving army, and Joan rode out to meet them.[34] To Jean d'Aulon the fact that with Joan's escort they were able to enter the city "before the enemy's eyes" without opposition seemed almost miraculous.[35] Why did the English not attack the relieving force? British military historian J. F. C. Fuller speculates that their disposition, deployed in their several forts, prevented them from concentrating for an attack.[36] The English system of "circumvallation"—encircling with separate bastilles—was later described by Jean de Bueil, author of the late-fifteenth-century semifictional account of the Hundred Years War, *Le Jouvencel,* as outdated, and it appears to have been tactically ineffective, since it neither cut off the city nor facilitated an assault.[37]

That day Joan and Jean d'Aulon shared their noon meal in her lodgings. Afterward Dunois came to tell her that he had learned that Sir John Fastolf was en route from Paris with reinforcements and provisions for the English army. He had reached Janville, thirty-five kilometers to the north. Far from being alarmed, Joan was delighted (according to d'Aulon) and answered, "Bastard, Bastard, in the name of God, I order you that as soon as you hear of the arrival of Fastolf you will let me know, for if he gets through without my knowing it, I promise that I'll have your head cut off." Dunois took this ferocious threat in good part, and merely answered that he didn't doubt it for a moment, and that he would certainly let her know.[38]

When Dunois had left, Joan lay down in her room on the second floor of the house to nap, sharing the bed with her hostess, Jacques Boucher's wife, while Jean d'Aulon stretched out on a couch nearby. Just as he dozed off, Joan sprang out of bed and wakened him. "In God's name, my Counsel has told me that I must attack the English; but I don't know whether I must go to their bastilles or against Fastolf, who is to provision them." D'Aulon rose immediately and helped Joan with her armor.[39]

Downstairs, she found her page Louis de Coutes and scolded him: "Oh, wicked boy [*sanglant garçon,* literally, bloody boy], why did you not tell me that French blood is being spilled?" and ordered him to fetch her horse.[40] At that moment, d'Aulon reported, they heard "a great noise and loud cries from the citizens, saying that the enemy was doing great harm to the French."[41] While he put on his own armor, Joan ran into the street, calling to Louis to bring her standard from upstairs.[42] He handed it out through the window as she mounted her horse to gallop off to the Burgundy gate—"sparks flew from the pavement," recalled an eyewitness.[43] Louis and Jean followed their headlong mistress.

Without notifying Joan, Dunois had launched an attack against the English garrison in the fortified church of St. Loup, two kilometers east of town. Isolated from most of the other English strongholds, St. Loup was the most vulnerable fort in the besiegers' line. Its fall would free the road east and make easy the future supply of the city. That Dunois had kept his plans from Joan doubtless reflects fear for her safety, but it also indicates that he and the other captains still did not really take her seriously.

At the Burgundy gate Joan met a party carrying a wounded man, and exclaimed, according to d'Aulon, that she never saw French blood spilled without feeling her hair rise in horror.

Joan, d'Aulon, and others who had joined them galloped on through the gateway and soon saw the battle raging in the distance. According to the account in the *Journal du Siège,* Dunois had been pressing the assault when a force of English from their nearest neighboring fort, St. Pouair, arrived and attacked the attackers. Joan's reinforcements, apparently city militia, fell on these English. D'Aulon said that he had never seen so many soldiers of their side at one time before.[44] On catching sight of Joan, the embattled French gave a cheer, renewed their assault, and the English in St. Loup suddenly yielded. Inside the church, according to the *Journal du Siège,* 114 English lay dead, leaving only forty to be taken prisoner. The attackers "leveled, wrecked, and burned the whole fort from top to bottom."[45]

The following day, Thursday, May 5, was Ascension Day, and Joan informed Pasquerel that she would "wage no war and bear no arms." She issued two orders: any soldier who intended to fight on Friday must go to confession, and no camp followers should accompany the army, "as it was for such sins that God would let us lose the war," Pasquerel reported, adding, "and it was done as Joan had ordered."[46]

Dunois now called a council of war to discuss future strategy. This time Joan was included, along with the other captains—Raoul de Gaucourt, La Hire, Xaintrailles, Gilles de Rais—and the decision was made to attack the Tourelles and the other fortifications at the southern end of the bridge.[47]

According to Jean Chartier's chronicle (late and secondhand) Joan was summoned to the council only belatedly, after it had been decided to have her lead a feint against St. Laurent and the other English forts on the Orleans side of the river, letting her think that this was the principal attack. Joan was reported angry at being excluded from the decision making and, when Dunois finally explained the plan to her, at being assigned a secondary role.[48] None of the eyewitnesses mentions the incident, however, and there is no record of the diversionary attack—though modern attempts to account for the failure of the English in the western forts to intervene at the Tourelles have inspired speculation that it may nevertheless have been made.

Joan dispatched a final summons to the English commanding them to go home or "I will give you such a *hahay* that it will be forever remembered." A postscript explained that she could not use normal channels for delivering messages, since "you seize my messengers, and have held my envoy Guyenne." If Guyenne was returned, she would send them in exchange some of the prisoners taken in the attack on St. Loup. Tying the letter to an arrow, she handed it to a bowman to shoot across the broken span of the bridge to the English in the Tourelles, crying out to them, "Here's news for you! Read it!" The English replied with the usual insults—"Here's news from the Armagnac whore!"—to which Joan responded with angry tears.[49]

Early on Friday morning, May 6, Joan confessed to Pasquerel and, in company with her household, heard him say mass. Then she rode out of the city once more by the Burgundy gate, with Dunois, La Hire, Gilles de Rais, and other captains, knights, and squires, at the head of a large force (4,000 men-at-arms, according to the *Journal du Siège*). The troops forded the shallow near arm of the river to the small Île des Toiles, whence a pontoon bridge supported by two boats had been built to the southern bank.[50]

Assembled across the river, the attackers confronted two obstacles between themselves and the Tourelles: the little fortress of St.-Jean-le-Blanc, to the east of the bridgehead, and the fortified monastery of the Augustins, directly south of it. The Tourelles itself was now fronted with a large bridgehead fortification crowned with a palisade and surrounded by a moat, built by the English to protect the drawbridge.

On the approach of the French, the English in St.-Jean-le-Blanc withdrew into the Augustins.[51] This fortress and the bridgehead fortifications, with their moats and high palisades, so impressed Alençon when he examined them later that he felt they must have been captured "by a miracle rather than by force of arms," and concluded that they offered such protection that a few defenders could resist many times their number of attackers.[52]

An advance party of the French, arriving at the Augustins, "perceived that they were not strong enough to take it," according to Jean d'Aulon, and fell back toward the main body. Seeing them give way, the English burst out of the fortification with loud cries and charged. At that moment Joan and La Hire, who had just crossed the river in boats with their horses, following the main body of the army, galloped up and joined the melee.[53] "Let us go boldly in the name of the Lord" was Joan's rallying cry, according to Simon Beaucroix, a knight.[54]

Jean d'Aulon described an incident in the battle: he had been detailed to guard Joan's passage to the Augustins with other soldiers, including a Spaniard named Alfonso de Partada, and called out to a knight, "a handsome man, tall and well-armed," to join them. The knight refused, considering it dishonorable to remain in the rear. After an exchange of "arrogant words" between the knight and Alfonso, the two agreed, according to d'Aulon, "to ride together side by side against the enemy, to prove which was more valiant and which performed his duty better." Clasping hands, the pair galloped in tandem at top speed toward the Augustins and reached the foot of the palisade.

Despite the impetuous onslaught of the two knights and the other attackers, the fortifications held. Inside the palisade d'Aulon caught sight of a "big, strong, and powerful Englishman," well armed and equipped, who was putting up such a resistance that the knights could not enter the enclosure. D'Aulon pointed him out to a famous gunner of the royal army, Jean de Montesclere, known as Jean the Lorrainer, telling him to fire at the Englishman who was causing such havoc. The gunner aimed his weapon, a culverin—in effect, a hand cannon or giant musket—and fired. The Englishman toppled over. "And then the two knights gained passage into the enclosure, followed by all the others of their company." A furious battle raged briefly inside the enclosure. Then the English survivors abandoned the Augustins and retreated over the drawbridge into the Tourelles.[55]

Night fell, with the French in possession of the Augustins and the English in the Tourelles on the bridge, between the French and the city.

Joan was exhausted (the *Chronique de la Pucelle* says that she had been wounded in the foot by a calthrop, a spiked iron ball planted on the ground to impede cavalry—though no other source mentions this detail), but she resisted return to the city.[56] "Are we to abandon our people?" she asked, according to Simon Beaucroix.[57] She was finally persuaded to go back to town, with some of the soldiers, while all night long the people of Orleans ferried provisions across the river to those remaining on the southern shore—2,388 large loaves of bread, according to municipal accounts, seven barrels of wine, oats for the horses.[58]

Joan had intended to fast that day—a Friday—but was too weary and too hungry. She ate supper, and afterward a knight came to tell her that the captains had decided that, considering their numbers, the victory that God had already granted them, and the fact that the city was now well supplied with food, it would be wiser not to fight on the following day, but to wait for further reinforcements. Joan replied: "You have been in your council, and I in mine; and believe me, the council of the Lord will be carried out and will endure, and your council will perish." Then she told Pasquerel, "Get up early tomorrow, even earlier than today, and do your best. Keep close to me, because tomorrow I will have much to do, more than ever before, and I will be wounded above the breast."[59]

During the night the English evacuated the little fortress of St. Privé which protected the Tourelles on the west as St.-Jean-le-Blanc had protected it on the east.

On Saturday, May 7, Joan followed her advice to Pasquerel and rose early. A witness reported that someone brought her a shad from the river for breakfast, but she told Jacques Boucher, "Keep it until tonight, and I'll bring you back a *godon,* *" adding, "and I will come back by the bridge"—in other words, after capturing the Tourelles.[60]

An incident that morning which bore out the unknown knight's report of the night before was narrated by Simon Charles, the royal officer who described Joan's arrival at Chinon.† The commanders had decided not to continue the assault, and when Joan reached the Burgundy gate she found Raoul de Gaucourt, second only to Dunois in prestige and author-

*An Englishman, supposedly from "god damn," the favorite imprecation of the English soldier, though this derivation has been questioned.

†Simon placed the incident a day earlier (Friday, May 6), which, however, does not square with logic or other known facts, e.g., that Raoul de Gaucourt was at Thursday's council and agreed to Friday's attack.

ity, stationed there to halt soldiers from going out. Joan was furious at this cautious decision, and her view that the advantage should be pressed was shared by "many soldiers and men of the city." Joan said that Gaucourt was a bad man, and told him, "Like it or not, the soldiers will go out and they will win as they have won before." The garrison and town militia rallied to Joan's orders with an enthusiasm that caused Gaucourt, who stood aside and allowed the troops to pass out of the city, to declare afterward that his opposition to Joan had placed him "in the greatest danger."[61]

Once more crossing the river and reaching the Augustins, Joan summoned "all the lords and captains," according to Jean d'Aulon, to plan the attack, first against the great outwork—palisade, moat, and earthworks—which the English had built to protect the drawbridge leading to the Tourelles.[62] The French surrounded the rampart and assaulted it from three sides. The English above showered them with arrows, missiles, and cannonballs. As the French placed their scaling ladders, the defenders hurled the assailants down and battled them with axes, lances, maces, guisarmes,* and even with their fists.[63] Early in the fighting, Joan was wounded, as she had foretold, by an arrow that pierced her shoulder. She "was afraid, and wept, and was comforted," Pasquerel reported, as the wound was dressed with olive oil and lard. Some soldiers wanted to use a spell to heal the wound, but she refused, saying that it was a sin to use magical cures.[64]

Dunois and the other captains advised suspending the assault until the next day. Joan would hear none of it. "In the name of God, you will soon enter the fortress, never doubt it, and the English will have no more strength against you. Rest for a while, eat and drink." They did as she bade; after which she told them, "Return to the assault, before God, for the English will have no more will to defend themselves, and their Tourelles and their ramparts will be taken."[65]

The attack was renewed. The English fought, said the *Journal du Siège,* as if they believed they were immortal.[66] At sunset the leaders of the army were once more ready to sound retreat. Exactly what followed is uncertain in detail but clear enough in its general sense. According to Dunois, Joan again asked him to wait. Mounting her horse, she withdrew into a nearby vineyard, where she prayed for eight minutes.[67] Returning,

*Spears with scythe-shaped heads.

she seized her standard and took up her position on the outer edge of
the moat, declaring (as Louis de Coutes reported) that when the wind
blew her standard toward the rampart, it would be theirs.[68]

Jean d'Aulon gave a somewhat different and very circumstantial account: retreat had already been sounded and the army was withdrawing,
when he saw Joan's standard-bearer, exhausted, hand her standard to a
man known as the Basque. D'Aulon conceived the idea that if Joan's
standard were carried forward, the French would rally behind it and
might still succeed in taking the fortification that night. He asked the
Basque if he would follow him if he ran toward the rampart, and the
Basque promised to do so. Leaping into the moat, d'Aulon approached
the farther bank, holding his shield to ward off the English missiles, and
expecting the Basque to follow. But when Joan saw her standard in the
Basque's hands, she seized the shaft, crying, "My standard! My standard!" and shook it so vigorously that d'Aulon believed the others must
think she was signaling. He shouted, "Oh, Basque! Is this how you keep
your promise?" Whereupon the Basque wrenched the standard from
Joan's hands and brought it to d'Aulon, while Joan's company rallied
again and stormed the rampart.[69]

The *Journal du Siège* reported that Joan said to a knight who was
standing nearby, "Watch for the moment when the tip of my standard
touches the wall." When he cried, "Joan, the tip is touching!" she replied,
"It's all yours, go in." And the troops burst into the rampart.[70]

The English tried to retreat into the Tourelles, but the French attack
now closed in on them from both directions. Some of the Orleans militia
that had remained in the city had organized an assault from the northern
bank. They moved onto the bridge, bringing ladders and pieces of
troughs (perhaps from the eaves of houses) to rig a temporary span over
the broken arches and threaten the Tourelles from this side. The troughs
proved too short, but a carpenter fashioned a scaffold that reached the
farther arch, and a knight of the order of Rhodes ventured out on it. His
example was at once followed—"a greater miracle than any other performed by our Lord that day," the *Journal du Siège* thought, considering
that the scaffold was "marvelously long and narrow, and high in the air,
without any support."[71]

Simultaneously, as the French poured into the outwork from the
southern bank, the English tried to retreat across the drawbridge, but the
French had set fire to a boat and floated it down the river. It came

accurately to rest against the drawbridge, setting it ablaze. Many of the English (four or five hundred, said the *Journal du Siège*) fell into the river and were drowned, among them Sir William Glasdale, the commander of the Tourelles. The handful of remaining defenders were soon compelled to surrender.[72]

Pasquerel, in an echo of his story about the soldier at Chinon who had insulted Joan and later drowned, reported with satisfaction that Joan had shouted to Glasdale, "Clasdas, Clasdas, yield to the King of Heaven! You have called me a whore, but I have great pity for your soul and the souls of your men." When Glasdale and his men drowned, Joan wept for their souls.[73] The *Journal du Siège* expressed a more practical regret: all the enemy lords were killed, leaving only common soldiers to be taken prisoner, which was a great misfortune, since they brought no ransom.[74]

The dramatic reversal of the war's fortune, swiftly reported in Paris, struck dismay to the hearts of the Anglo-Burgundians, and lent credence to the idea that Joan was a witch. "It was said that she told an English captain to leave the siege with his company or evil would come to them all," recorded the *Journal d'un Bourgeois de Paris.* "He cursed her, calling her whore and tart; she told him that in spite of themselves they would all very soon depart, but that he would not see it, and that many of his men would be killed. And so it happened." The Bourgeois added funerary details: "Afterwards [Glasdale] was fished up, cut in quarters, and boiled, and embalmed"; the body spent a week in a chapel in Paris before it was shipped to England for burial.[75]

In Orleans the bells rang, and clergy and people sang the "Te Deum Laudamus." The *Journal du Siège* reported that Joan remained with a part of the army that camped south of the river,[76] but more probably, as Dunois says, she returned with him to Orleans by the bridge, as she had promised they would. They were received with "transports of joy and thanksgiving." Joan went to her lodging to have her wound dressed, and supped on bread dipped in wine mixed with water—the first meal she had eaten all day. (Someone else must have eaten the shad.)[77]

Early on Sunday, May 8, the English in the western forts at last stirred. Abandoning their forts, they assembled in battle array in the open, as if to challenge the French. Joan donned a coat of mail—her wound prevented her from wearing her plate armor—and rode out of town with the other captains and knights, men-at-arms, and citizens of Orleans, ranging themselves in order of battle facing the enemy.[78] The English, practicing their usual tactic of standing on the defensive, awaited attack, perhaps hoping to retrieve their defeat with an eleventh-hour Agincourt. But Joan (undoubtedly in agreement with Dunois, Gaucourt, and the others) forbade the French to charge, and for an hour the two forces faced each other without a blow being struck. The *Journal du Siège* attributed Joan's prudence to her reluctance to fight on the Sabbath, but on other occasions she did not scruple to fight on holy days.[79]

The *Chronique de la Pucelle,* a compilation of other chronicles made some twenty years after the event, described Joan as sending for an altar and vestments and having two masses said for the French army. Then she asked whether the English were still facing them. "No, they are turned toward Meung." She is supposed to have replied, "Let them go —our Lord does not want us to fight them today; you will have them another time."[80] Eyewitnesses, however, merely say that after an hour the English began to depart—Jean d'Aulon says "discomfited and in confusion,"[81] the *Journal du Siège,* more credibly, in good order, to take refuge in Meung and Beaugency, the two towns they held on the river west of Orleans. The French harried their rear guard and captured bombards, cannons, bows, and crossbows. The *Journal du Siège* added a symbolic incident: among the retreating English was an Augustinian monk, Talbot's confessor, who dragged a French prisoner in fetters. The Frenchman overpowered the monk and forced him to carry him on his shoulders back to Orleans "and thus escaped his ransom."[82]

Miraculously, as it seemed, the siege of Orleans was raised. Joan, the captains, and the soldiers returned triumphantly to the city, where the day was celebrated with "a solemn procession and a sermon." The joy and the solemnity were justified. The turning point in the Hundred Years War had at last arrived.

6. The Loire Campaign and the Battle of Patay

MODERN (MALE) HISTORIANS have generally disparaged or minimized Joan's military talents. Anatole France in his biography of Joan (1908) pictures her as little more than a mascot, forever praying or in ecstasy, paying no attention to such practical considerations as terrain, roads, fortifications, weapons, and enemy forces, and substituting for tactics a ban on prostitution and blasphemy. "She thought that if [the army] fought in a state of grace they would win. That was her entire military science, aside from her lack of fear." The lack of fear, however, was significant in Anatole France's estimation, since it provided inspiring example.[1]

Edouard Perroy, the leading twentieth-century authority on the Hundred Years War, came to a similar conclusion: Joan "knew nothing about the art of war, and thought that abstaining from oaths and brothels was enough to earn victory for the soldiers. . . . Despite her ascendancy over the troops, Joan did not lead them. She left that duty to the captains, such as Dunois, Alençon, and Richemont. Though their decisions were often contrary to her wishes, she finally gave in to them. She was content to exhort the combatants, say what advice her voices gave, step into the breach at critical moments and rally the infantry."[2]

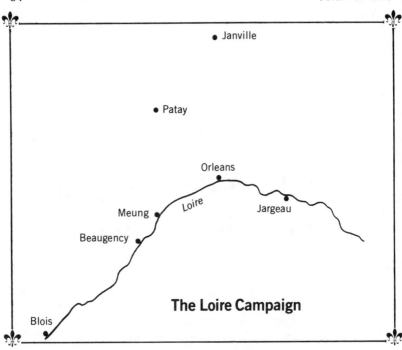

The Loire Campaign

Numerous other modern writers, both French and English, echo Anatole France and Perroy. Yet the repeated testimony of Joan's contemporaries expresses a different view. Dunois gave her high marks for skill and judgment. Her disposition of the army on one occasion* was in his eyes "so admirable that even the two or three most famous and experienced captains would not have made as good a plan."[3] Alençon too asserted that "everyone was astonished that she acted with such wisdom and clear-sightedness in military matters, as cleverly as a great captain with twenty or thirty years' experience."[4] Thibaut d'Armagnac, a knight who fought at her side at Orleans, declared that "in the leading and drawing up of armies and in the conduct of war, in disposing an army for battle and exhorting the soldiers, she behaved like the most experienced captain . . . one with a whole lifetime of experience."[5]

In judging both the contemporary and latter-day views, it must be kept

*At Troyes.

in mind that generalship in the modern sense scarcely existed in the fifteenth century. Anatole France conceded that "many leaders, especially princes of the blood, did not know much more" about war than Joan.[6] And Perroy says, "At that time, the art of war did not amount to much. Courage, confidence and boldness readily made up for it."[7] Joan's ignorance of the roads leading to Orleans is understandable enough in the absence of maps. Limited geographic and topographic information discouraged if it did not prevent the planning and coordinating of marches and maneuvers. The armies themselves were ill-adapted to sophisticated strategy or tactics. Though the collection of independent companies that formed Charles VII's army represented a historic advance over the old assemblage of private military parties of Agincourt and Crécy, it still lacked a critical element in modern military organization, the echelon. In the absence of higher headquarters (regiments, divisions, corps), each of twenty-odd captains had to be given instructions, which necessarily came down to such simplicities as direction of march, objective, and to attack or not to attack.

The command function had hardly progressed from the feudal pattern. The absence of echeloned units meant a corresponding absence of echeloned rank. Though for the forthcoming campaign Alençon was accorded by Charles the designation of "lieutenant general," there was no implication of his assuming command over Dunois, or even over La Hire and Xaintrailles. Command decision was by consensus, arrived at by council. It was this very combination of the simplicity of order giving and consensus decision making that gave scope to an outsider armed with prestige, ability, and determination.

Even the English, whose army had been recruited on a professional basis since Edward III's time, lagged behind the Roman army of the Caesars in organizational sophistication. The famous longbow gained its spectacular victories thanks to the accommodating tactics of the enemy, whose massed charges presented the target it needed. Matched against the solitary French feudal field tactic of advancing in "battles"—two or three massive lines—the solitary English tactic of forming a defensive line of archers behind pointed stakes was very effective. But if an enemy grown prudent refused to attack, as the French refused in the confrontation following the relief of Orleans, the tactic was useless. It was also useless against an enemy who attacked before the archers had time to form up and drive their stakes, as was about to be shown.

Thus, despite the longbow, the art of war had remained essentially static. But at the very moment of Joan of Arc's appearance, the novel element of gunpowder was making its potential felt. Technical and economic problems had slowed the maturing of the new weapon, but by 1429 purchases of gunpowder by the French royal treasury were in thousands of pounds instead of the hundreds of the previous century.[8] In the campaign against the English strongholds on the Loire, the artillery proved a conspicuous factor in French success. Therefore it is interesting that Alençon singled out Joan's grasp of this arm in his encomium on her military ability: "and especially in the placing of artillery, for in that she acquitted herself magnificently."[9]

Given the picturesquely transitional character of military science in 1429, with armored knights, archers, and gunners simultaneously on the battlefield, it may well be that Joan, bringing to warfare the fresh eye of an amateur, better perceived the potential of gunpowder than did captains handicapped by "a lifetime of experience."

Her peasant origin may also have helped. The lords and knights who foolishly charged the English lines at Agincourt were considered even by their contemporaries to be obedient to an out-of-date tradition of chivalric warfare. The tradition was rooted in part in a view of war as sport, a sort of grand-scale version of the knightly tournament. Such a view obscured political content. Joan's emphatic reiteration of the war's political meaning—that Charles should be king and that the English should quit France—is the practical ideology of a peasant or bourgeois.

Her attitude toward combat was correspondingly practical. To insist on the soldiers' "abstaining from oaths and brothels" (she even rebuked Alençon for blasphemy) or to ban camp followers (whom she personally drove off with blows of the flat of her sword) was perhaps less worthy of ridicule than Anatole France thought. Both rules of conduct were conducive to military discipline, a quality more needed than found in a fifteenth-century army. Her conviction that God was on her side did not lead her into the fatal illusion that God would do the work. She understood, and made it clear to the soldiers, that the army had to fight, and fight with determination, renewing the attack as often as necessary, and then God would give the victory.

Perroy and other modern writers notwithstanding, Joan did not leave to the captains the military decisions she considered important. At Orleans, Joan's advice was at first disregarded, but later taken into account. According to at least two witnesses—Pasquerel and Simon Charles—the decision to attack the rampart before the Tourelles was hers. When others wanted to suspend the assault, Joan, despite her wound, again intervened, and again decisively. That she sometimes bowed to the decisions of others in no way detracts from her leadership and independence of judgment.

The emphasis that both contemporary and later writers have laid on Joan's contribution to morale has somewhat obscured the sense of the contribution. Dunois's testimony has been frequently quoted: "I swear that the English, two hundred of whom had previously been sufficient to rout eight hundred or a thousand of the royal army, [from the moment of Joan's arrival] became so powerless that four or five hundred soldiers and men-at-arms could fight against what seemed to be the whole power of England."[10] In similar vein, information from the English side testified to the "panic" she caused: a letter from the duke of Bedford to his royal nephew Henry VI three years later ascribing his defeats in France to the "fear that [the army] had of a disciple and limb of the Fiend, called the Pucelle, that used false enchantments and sorcery, which stroke and discomfiture not only caused in great part the desertion of a number of your people there, but also diminished the courage of the remaining in marvelous wise, and encouraged your adverse party and enemies to assemble themselves forthwith in great numbers."[11] But the "diminished courage" of the English was not evident to eyewitnesses at Orleans, where they fought "as if they thought they were immortal." Desertions doubtless occurred in the Anglo-Burgundian ranks, but the English problem at Orleans was less morale than faulty strategy and the inherent weakness of their position.

Contemporary Burgundian chronicler Enguerrand de Monstrelet asserted that Joan's enemies "feared her more than any captain, or commander."[12] Again, there is no factual evidence of panic in the Burgundian ranks.

Morale aside, the French leaders were inclined to view Joan's role as providential rather than practical. "From what I have heard from the soldiers and captains who were [at Orleans]," Alençon said, "they all regarded almost everything that happened at Orleans as a miracle from God and considered it to have been the work of no human hands but to have come from on high."[13] Her squire Jean d'Aulon thought "all the Maid's exploits rather divine and miraculous than otherwise."[14]

Yet divine intervention might have been secured by a Maid who did no more than pray and fast. Joan participated as well as prayed, and her participation had a large significance. What she offered was leadership, the ability to get soldiers and captains to listen to her and do as she wanted them to do. This she achieved through her self-confidence, her determination, and her courage, a contribution recognized by freethinkers like Anatole France, but not given enough weight by them. It was Joan's success in rallying and exhorting the soldiers at Orleans, under fire and even wounded, that made victory possible. Her courage was not rooted in any illusion of immunity. When she heard it said that she was not afraid because she knew she would not be killed, she replied that she "had no more assurance of that than any soldier."[15]

Joan was far from being the first medieval woman to command men in battle. Neither was she the first to take part in combat. Throughout the Middle Ages queens and great ladies had, when necessity dictated, worn armor, ridden chargers, led armies, and defended castles and lands. Women of lesser rank had joined men in resisting invaders and marauders. The women of Orleans had already played an active part in the defense of the city before Joan arrived on the scene. According to the *Journal du Siège,* women helped defend the Tourelles, pouring hot ashes and boiling oil and wielding lances.

Yet Joan was the first woman of the people to assume a leadership role. The English gibe of "cow wench" was aimed less at her sex than at her class,[16] which probably provided a better physical preparation for military life than an aristocratic one, particularly in the late medieval atmosphere of increasing luxury among the nobility. Even Joan's native common sense, emphasized by Michelet and Shaw, was a quality that came more naturally to a peasant woman than a countess.

On Monday, May 9, Joan left Orleans, in company with Dunois, Gilles de Rais and several knights, squires, and men-at-arms, to report to the king. The *Journal du Siège* recorded that the people of Orleans wept as they thanked her, "offering their goods and persons for her to use as she saw fit." Joan cheerfully returned their thanks. The first task of her mission had been fulfilled: the siege of Orleans had been raised, "during which," commented the *Journal,* "had been accomplished many fine feats of arms, skirmishes, assaults, and numerous engines were seen, new contrivances, and subtleties of war."[17]

Two not very reliable sources (the *Chronique de la Pucelle* and the chronicle of Eberhard Windecken, German emperor Sigismund's treasurer) say that Joan went directly to Tours. Windecken describes a charming scene, which seems like the way Joan's meeting with the king after her great victory should have happened: Joan arrived in the city before the king and, taking her standard in her hand, rode to meet him. She bowed low in the saddle before him, and he raised her up, and "was so joyful that people thought he would like to have kissed her."[18]

Dunois's eyewitness account, however, says that the meeting took place at Loches, 150 kilometers southwest of Orleans, where a royal castle, somewhat larger than Chinon, rose on an eminence above the river Indres—like Chinon, a 300-year composition, from the huge square eleventh-century donjon built by the counts of Anjou to the fourteenth-century royal palace.

Joan's purpose, fully shared by Dunois and the others, was clear. It was to ask the king for troops "with which to recover the castles and towns on the Loire," as Dunois explained, "that is to say, Meung, Beaugency, and Jargeau, so as to clear an open and safe road for him to go to Reims for his consecration." Joan and her companions found the king closeted with his council. Joan knocked, and as soon as she was admitted, fell on her knees and embraced Charles's legs, saying, as Dunois remembered it, "Noble dauphin, do not hold such lengthy and protracted council; but come to the city of Reims to receive your worthy crown."

One councillor, Christopher de Harcourt, asked her whether her voices had told her to make this demand. She replied, yes, that she was receiving pressing advice on the matter. Then Christopher said, "Will you not tell us here, in the presence of the king, how your counsel speaks to you?" Dunois tells us that Joan's face reddened, but she answered, "I understand well enough what you want to know, and I will freely tell you." The king added his voice to the request: "Joan, please tell us what he asks, in the presence of those who are here."

Then Joan explained that when things were going badly because the others did not have confidence in her counsel from God, she drew apart from them and prayed, telling God that those to whom she spoke did not easily believe her; and when she had prayed, she heard a voice saying to her: "Daughter of God, go, go, go. I will help you, go!" When she heard the voice, she felt a great joy and wanted to remain forever in that state. Dunois reported that when she thus repeated the words of her voices, "she exulted in marvelous fashion, raising her eyes to the heavens."[19]

King and council gave in to Joan's pleas, and the army's mission of clearing the enemy from the Loire strongholds was confirmed. Alençon was placed in command, but Joan's role was far less ambiguous than a month earlier. The *Journal du Siège* perhaps exaggerated it: along with "a great number of soldiers and artillery," the king "placed the Maid in [Alençon's] company, commanding him expressly to behave and act entirely at her advice."[20]

Alençon accepted Joan's help without reservations. When he had "left his wife to come to the army with Joan," as he himself expressed it, Jeanne d'Alençon confided to Joan her worries about her husband.* She feared for his life, though not for that alone. When the young lord had been captured at Verneuil in 1424, the duchess had had to sell part of their lands to pay his ransom. Joan reassured her: "My lady, have no fear. I will return him to you safely, in the same state as he is now or better."[21]

The townspeople at Loches were nearly as enthusiastic over Joan as the inhabitants of Orleans. They "seized her horse by the legs and kissed her hands and feet," as prelate Pierre de Versailles recalled, so that he felt called upon to rebuke her. "It was wrong of her to permit this, it was not seemly, she must beware of this sort of thing, for it drove men to idolatry." Joan answered, "In truth, I should not know how to protect myself from such temptations, if God did not protect me."[22]

A valuable effect of her celebrity was the recruitment of volunteers to the army. Among them were two young Breton noblemen, Guy and André de Laval. A letter dated Wednesday, June 8, 1429, from Guy to his mother and grandmother, gives an eyewitness picture of Joan's activities just before the Loire campaign, and a sense of the excitement that her presence stirred.[23]

On Sunday, June 5, Guy and his brother André arrived at St. Aignan, south of Blois, to offer their services to the king, whom the next day they accompanied to Selles-en-Berry, a short distance to the east. Joan, already in Selles, was summoned before the king. "I was told by some that this was for my sake, so that I could see her," Guy wrote his mother. Arriving clad in armor but bareheaded and carrying a lance, she "welcomed my brother and me." Later in the day, Guy called on Joan at her lodgings. "She sent for wine, and told me that she would soon have me

---

*There is no indication when this conversation occurred. The Alençon chronicler says it was shortly after Joan's arrival at Chinon, at St. Florent, near Saumur, but more probably it was later, since Alençon did not join Joan's army until after the relief of Orleans.

drinking in Paris." To the young man "it seemed an entirely divine thing
—not only her deeds, but to see and hear her." Joan told him that three
days before his arrival she had sent "a very small gold ring, a very small
thing, and she wished it had been better" to his grandmother, Anne de
Laval, who in her youth had been married to Bertrand du Guesclin,
Charles V's redoubtable constable.

That day at vespers (6 P.M.), Joan left for Romorantin, northeast of
Selles. "I saw her mount her horse, entirely in white armor [*vermeil*], but
without a helmet, a small axe in her hand," Guy reported. At the door
of her lodgings, the horse, a great black charger, shied violently and
would not let her mount. She told the men who were holding him to take
him to the cross that stood in front of the church. "And then she
mounted, while he stood as still as if he were tied. And she turned toward
the door of the church and said in a womanly voice, 'You, priests and
people of the church, make a procession and offer prayers to God.' And
then she went on her way, calling, 'Forward, forward!', her standard
unfurled, carried by a gracious page, and she with her small axe in her
hand. And one of her brothers [Pierre], who came a week ago, left with
her, also in white armor."

That same day, Guy de Laval reported, Alençon arrived in Selles with
"a very great company." On Wednesday Guy engaged the duke in a
game of tennis and beat him; later that day Guy's cousin Gilles de Rais
appeared, "to swell my company." Guy wrote: "Never have men gone
into an enterprise with better will than this one." What was lacking was
money: "There is none at all at court." Guy entreated his mother to sell
or mortgage land, or do whatever necessary to raise funds.

Constable Arthur de Richemont was also expected, with an additional
thousand men, but his role in the coming campaign was in doubt. He had
capped his history of changes of allegiance the year before by a rebellion
against the king.

Alençon, Dunois, and Gaucourt were to leave Selles that day, Guy
wrote, to join the Maid; the king wanted to keep Guy with him until the
English strongholds on the Loire had been taken and the road to Reims
cleared, "but God forbid that I should stay with the king until we go to
Reims and not join in the siege of those places. He who remains behind
will be lost."

On Thursday, June 9, Alençon and Joan and the rest of the army
re-entered Orleans, to be received "with very great joy by all the citi-

zens."[24] The campaign began next day, aimed at the English garrisons that, reinforced by contingents from the English besieging army at Orleans, held the three towns with their stone-arch bridges: Jargeau, east of Orleans, and Meung and Beaugency west. The frequently reported English relief force from Paris was still expected at any moment. The decision was made to strike first at Jargeau, to the east. The army marched as usual under its individual commanders. The force under Alençon's personal command, numbering 600 "lances,"* 1,800 to 2,400 men, took the lead, bivouacking Saturday night (June 11) in a wood near Jargeau. Dunois and mercenary captain Florent d'Illiers joined them there on Sunday with another 600 lances.[26] There may have been other infantry, in addition to the artillery, which followed by boat. The *Journal du Siège* stated that the French army numbered "about 8,000 combatants, on horseback and on foot, some carrying guisarmes, axes, crossbows, others maces."[27] The number is probably exaggerated; a fresh report of the approach of the English relief army under Sir John Fastolf estimated it at only 2,000 men, but the council of war that assembled indicated a fear that the French were outnumbered by the combined English forces. "Some were of the opinion," Alençon recalled, "that an assault should be made on the town, while others held the contrary, asserting that the English had great power and large numbers." Finally Joan intervened, and decisively. She declared that they should not fear any numbers, nor hesitate to attack the English, for God was conducting the campaign. If she were not sure of this, she would rather be minding her sheep than exposing herself to danger.[28]

Won over by her confidence, the captains agreed to an immediate advance on the suburbs of Jargeau. The English sallied out and drove back the attackers. Joan seized her standard and led a counterattack, exhorting the soldiers to be of good courage, and drove the English in turn back inside the town walls. The French occupied the suburbs, which permitted bombardment of the town by the artillery throughout the following day and night.

Disagreement again arose. In the midst of a council, word came that La Hire, on his own, was parleying with the English commander, the earl

---

*A lance at full, or paper, strength consisted of a group of four to six men: an armed knight, plus two archers and sometimes a swordsman, plus one or two valets or pages armed with daggers. But like all military formations, lances must have been typically under strength.[25]

of Suffolk, who offered to surrender Jargeau if he were not relieved within fifteen days. Believing that Fastolf was close by, the French captains refused, but expressed their willingness to agree to a surrender of the town that would allow the English to depart with all their equipment. Joan vetoed this prudent proposal, stipulating that they must leave "in their doublets and tunics"—without armor or weapons. Suffolk refused the terms.[29]

La Hire "was sent for, and came," and an attack was agreed upon. The heralds cried, "To the charge!" and Joan called to Alençon, "Forward, gentle duke! to the assault!" Alençon had misgivings, but Joan told him, "Do not doubt; when God pleases, the time is ready." They must act when God willed it. "Act and God will act. Ah, gentle duke, are you afraid? Do you not know that I promised your wife to bring you back safe and sound?"

Joan addressed Alençon, a prince of the royal blood, with the familiar *tu* and in a playful tone as *gentil duc, beau duc.* Alençon, who was perhaps six years older than Joan, evidently inspired her affection with his frank admission of his own doubts and fears, and appreciation of her firmness and confidence.

At the beginning of the attack Joan warned Alençon to move from the spot where he was standing, or "that engine [pointing to a cannon on the town wall] will kill you." Alençon followed her instructions, and recalled that "a little later on that very spot a man named my lord de Lude was killed."

As the French carried their scaling ladders into the moats, the earl of Suffolk directed his herald to call to Alençon that he wanted to parley. But, said Alençon, "he was not heard," and the assault went on.[30] One of the defenders on the walls, "very big and fat," according to the *Journal du Siège,* and fully armed, wearing a helmet, was hurling "marvelously big iron balls" and knocking over ladders and the men climbing them. Once more Master Jean the gunner, the hero of the attack on the Augustins, was called on. Master Jean aimed his culverin at the Englishman, striking him unerringly in the chest and hurling him down inside the walls.[31]

Joan had mounted a ladder, her standard in her hand, when she was struck on the head by a stone, which cracked her helmet. She fell to the ground, but struggled to her feet, calling out, "Friends, friends! Up, up! Our Lord has condemned the English! This hour they are ours, be of good heart!"[32] The assault swept over the wall, and the English, including Suffolk and his two brothers, fled toward the bridge, pursued by the French. One of Suffolk's brothers, Alexander de la Pole, was thrown into the Loire and drowned. The other, John, was taken prisoner, along with Suffolk himself. A story told by the chronicler known as the Herald of Berry and repeated by other chroniclers credits Suffolk's capture to a squire from Auvergne named Guillaume Regnault. Suffolk asked Regnault whether he was a gentleman. Regnault said yes. Was he a knight? No. Whereupon Suffolk first knighted him and then surrendered to him.[33] (The scribe of La Rochelle, on the other hand, claimed that Suffolk refused to surrender to anyone but the Maid, who, he is supposed to have said, "is the bravest woman in the world and who has subjugated us all and put us in confusion," a most improbable speech, considering the English view of Joan.)[34]

Alençon said that more than 1,100 English were killed.[35] Prisoners were taken back to Orleans by water, according to the *Journal du Siège,* "to prevent their being killed, for several others were slain on the way when some of the French began to quarrel [over their ransom]. As for the town of Jargeau, and even the church where goods had been stored for safety, everything was pillaged."[36]

That night Alençon and Joan led the army back to Orleans, leaving a garrison at Jargeau. During the next two days, the *Journal du Siège* tells us, "the king's army grew swiftly, for every day people arrived from every part of his realm."[37] But there was no time to lose. On July 14 at vespers, according to the Alençon chronicler, Joan called the young duke to her and told him, "Tomorrow after dinner I want to go to Meung. Have the company ready to leave at that hour."[38] Next day, headed by Alençon and Joan, the army marched downriver, followed by a train of supplies. The artillery, again loaded on boats, went by river.

At Meung, on the northern bank of the Loire, twenty-one kilometers west of Orleans, the English had fortified the bridge, which lay outside the town. The French at once assaulted and took the bridge, leaving the English in possession of the town. Alençon spent the night (June 15) on guard in a neighboring church with a handful of soldiers, while Joan and the rest of the army bivouacked in the fields.[39] The next morning, June 16, leaving a garrison to hold the bridge, the army marched downstream to English-held Beaugency, also on the northern bank. The reason for the maneuver is not clear. An operation against Beaugency, farther west, may have seemed preferable to an assault on Meung because of the threatened arrival of the English relief army. On the approach of the French, the English garrison in Beaugency withdrew to a rectangular twelfth-century donjon that dominated the bridge, leaving a few soldiers in ambush in the houses of the town. After wiping out these pockets of resistance, the French began bombarding donjon and bridge.

Thus in Meung the English still held the town, but the French commanded the bridge, while eight kilometers west at Beaugency the situation was reversed, with the English holding the bridge (and the donjon) and the French the town. On this same day (June 16) the long-awaited English relief army from Paris reached Janville, thirty kilometers due north of Orleans, about fifty kilometers from Beaugency.

At this critical moment word came that the out-of-favor constable Arthur de Richemont was approaching from the west (from Brittany), at the head of a strong company. The news was received with mixed feelings by Dunois, Alençon, and the other captains, who had been given strict orders to have nothing to do with this ex-rebel. Some even talked of abandoning the siege. Alençon told Joan that if Richemont appeared, he himself would leave. Joan kept her head. Most of the witnesses and chronicles agree that it was she who persuaded the others to accept Richemont if he would swear to serve the king loyally. "Ah, *beau connétable,* I did not ask you to come, but since you have come, you shall be welcome."[40] Richemont's biographer alone told a different, and improbable, story: that La Hire and some other captains announced that "they would prefer [Richemont] and his company to all the Maids of the kingdom of France," that Joan then rode to meet Richemont, dismounted, and embraced his legs, and that Richemont told her that whether she was from God or the devil, he did not fear her.[41]

The English relief army was in a position to effect a junction with the English garrison in Meung. It could not, however, make contact with the English garrison in Beaugency, which was now isolated in the donjon at the north end of the bridge, and on the bridge itself. Neither could that garrison join the main English body by marching south of the river to Meung, since the Meung bridge was in French hands.

Whether the English in the donjon realized that the relief army was near is doubtful. In any case, that night they put an end to the strategically awkward situation by surrendering.* Unlike the Jargeau garrison,

*Their surrender may possibly have come on the following night; the chroniclers and witnesses are in conflict on this point.

The donjon at Beaugency where the English garrison took refuge when Joan captured the town

they were permitted "terms," which meant keeping "their bodies, horse, and armor" (according to the Alençon chronicler), and were given a safe conduct signed by Alençon. At that moment a scout from La Hire's company brought word that the relieving English army was at last approaching.[42] Many of the French were afraid, Alençon said, but Joan told them, "In the name of God, we must fight them, and even if they were [so numerous as to be] hanging from the clouds we would beat them, for God has sent them to us so that we may punish them. Today the gentle king will have the greatest victory he has ever had. And my counsel has told me that they will all be ours."[43]

The English army rode across the fields "in very fine order," according to the Burgundian mercenary captain Jean Wavrin, whose company formed part of it and who wrote the most important eyewitness account of what followed.[44]

On arriving in Janville on June 16, Sir John Fastolf, commanding the relief army, had learned of the fall of Jargeau and the siege of Beaugency, news which caused the English captains "very great displeasure," according to Wavrin. They had been holding council when Sir John Talbot arrived with an additional "forty lances and two hundred archers," and the English had been "most joyous at the coming of . . . the wisest and most valiant knight of the realm of England." The captains had sat down to their noon meal, and afterward returned to council. Fastolf had advanced a counsel of prudence: because of their losses at Orleans and Jargeau, they should abandon Beaugency and Meung and take "the best treaty [truce] they could get" from the French, temporizing until the duke of Bedford could send reinforcements from Normandy and England. The other captains, and especially Talbot, wanted to fight. Talbot insisted that, with his own people and whoever chose to follow him, he would go to fight the French "with the aid of God and *monseigneur* St. George."

On the morning of June 17, the English army drew up outside Janville with their "standards, pennons, and guidons." But Fastolf was still arguing with the captains, advising them, according to Wavrin, that "they were only a handful in comparison to the French, assuring them that if fortune turned against them, everything that the late King Henry [V] had conquered in France with great labor and over a long period of time would be lost, and that it would be better to wait for reinforcements." No one listened to him, and according to the consensus, Fastolf ordered his men to march toward Meung.

At a point "a league [five kilometers] from Meung and fairly close to Beaugency" the English army found itself face to face with the French, ranged in battle on a ridge (*une petite montaignette,* said Wavrin). The English men-at-arms quickly dismounted, and the archers planted their pointed stakes in the ground, as at Agincourt. But once more, as at Orleans, the French refused the bait. Again the two armies stood face to face, just out of bowshot, each challenging the other to attack. Finally the English sent heralds with a proposal for an old-fashioned chivalric duel: three English knights to fight three French. The French captains were not interested. For reply they bade the English, "Go and find lodgings tonight, for it is late; but tomorrow, if it please God and our Lady, we will see you at closer quarters."[45]

The English withdrew to Meung, where they spent the night. Thus two parts of the scattered English forces were joined. The third English force, the garrison that had been allowed to quit Beaugency after surrendering, is not again mentioned by witnesses or chroniclers, but that it did not join the main body is evident from the fact that Talbot and Fastolf were unaware of Beaugency's fall. That night they bombarded the French-held Meung bridge with the intention of recapturing it and opening a route on the southern bank for the relief of Beaugency. In the morning their captains heard mass and prepared to make an assault on the bridge. Suddenly a messenger arrived with the news that Beaugency had surrendered and that the victorious French were advancing on Meung. At once abandoning both bridge and town of Meung, the English army assembled in the fields north of town "in fine battle order," and took the road north, toward Paris.

The English Loire offensive, begun ten months earlier with serious hope of putting an end to the war, was finished. Yet the English army, if in retreat, remained intact and dangerous. In accordance with medieval practice, it marched north in three detachments. The advance guard was led by an English knight carrying a white standard, followed by artillery, provisions, and supplies; next the main body of troops, commanded by Fastolf and Talbot; and finally the rear guard.[46] The French, drawn up for battle west of Meung, learned that the English had gone. Should they be allowed to depart in peace? Dunois asked Joan what she thought. "Have good spurs," was her cryptic answer. The French captains were taken aback. "What are you saying? Are we to turn our backs on them?" Joan replied, "No, it is the English who will not be able to defend themselves and who will be conquered, and you will need good spurs to overtake them."[47] The French took up the pursuit; Louis de Coutes tells us that La Hire led the advance guard, which "greatly annoyed Joan, who liked to command it herself."[48]

According to Wavrin's narrative, which contains the only eyewitness story of the battle, La Hire overtook the English rear "about a league" from Patay. English scouts reconnoitered to discover the enemy strength. The English captains ordered their vanguard, supply wagons, and artillery to take up a position on top of a gentle rise, guarded by a line of hedges. The main body followed. When Talbot reached a place where a pair of thick hedges bordered a narrow passage, he dismounted and told 500 archers of the main body to position themselves in this advantageous site, with the hedges protecting their flanks, the rest of the main body behind them. "He hoped [later] to rejoin the main body," explained Wavrin, adding, "but it turned out very differently."

Talbot's archers were hammering their pointed stakes into the ground, their position still not set, when a stag burst out of the woods and bolted straight into the main body of the English, who "raised a loud cry." The French scouts heard it, sighted the enemy, and sent back word to their own advance guard, which spurred forward, closely followed by the French main body. The main body of the English army hastened up the little ridge; but by the time the two English forces joined, the French had galloped into the passage between the hedges and overpowered Talbot's archers. In a moment they had "thrown the Lord de Talbot to the ground and taken him prisoner and killed all his men, and were at such advantage in the battle that they could kill and capture at will." Fastolf galloped back toward the ridge, intending to rally his men there, but they instead interpreted the action as flight. The captain of the vanguard, white standard and all, fled, abandoning the ridge, followed by his men.[49]

A slaughter like a reverse Agincourt followed. "Almost all the English were killed," Louis de Coutes reported.[50] The prisoners, as usual, were the ransom-worthy—Talbot, Lord Thomas Scales, and other nobles. The slain were all "people of small or middling estate," wrote Enguerrand de Monstrelet, "such as were usually brought from their country to die in France."[51]

"Thus the French obtained the victory at Patay," wrote Wavrin, ". . . the place by whose name the battle will forever be known: the day of Patay."[52]

The battle was over so quickly that Joan, arriving with the rear guard, missed most of the fighting. Louis de Coutes said that she "had great pity for such slaughter," and went on to tell how she saw a French soldier strike an English prisoner on the head so that he fell down as if dead; Joan dismounted and heard his confession, holding his head and comforting him.*[53]

Fastolf, advised to save himself, protested, according to Wavrin, that he would rather be dead or a prisoner than to "flee shamefully and abandon his men," but he finally left "with a very small company, uttering the greatest lament that I have ever heard a man make."[54]

The radical discrepancy in casualties so typical of medieval field engagements reached an almost incredible level. The victors suffered practically none—three men, according to Perceval de Boulainvilliers, one, according to Thibaut d'Armagnac. On the English side, Dunois es-

*The incident may have taken place elsewhere; Louis de Coutes does not make clear that it occurred at Patay.

timated the dead at 4,000, Wavrin and the *Journal du Siège* 2,000, and 200 prisoners.

Fastolf took the road to Étampes, south of Paris, "and I followed him as my captain," Wavrin wrote, "whom the duke of Bedford had commanded me to obey and serve." The next day they joined Bedford at Corbeil.[55] Bedford reproached Fastolf for the disaster, and stripped him of the Order of the Garter. Fastolf defended his conduct and eventually recovered his decoration, but was portrayed by Shakespeare in *Henry VI, Part 1,* under his own name, as deserting Talbot and fleeing the field to save his own skin; later he metamorphosed into the cowardly buffoon Falstaff.

The stunning victory had immediate repercussions. The English commander of the garrison at Janville, which Talbot had long made his headquarters, switched to the French side, while many English garrisons of other small fortified towns south of Paris fled to the capital.

Though she had not even been present until the battle was almost over, Joan had contributed significantly to its outcome. Wavrin thought her effect on English morale played an important part. "By the renown of Joan the Maid the courage of the English was much altered and weakened. They saw, it seemed to them, the wheel of fortune turn harshly against them, for they had already lost several towns and fortresses which had returned to the obedience of the king of France, principally by the enterprises of the Maid, some by force, others by treaty; they saw their men struck down, and found them no longer of such firm purpose and prudence as they had once been; thus they all were, so it seemed, eager to retreat to the marches of Normandy, abandoning all they held in the Île de France and thereabouts."[56]

The French army occupied Patay. The night was warm, and Richemont and many of the others slept in the fields, but Joan and Alençon spent the night in town. Talbot was brought before them, and youthful Alençon expressed to veteran Talbot his astonishment at how the battle had turned out, to which Talbot stoically replied that such were the fortunes of war.[57]

The fortunes of war had in fact taken a decisive turn.

7. The Coronation Journey

TRADITIONALLY JOAN HAS BEEN PICTURED as conducting to his coronation at Reims a king too lazy, frivolous, and cowardly to act for himself or even to recognize that she knew what was best for him. This version, enhancing Joan's memory at the expense of Charles's, gives Joan's paramount role in the coronation journey an embellishment it does not need.

In the wake of Orleans-Patay, three different strategies were possible. An attack on Paris was the most obvious, at least to the Parisians. The *Journal d'un Bourgeois de Paris* reported that "on the Tuesday before St. John's Day [June 21, three days after Patay] there was a great disturbance in Paris, and the Armagnacs were said to be about to enter the city that night, but nothing happened. After that, the Parisians enforced a strict watch day and night without pause, and the walls were strengthened, and many cannons and other artillery were placed on them."[1] At Charles's court, however, the idea of an immediate move on Paris was given little consideration. The city's large population (about 100,000) supplied it with a numerous militia to man its strong walls even in the absence of a large professional garrison. Instead, in opposition to Joan's project of the coronation at Reims, several of the captains and princes, according to Dunois, favored an invasion of English Normandy.[2]

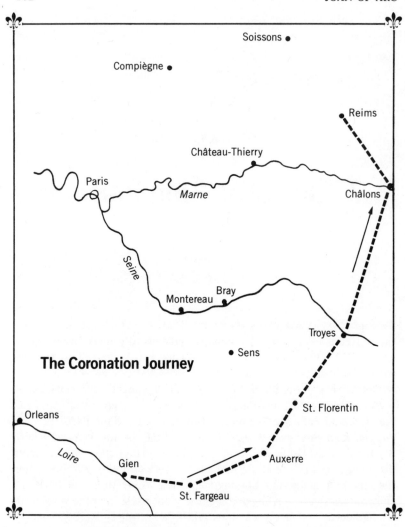

The Coronation Journey

Militarily the captains had some reason on their side. Normandy was the center of English power, now vulnerable owing to the rout of the English field army. Further, the duke of Burgundy was unlikely to intervene seriously, whereas he might be expected to be sensitive to a march to Reims, necessarily through territory under his political control.

Even in a military sense, however, the reduction of the strongholds where the English had been so long established might have been difficult and costly both in lives and—the commodity always in short supply—money.

In any case Joan had political sense on her side. She believed the coronation ceremony crucial as God's recognition of Charles's kingship. "When the king is crowned and consecrated," she told Dunois, "the power of his enemies will always be lessened, nor will they ultimately be able to harm him or the kingdom."[3]

Joan was well acquainted with the legend of Reims, where nearly a thousand years earlier, on Christmas Eve in 496, St. Rémi, for whom Domremy was named, had baptized Clovis, the king of the Franks. During the baptism St. Rémi had found his supply of holy oil dangerously diminished. A dove descended from the heavens bearing the sacred ampulla containing the Holy Chrism (consecrated oil), with which the ampulla thereafter miraculously refilled itself.

St. Rémi and Clovis notwithstanding, the sacred ampulla used in fifteenth-century coronations in all probability dated only from the twelfth century, and the tradition of holding coronation rites at Reims was actually due to the political obligation that Hugh Capet, founder of the Capetian dynasty in 987, owed to Archbishop Adalbero, who had intrigued to get Hugh elected king. Hugh himself was crowned at Noyon, but his successors were crowned at Reims, beginning in 1026, in a ceremony whose form became fixed in the twelfth century and was therefore a revered tradition by 1429.

The expedition to Reims, as opposed to an assault on Paris or an invasion of Normandy, suited Charles's style as it did Joan's, though for rather different reasons. A peaceful progress to Reims, marked by diplomatic transactions with the cities along the way, in which general amnesties could be bartered for allegiance, was thoroughly congenial to Charles, and anticipated his treatment of all the towns and districts later liberated from the English. Pacific measures he invariably "preferred to shedding blood."

On Sunday, June 19, Joan returned to Orleans from the battlefield of Patay. She found that the king had withdrawn to Georges de la Tremoille's castle at Sully, on the Loire east of Orleans, to avoid meeting Richemont. Richemont had sent envoys to beg Tremoille, who had replaced him as the king's chief minister, to "let him serve the king, and he would do anything he wanted." Tremoille feared, not without reason, that allowing Richemont to return to court would endanger his own position, and persuaded Charles to send back a message that Richemont should depart, and that "he would prefer never to be crowned rather than have [Richemont] there."[4] According to the *Journal du Siège*, Richemont solved the problem by taking his company off to besiege Marchenoir, a town near Beaugency, and presently returned to his own estate at Parthenay, west of Poitiers.[5]

Meantime in Orleans Joan received a gift from England. Charles of Orleans, still in comfortable detention, sent a letter ordering a robe and a *hucque* made for her, in gratitude for her "good and agreeable services against the English, old enemies of my lord the king and of us." The garments were to be in his colors: the robe of fine crimson Brussels cloth and lined, the *hucque* of dark green. A merchant, Jean Luillier, was to furnish the cloth, a tailor, Jean Bourgeois, to make the garments, for which Charles of Orleans ordered his treasurer Jacques Boucher, Joan's host, to pay thirteen golden crowns.[6]

During the week, Joan had an emotional reunion with the king at St.-Benoît-sur-Loire, west of Sully, where the king spoke "very high praise of her," according to Simon Charles, but upset her by expressing his sorrow at the hardships she had endured and ordering her to take a rest. Grateful though he felt toward her, the implication was that he was not unwilling for her now to retire. Joan burst into tears and told him that "he must have no doubts and that he would have his whole kingdom and would be crowned within a short time."[7]

Charles evidently was persuaded. A few days later he moved to Gien, on the Loire, farther east, almost in Burgundy, and a good point of departure for Reims, to the northeast. Alençon and Joan joined him there on Friday, June 24. The Alençon chronicler tells us that that morning Joan addressed her *beau duc:* "Have the trumpets sounded and mount your horse. It is time to go to gentle king Charles to set him on his way to his anointing at Reims."[8]

From Gien both the king and Joan dispatched letters with news of the Loire victories. The king's were to his "good towns" and all his great vassals inviting them to the coronation. Joan's letter was to the citizens of Tournai, like Domremy and Vaucouleurs an island of resistance loyal to the king. Inviting the town's citizens to Reims, "where we will arrive shortly," she informed the "gentle loyal French of the town of Tournai" that in eight days she had driven the English out of their strongholds on

the Loire, "by assault or otherwise." She listed the noble prisoners taken
—Lord Talbot, Lord Scales, Fastolf (erroneously, apparently through a
confusion of names), the earl of Suffolk and his brother—and those slain
—Glasdale and Suffolk's other brother.[9] Her tone was certainly devoid
of false modesty. On the other hand, in claiming the victories for herself,
she believed she was claiming them for God; a citizen of Orleans remarked that the people of that city "never saw any signs that Joan
attributed any of her achievements to her own glory. They say that she
attributed all things to God."[10]

At the same time, in preparation for the expedition through Burgundian territory, Joan wrote a letter to the duke of Burgundy, urging him
not to "make war on them," but to join them at the coronation. In spite
of her anger at the Burgundians, she realized that the Armagnac-Burgundian quarrel had opened the door to the English—the murder of John
the Fearless was "a great tragedy for France," she said at her trial—and
fully recognized the importance of a reconciliation between the two
French factions.[11]

The Alençon chronicler tells us that Joan became very restless over
the delay at Gien while Charles weighed conflicting advice. Some of his
councillors wanted him to first complete the clearing of the Loire by
laying siege to the Burgundian-held crossings at Cosne and La Charité,
to the southeast of Gien, before setting out for Reims. Others warned
him that the coronation journey would be dangerous, since "many cities,
towns, castles, and fortresses" between Gien and Reims were strongly
garrisoned with Burgundians and English. Finally, there was the shortage of money.[12] Joan overrode the councillors as she had the captains,
persuasively assuring Charles that if they went boldly forward "everything would turn out well, and that they should not be afraid, for no one
could harm them, or resist them, and that they must not doubt that they
would have enough men, for many would follow her."[13] And in fact,
although the king could not pay them, there flocked to Gien "knights,
squires, men-at-arms, and common people" eager to serve the king on
this expedition "in the company of the Maid, saying that they would go
wherever she wanted to go."[14] "Two or three francs" were scraped
together to pay each soldier; knights served at their own expense, and
some gentlemen, lacking the means to buy suitable mounts, rode "little
horses," of the sort that were used by archers and common soldiers.[15]
The *Journal du Siège* asserts that the army numbered about 12,000, a
figure that must have included noncombatants.[16]

On Monday, June 27, as if to draw the cumbersome procession forward by her example, Joan left town and camped in the fields.[17] Two days later the army got on the road, marching for Auxerre, eighty-seven kilometers to the east, well inside Burgundian territory, where four months before Joan had paused to hear mass in the cathedral. They arrived before Auxerre on July 1. The gates were closed. Envoys were sent to summon the citizens to receive the king as their "natural and rightful lord." The gates remained closed while envoys negotiated, passing back and forth for the next two days between the army outside the walls and the citizens within. Meanwhile, according to several chroniclers, Tremoille accepted a secret bribe of 2,000 crowns in return for leaving the town unharmed.[18] However that might be, a treaty was ultimately concluded which amounted to effective neutralization of Auxerre, whose citizens promised that they would submit to the king if Troyes, Châlons, and Reims did, and for the present agreed to sell the army much-needed supplies.[19] Joan and some of the captains wanted to attack the town and were "very unhappy" at the decision to depart in peace, which they blamed on Tremoille.[20] But the army departed for St. Florentin, to the north, which surrendered to the king without difficulty. On July 4 the royal host arrived at the castle of St. Phal, a few kilometers southwest of Troyes.

Troyes, long a home of the great international Champagne Fairs, was still an important center of commerce, and generally Burgundian in sympathy. It had served as temporary capital of the Burgundian-dominated government of Queen Isabelle, and had been the scene of the treaty of 1420 that disinherited Charles. But Charles had succeeded in making contacts with prominent citizens and churchmen of the city, promising to safeguard bourgeois liberties and Church property.[21] Half won over, the wealthy merchants and prelates hesitated. The weavers and small merchants, like those of Paris, remained strongly Burgundian; and Troyes had to consider its Burgundian neighbors. Finally, to complete the dilemma, the city had an Anglo-Burgundian garrison which was too weak to protect it against the royal army but strong enough to make it impractical for the citizens to surrender.

As the French approached, the garrison sallied out to skirmish, then withdrew and closed the gates, which remained shut while the town council deliberated and a delegation ventured out to parley.[22]

At its head was a Franciscan monk named Brother Richard, a popular preacher who had just returned from a triumph in Paris, where he had preached ten all-day sermons to crowds of thousands. Brother Richard —a disciple of Vincent Ferrier and Bernardine of Siena, who taught that the end of the world was at hand, and that salvation could be achieved by worshipping the holy name of Jesus—had preached so movingly against Parisian frivolities that "in less than three or four hours you would have seen more than a hundred fires in which men were burning chess and backgammon boards, dice, cards, balls, and sticks . . . and all things that can give rise to anger in covetous gaming," reported the Bourgeois of Paris. Women burned their elaborate headdresses, their trains, and "many [other] of their vanities." Like other eschatological doctrines on the fringes of established religion, Brother Richard's beliefs verged on the heretical, and his departure from Paris had been abrupt. He had scheduled a sermon at Montmartre, and "over six thousand people" had thronged there the night before, sleeping in huts or on the ground, but he had vanished, evidently after getting word that the University of Paris threatened to scrutinize his orthodoxy.[23]

At her trial Joan told the story of her meeting with Brother Richard. He approached her making the sign of the cross and sprinkling holy water in a gesture of exorcism. Instead of rebuking him, as she had the priest brought to her by Robert de Baudricourt at Vaucouleurs, she remarked good-humoredly, "Approach boldly. I shall not fly away." A chronicler reported that Brother Richard knelt to Joan, and that she then fell on her knees too; they talked for a long time, and he was so completely won over by her that he returned to the town to preach a sermon admonishing the people to submit to the king.[24]

He also carried a letter from Joan advising the people of Troyes to "come out to meet King Charles . . . and fear not for your persons or your property . . . and I promise you and certify on your lives that with the help of God we shall enter all the towns which should be part of the holy kingdom, and there make a good and firm peace."[25]

Brother Richard's intercession notwithstanding, Joan's letter got a poor reception from the town council. The aldermen derided it as being from "a madwoman full of the devil," and having "neither rhyme nor reason," and burned it without answering.[26] They wrote to the citizens of Reims and Châlons (halfway between Troyes and Reims) warning them that "the enemies of King Henry and of the duke of Burgundy were coming to besiege them," and asking for help. But in a significant passage, they confessed, "Whatsoever we decide, we must consider the [Anglo-Burgundian] soldiers who are in town, and who are stronger than we."[27] As businessmen they were reluctant to fight and had no desire to see their city besieged and pillaged. Probably they expected no help from their neighbors, and they received none.

Yet the moment was critical for the French. The army was a long way from its base, deep in enemy territory. Not only were food and money in short supply, but it had been impossible to bring along artillery and ammunition for a siege operation. To bypass Troyes along with Auxerre invited Châlons and Reims to shut their gates. Once more, as at Orleans and Patay, the entire enterprise hung in the balance, and once more Joan's voice was decisive. The king held a council of war (apparently at St. Phal) attended by the members of the great council as well as by the captains of the army, Joan pointedly not included. The council came to no decision. We are told by the chroniclers that chancellor Regnault of Chartres advocated retreat. Then another councillor, Robert le Maçon, demanded that Joan's advice be sought. They sent for her; she "knocked loudly on the door of the room," and when she had entered, the chancellor explained the dilemma to her. Her response, according to Dunois, was "Noble dauphin, command your people to come and besiege the city of Troyes, and debate no longer, for, in God's name, within three days I will lead you into the city of Troyes by love or by force or by courage, and false Burgundy will be amazed."

Joan's counsel of action prevailed. Under her direction, the army deployed outside Troyes's walls and spent the day gathering timber and brush to bundle into fascines for filling the moat. From their parapets the apprehensive townsmen watched the operation. When the following morning Joan gave the command for the assault and the soldiers began flinging the fascines into the moat, the citizens were convinced. Emissaries hastened from the city to negotiate surrender. In Dunois's words, "The bishop and the citizens made their obedience to the king, shaking and trembling."[28]

Early on the morning of Sunday, July 10, Joan and Charles rode into Troyes side by side.[29] The bloodless victory was almost as startling and almost as valuable as that of Orleans.

The Anglo-Burgundian garrison was allowed to leave, taking their arms and baggage. The latter stipulation was interpreted to include prisoners held for ransom. When Joan found this out, she hurried to the gate where the departing garrison had gathered and called on them to release their prisoners. She received only derision for her pains, but when Charles learned of the controversy, he directed that the prisoners' ransoms be paid.[30]

During the brief stay at Troyes, Joan was asked to serve as godmother to at least one baby—a request that was repeated subsequently in several towns. She named the boys Charles, after the king, the girls, at their mothers' unvarying request, Joan.[31]

When the army left Troyes on July 12, Brother Richard accompanied it. On July 14 they arrived before Châlons, whose town council, in a letter informing Reims of the surrender of Troyes, had declared its intention of standing firm. But the king's army had no sooner appeared than the bishop and "a great number of bourgeois of the town" rode out to meet them, bringing the keys of the city and promising obedience to the king. They wrote a second letter to their compatriots at Reims announcing their surrender and declaring that the king was gentle, compassionate, and a "handsome person."[32]

News of the king's progress aroused widespread excitement. Along the roads toward Reims parties of travelers converged from all the neighboring regions. Among them were a number of villagers from Domremy, who had traveled a distance of 200 kilometers. Joan's godfather Jean Moreau found her in Châlons, where he had gone because "it was said that the king was going to Reims to be crowned," and where Joan made him a present of a red coat that she was wearing.[33] Gerardin of Épinal, husband of her childhood friend Isabelette, with four other people from the village, also met her in Châlons and remembered Joan's telling him that she was "afraid of nothing but treason."[34]

As the king's army left Châlons and headed north, the two Burgundian captains of the garrison at Reims assembled the citizens and promised that if they could hold out for six weeks, a relieving army would arrive. But the atmosphere was now radically changed. After a short consultation, the citizens declared their intention of surrendering to the king, and the Burgundian captains tamely led their soldiers away, taking the road west for Château-Thierry and Paris.[35]

On Saturday, July 16, the king arrived at Sept-Saulx, a castle belonging to the archbishop of Reims. There he received a delegation bringing the keys to the city.[36]

Coronations were traditionally held on Sunday, and preparations were rushed to perform the ceremony the following day. As Joan later explained, it was necessary to proceed quickly because the citizens protested that they could not afford to quarter the army for a whole week. Therefore on Saturday afternoon the king made his triumphal entry, accompanied by Joan, "who was the cynosure of all eyes," and followed by the army; the citizens lined the streets, crying, "Noel!"[37] Also waiting in the city were a number of leading nobles who, persuaded by the royal victories, had decided to transfer their allegiance from the duke of Burgundy to the king. Among them were René of Anjou, son-in-law and heir of Duke Charles of Lorraine, whom Joan had tried to enlist in her enterprise on her visit to Nancy, and the damoiseau de Commercy, the robber baron who had extorted protection money from the inhabitants of Domremy.[38] In the crowds of less exalted folk were many of Joan's relatives and friends, including her father and mother, who were put up at the town's expense at an inn facing the cathedral.[39]

On Sunday morning, four dignitaries—Gilles de Rais, the Marshal de Boussac, the Lord de Graville, and Admiral de Culan—fully armed and carrying their banners, rode to the ancient abbey of St. Rémi, burial place of the baptizer of Clovis, where was kept the sacred ampulla containing the Holy Chrism. After swearing solemn oaths to transport the ampulla safely, they escorted the abbot, in his priestly robes and protected by a canopy of gold cloth, to the cathedral, where the archbishop joined him, took the ampulla, and carried it to the altar. The abbot and his escort then rode their horses into the cathedral, passing through the nave and dismounting at the entrance to the choir.[40]

Although the cathedral floor was crowded, there were some noteworthy absences. Traditionally the ceremony was attended by the "twelve peers of France," six great nobles, six prelates. Because several of the ancient domains now belonged to the crown and others were in English hands, only the duke of Burgundy—who was also the count of Flanders and therefore represented two of the peerages—remained of the six great nobles, and though invited by Joan, the duke was of course missing. Of the six ecclesiastical peers, only Regnault of Chartres, archbishop of Reims, and the bishops of Laon and Châlons* were present. The bishoprics of Langres and Noyon lay in occupied territory, and the sixth prelate, the bishop of Beauvais, was Pierre Cauchon, an enthusias-

---

*The damoiseau de Commercy was his nephew.

tic supporter of the English. The places of the missing peers, lay and ecclesiastical, were taken by substitutes—Alençon for the absent duke of Burgundy; the king's cousin, the count of Clermont, for the nonexistent duke of Normandy; another cousin, the count of Vendome, for the English duke of Aquitaine; young Guy de Laval, Georges de la Tremoille, and the sire de Beaumanoir for the counts of Flanders, Toulouse, and Champagne. Prelates took the places of the three missing ecclesiastical peers. Since Arthur de Richemont had been excluded from the expedition, his place as constable of France was taken by Georges de la Tremoille's brother Charles d'Albret. Missing too were some of the trappings of coronation kept at the abbey of St. Denis, near Paris, in enemy hands: the crown, the sword of Charlemagne, the golden spurs and scepter, and the ivory hand placed on the altar to hold the king's baton. Substitutes were found in the Reims cathedral treasury.

The ceremony took place in three parts: the oath, the unction, and the bestowing of the insignia of royalty. First, while litanies were sung, the king prostrated himself before the altar, remaining prone until the bishops raised him to his feet. The archbishop administered the oath: to uphold the faith of his ancestors, to defend the Church, and to adhere to the justice of his forefathers in ruling the kingdom which God had entrusted to him. The king was then knighted by Alençon.

Removing his garments except for a silken tunic with openings, closed by silver cords, at the spots where the oil would be applied, the king knelt before the archbishop. With a golden needle, the archbishop lifted a drop of the Holy Chrism from the ampulla, mixed it with other consecrated oil on a special paten (communion plate) from the abbey of St. Rémi, untied the silver cords, and anointed the king in five places: the top of the head, the chest, the back, the shoulders, and the elbows. The congregation chanted the anthem "They Are Anointing King Solomon." The cords were retied, and the king was dressed in a violet tunic and cope decorated with golden fleurs-de-lis.

The archbishop then placed the scepter in the king's right hand and the baton in his left. The twelve peers were summoned; the archbishop took the crown from the altar and placed it on the king's head; and each peer placed a finger on the crown, symbolically supporting it, as the archbishop led the king to the throne. (The duke of Burgundy, in token of his importance, was allowed to place two fingers on the crown, and presumably Alençon followed this custom.) Before the throne, the archbishop removed his miter in sign of respect and bowed before the king, kissing first his hand and then his cheek; the peers followed the same ritual.

After the concluding prayers and benedictions, the king distributed honors, bestowing the title of count on Guy de Laval and Georges de la Tremoille, and that of marshal on Gilles de Rais. Alençon and the count of Clermont knighted several young men, including René of Anjou and the damoiseau de Commercy.[41]

During the long ceremony—from 9 A.M. to 2 P.M.—Joan stood beside the king. "And it was a fine thing to see the goodly demeanor of the king and the Maid," reported an eyewitness. Conspicuously at hand and even somewhat obtrusive in the setting was her standard, held either by herself or by another; Brother Richard may have held it part of the time.[42]

The ceremony over, "everyone cried, 'Noel!' and the trumpets sounded so loud that it seemed as if the vaults of the church would burst."[43]

A chronicler tells us that after the coronation, Joan knelt before the king and embraced his legs, weeping and saying, "Gentle king, now is executed the pleasure of God, who wanted the siege of Orleans to be raised, and who has brought you to this city of Reims to receive your holy consecration, showing you that you are the true king, and that the kingdom of France belongs to you." The chronicler concluded: "And this very much moved all those who saw her."[44]

Two great goals had indeed been achieved in the relief of Orleans and the coronation. At the king's side, her standard in her hand, in the center of the vast cathedral crowded with dignitaries, comrades-in-arms, townspeople, and peasants from a hundred villages, including her native Domremy, Joan stood at the pinnacle of her brief career.

8. The Road to Paris

THE RELIEF OF ORLEANS and the Loire campaign were victories for Joan's activist policy; the coronation journey was a happy convergence of Joan's and Charles's inclinations. After the coronation these elements began to diverge, with tragic consequences for Joan. At Orleans the political and military problems had been clear-cut and the aims of the king's party reasonably harmonious, a situation that held throughout the Loire campaign. Despite some dissension among French leaders before and during the march to Reims, Joan and the king had remained essentially in agreement. But after the coronation, Joan's single-minded militance was increasingly challenged by the promises and prospects of Charles's diplomacy.

At the same time, though Joan's career after Reims is usually regarded as downhill (she probably so regarded it herself), the campaign was nevertheless of great importance in the growing ascendancy of French national power in the war.

Joan was not blind to the value of diplomacy. On the day of the coronation, she wrote a second letter to the duke of Burgundy urging in the name of the King of Heaven that he and Charles should "make a good firm peace, which will last a long time. Forgive each other with

113

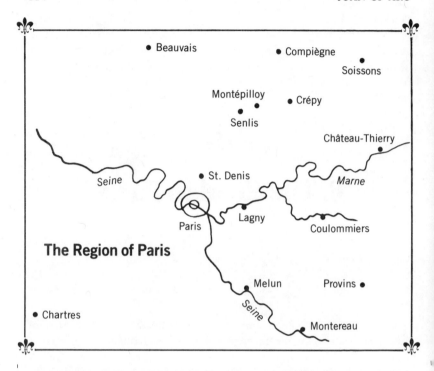

The Region of Paris

good heart, wholly, as faithful Christians should; and if you want to make war, go to fight the Saracens. Prince of Burgundy, I pray you, I beg, and require, as humbly as I can, that you no longer make war on the holy kingdom of France, and that you immediately withdraw your men from the towns and fortresses of that holy kingdom. . . . All those who make war against the holy kingdom of France are making war against King Jesus, King of Heaven and of the whole world." She begged him "with clasped hands," assuring him that "no matter how many men you bring against us, they will gain nothing, and it will be a great pity, the great battle and the blood that will be shed there by those who come against us." Reminding him that she had already written him a letter and had sent it by a herald, she complained that she had had no answer, and no news of the herald (it was a dangerous affair to be Joan's herald).[1]

One of the accusations made at her trial in Rouen was that Joan "dissuaded the king and his men from making any kind of peace treaty or accommodation with his enemies, always inciting them to killing and the spilling of human blood, saying that there could be no peace except at the point of lance and sword, and that it had been ordained by God, because otherwise the king's adversaries would not surrender the territory they occupied in the kingdom, which she said would be the greatest good possible in all Christendom."[2]

The accusation touched on one of Joan's aspects most galling to the Anglo-Burgundians and their sympathizers, her conviction that God was on the French-Armagnac side. Was not England a Catholic realm? Were not the Burgundians and Parisians good Catholics? Why should God be for Charles and the French and against Burgundy and the English? Joan never directly addressed this question, but her position might be defined: In the dynastic quarrel and feudal dispute, God might be neutral, but with the English occupation of northern France the issue had become (though the modern term did not yet exist) national liberation, which God's justice favored. And perhaps God might be favoring the English as well as the French in wanting them to quit France, where so many of their "people of small or middling estate" had been "brought to die."

At her trial, Joan responded to the charge of refusing to negotiate by saying that "as to the duke of Burgundy, she had required him both by letters and by ambassadors to make peace with the king; as for the English, the only peace that could be made with them was for them to return to their own country of England."[3] Thus a clear distinction existed in her mind between Burgundy and England, though the terms she proposed to the duke of Burgundy in her letter were essentially those she recommended for the English—the duke should withdraw his troops to Burgundy, and the English should go home to England.

Negotiations with Burgundy were in fact in progress, but Joan knew nothing about them. The same (coronation) day that she dictated her letter, Burgundian envoys arrived in Reims to confer secretly with the king.[4] Duke Philip could not fail to be impressed with Charles's progress, and he wanted to establish contact while still keeping his English connection.

On the English side, the duke of Bedford had been driven by Orleans and Patay to seek new ways to cement the Anglo-Burgundian alliance, now more indispensable to the English cause than ever. Early in July he had sent an embassy to Philip, and later 20,000 pounds Tournois were handed over to Philip's treasurer in Arras "for payment of men-at-arms and archers whom he will enlist to serve the king [Henry VI] against his enemies in France."[5]

A week before the coronation, Philip had arrived in Paris to preside (July 14) at the public reading of a letter reviving the case of his father's murder at Montereau, picturing John the Fearless as a martyr and "the dauphin and his accomplices" as treacherous assassins and violators of the peace. "After this letter had been read," reported the Bourgeois of Paris, "there was a great murmur and some who had been closely allied to the Armagnacs began to hold them in great hate." Bedford and the duke of Burgundy then called for "a show of hands from all who would be good and loyal to the regent and to the duke of Burgundy. And these lords promised them on their faith to guard the good town of Paris."

The Bourgeois also reported that the Parisians were angry to learn that their former favorite preacher, Brother Richard, was riding with the royal army and "using his eloquence to persuade the cities which had sworn faith to the regent of France or to his representatives to defect . . . They cursed him by God and his saints," and resumed all the frivolities Brother Richard had persuaded them to abandon—backgammon, bowls, dicing—although at his departure from Paris they had "wept as piteously and as bitterly as if they had been watching their dearest friends being buried."[6]

The Burgundian embassy kept the king in Reims for four days, after which he departed for Corbigny, south of Auxerre, to carry out a venerable post-coronation ritual, a pilgrimage to the abbey of St. Marcoul to heal the scrofulous (victims of tuberculosis of the lymph glands). The "king's touch" supposedly conferred by the coronation was not taken seriously by the sophisticated: "I have no actual evidence as to any cures performed during [the pilgrimage]," wrote skeptical Pope Pius II in his memoirs, "though the French think that anything that can conceivably happen, even by a miracle, does happen."[7]

From Corbigny, the king returned north, pausing at the village of Vailly, between Reims and Soissons, where he received delegations from Soissons and Laon bringing him the keys to their cities. At Soissons he was greeted enthusiastically and learned that Provins, Coulommiers, and several other towns had surrendered. The commanders of the 400-strong Burgundian garrison at Château-Thierry, finding that public opinion had swung to the king, retreated to Paris, leaving the town to surrender.[8]

From Château-Thierry the king, at Joan's request, sent an order (July

31) to the bailiff of Chaumont, in whose district Domremy and Greux were located, granting the two villages exemption from all regular and special taxes.*⁹

The king continued his progress to Provins, where he arrived on August 2. His negotiations with the Burgundian envoys had meanwhile resulted in a two-week truce. This fruit of Charles's secret negotiations was far from meeting with Joan's approval, and she expressed herself in caustic terms. Writing to the inhabitants of Reims (August 5) from "a stop on the road to Paris" she asserted that the truce had been made in return for a promise that Paris would peaceably surrender at the end of the two weeks. She was decidedly skeptical of such an outcome; the Rémois were not to be surprised if she did not enter Paris so soon, "because I am not at all pleased with the truce and I do not know if I will keep it; and if I keep it, it will be only to preserve the king's honor. However [the Anglo-Burgundians] will not abuse the royal blood, for I will maintain and keep the king's army together, ready to fight at the end of the two weeks, if peace is not made." She assured her "dear and perfect friends" that they would have no worries while she lived; they must guard and watch the king's good city, and let her know if anyone tried to do them harm, in which case she would come immediately to their aid.¹⁰

Paris was in Joan's eyes the main objective, and primarily in a military sense. Charles hoped the capital could be taken either by diplomatic maneuver or through action by his partisans within the city, but the separation of Philip of Burgundy from his alliance with the English remained the paramount aim of his policy. An assault on Paris, he feared, might ruin his diplomacy.

By the time the truce expired in mid-August, it was evident that Bedford had no intention of giving up Paris without a fight. He had been able to get quick reinforcements from England, thanks to the Hussites, the pre-Protestant reforming sect in Bohemia. Henry VI's great-uncle Henry Beaufort, cardinal of Winchester, had been raising an army in England to join a crusade against the Bohemian heretics, and Bedford commandeered the crusaders for the war in France. Beaufort landed at

---

*This privilege survived in Domremy until 1571, when the town became part of Lorraine. When Domremy was reunited with France in 1766, the village petitioned for its renewal, pointing out that Greux still enjoyed it, but the only result was that the privilege was withdrawn from Greux ten years later.

Calais early in July with 3,500 knights and archers, and arrived in Paris on July 25. Early in August, Bedford was able to lead a powerful force of English and Burgundians (both Monstrelet and the *Journal du Siège* said it numbered 10,000, Jean Chartier 10–12,000) south to Corbeil and Melun. The king and Joan left Provins on August 5 and marched to meet him with an army of equal size.

Once more the English stuck to their strategy of awaiting attack, and once more the French refused to accommodate them. The result was skirmishes and confrontations, but no battle. Near the castle of Nangis, halfway between Provins and Melun, Charles drew up his troops in battle order, but though they waited all day the English never arrived. Bedford had about-faced his army and returned to Paris. Charles decided to call an end to the campaign and retire to the Loire. He extracted from the town of Bray a promise of safe passage of the Seine, but the night before the army was to cross, a company of English seized the bridge, evidently a strongly fortified one, because its capture forced the king to abandon his plans. According to the chroniclers, Joan and many of the captains —among them Alençon, René of Anjou, and the Lavals—were delighted at the turn of events, which promised to keep the army north of the Seine.[11] It now returned to Château-Thierry, whence it turned west, arriving at La Ferté (August 10) and Crépy-en-Valois (August 11), some seventy kilometers northeast of Paris. "The people came out to meet [the king] rejoicing and crying, 'Noel,' " Dunois reported.

On the road between La Ferté and Crépy, Joan, riding between Regnault of Chartres and Dunois, remarked, "Here is a good people, and I have never seen people rejoice so much at the coming of such a noble king. And may I be fortunate enough, when I finish my days, to be buried in this ground!" The archbishop asked her, "Joan, where do you hope to die?" and she answered, "Wherever it pleases God, for I am sure neither of the time nor place, any more than you are; and would that it might now please God, my Creator, that I withdraw, laying down my arms, and go to serve my father and mother in watching their sheep, with my sister and my brothers, who would be very glad to see me."*[12]

Even before the coronation, Joan's mood had taken a somber turn,

---

*Anatole France ridiculed this speech, reported by Dunois, pointing out that Joan's family were not really shepherds and that her brothers were actually fighting at her side. Yet although Dunois's recollection of the exact words may have been faulty, he probably remembered the sense.

witnessed by the talk of treason to Gerardin of Épinal at Châlons. Probably the developing breach with the king was responsible, along with the strength of the peace party among his councillors. Alençon recorded that he sometimes heard Joan tell the king that she "would last a year and not much more"—whether she expected to die in a year, or to lose her influence is not clear—and that they must think how to use that year well in fulfilling her mission.[13]

At Crépy, the king received a letter from the duke of Bedford, truculent but with the bluster covering a peace offer. Written at Montereau on August 7, the letter challenged the king to fight (Bedford pictured himself as pursuing, Charles as avoiding battle), but also offered to parley —provided that Charles did not behave as he had at Montereau, where he had murdered "our late very dear and much-loved father [-in-law] Duke John of Burgundy." Addressing the king as "Charles of Valois, who called yourself dauphin and now, without justification, call yourself king," Bedford accused him of employing "superstitious and reprehensible people, such as a disordered and defamed woman, in male dress and of dissolute behavior, and also a mendicant friar, apostate and seditious [Brother Richard] . . . both of them, by the Holy Scripture, abominable to God."

Bedford described the situation as it appeared to him: Charles had deceived the "simple people" and seduced and abused the ignorant by telling them that he came to bring them peace and security. He had occupied "cities, towns, and castles" belonging to Bedford's "sovereign lord, Henry, by the grace of God, true, natural, and rightful king of France and England," and had subverted their inhabitants into treason and perjury, causing them to break their oaths and "violate the peace of the kingdoms of France and England, solemnly sworn by their former kings." Bedford summoned Charles to do battle, bringing with him "the said defamed woman and apostate and all the traitors"; or if he wanted to make a peace offer to Henry VI, represented by Bedford, that "good Catholic prince" would be ready to listen. Then the people of the kingdom might remain "in the long peace and sure repose which all Christian kings and princes must seek and demand."[14]

Bedford's stated eagerness for battle did not manifest itself in action. The French army now moved south from Crépy to Dammartin, leaving their advance guard there and continuing a short distance to Lagny, twenty kilometers east of Paris. Bedford's army was at Mitry, fifteen kilometers to the north. Patrols skirmished all day along a stream called the Biberonne, but in the evening Bedford once more led his army back to the safety of Paris. Charles returned to Crépy, whence he sent heralds to summon nearby Compiègne to return to his obedience, which it agreed to do "very willingly." Next, Beauvais, Pierre Cauchon's episcopal seat, welcomed the royal heralds with cries of "Long live Charles, king of France!"[15]

On August 14 the army marched west toward Senlis. Suddenly scouts reported clouds of dust on the Paris road signaling the approach of the English and Burgundians. Charles deployed his army in the fields between Montépilloy, where a castle topped a low wooded hill, and a stream, the Nonette, which ran past the walls of Senlis.[16] It was early evening by the time the enemy arrived and began to ford the Nonette, intending to bivouac. Two French captains, Xaintrailles and Loré, observed the first English troops enter the ford and, realizing that its narrow passage gave opportunity to attack, galloped to the king to report; but by the time the French army could change position, most of the English had crossed. Once more the two armies faced each other, "a culverin shot apart." Until the sun set, there were skirmishes, with "very fine feats of arms"[17] and a few casualties; but at nightfall the English and Burgundians camped on the riverbank near the abbey of Notre-Dame-de-la-Victoire, while the French remained to the east, below Montépilloy.

The following morning, August 15, the king deployed his army in the usual "battles": an advance guard under Alençon and the count of Vendome; the main battle under René of Anjou; the king's personal guard under the count of Clermont and Georges de la Tremoille; a group of skirmishers under Joan, Dunois, and La Hire; and the archers. During the night the English had been busy fortifying their position by digging ditches, arranging their supply carts, and fixing their pointed stakes, to which they added masses of thorn bush, a primitive version of barbed wire. The river protected their rear. The archers took their stand behind the stakes, protecting the main force of the Anglo-Burgundian army, the English on the left, the Picards and other Burgundians on the right. Over them flew the banners of France and England and the standard of St. George.

Joan rode up to the enemy fortifications, her standard in her hand, to issue a challenge, setting off a series of skirmishes. The day was sultry, and the clouds of dust stirred by the horses' hooves so obscured the scene that it was hard to tell friend from foe. Tremoille, spurring his horse, lance in hand, fell to the ground but was hastily helped to remount. Charles's Scots and Bedford's Picards particularly distinguished themselves in the bloody skirmishing. "Both parties felt great hate for each other," wrote Monstrelet, "and no man, of whatever rank, was taken for ransom, but they were all put to death without pity or mercy." The dead in this bitter but inconclusive battle were numbered by the Burgundian chronicler at about 300 from both parties.[18]

At nightfall, the two armies withdrew to their camps, and the king returned to Crépy.

The next morning, Joan and Alençon waited until noon at Montépilloy to see what the English would do. Some of Bedford's men wanted to pursue the French, but Bedford feared ambush. That afternoon the Anglo-Burgundian army once again took the road back to Paris, while the French returned to Crépy and then headed north to Compiègne. On August 17, the keys of Compiègne were handed over to Charles. From that city, the count of Vendome, the Marshal de Boussac, and Gilles de Rais were sent to accept the surrender of Senlis.[19]

Joan spent a restless week in Compiègne, impatient at what she saw as another delay. The Alençon chronicler reported that she called Alençon to her and said, "*Mon beau duc,* get your people and other captains ready. *Par mon martin,* * I want to go and see Paris from closer up."[20]

The day before Joan left Compiègne, an incident occurred that was to cause her embarrassment at her trial, but that also demonstrates her prestige. The count of Armagnac (Jean IV) wrote asking her advice on a sticky question: Which was the true pope? The "Babylonian Captivity" of 1309–1377, when the popes resided at Avignon, had ended in the Great Schism of 1378–1417, with first two and then three rival claimants to the papal throne; in 1417 Martin V had been elected by the Council of Constance. Anti-pope Clement VIII had abdicated in 1429, and Martin was now the generally accepted pope. The count, however, had backed another anti-pope, Benedict XIII, and had consequently been excommunicated by Martin. The count tried to enlist Joan's services as a kind of oracle; probably he hoped to use her advice as an excuse for

---

*A locution reported only by this chronicler, possibly meaning, "by my staff." Anatole France thought that the secretary who wrote down Perceval de Cagny's chronicle invented it.

transferring his allegiance to Martin. Joan sent him an offhand reply: she would tell him which of the three popes to obey "when I am in Paris or elsewhere and have time to spare, for I am at present too much pressed by the war; but when you hear that I am in Paris, send a messenger to me, and I will inform you in all truth which [pope] you should believe in, when I know it by the counsel of my rightful and sovereign Lord, the King of all the world."[21]

On August 23 Joan and Alençon, with a company of soldiers, rode south to Senlis, while the king remained at Compiègne to resume his talks with the Burgundians. The duke of Burgundy was at Arras, where French ambassadors visited him—Regnault of Chartres, Raoul de Gaucourt, Christopher de Harcourt. Burgundian ambassadors returned with them to Compiègne on August 27. Monstrelet wrote that "most of the principal councillors of the duke of Burgundy had great desire and inclination that the two parties become reconciled with each other."[22] The continued success of Charles's nearly bloodless campaigning had made its impression on Philip. The surrender of so many important towns in the neighborhood of Paris demonstrated the weakness not only of the English position but of the Burgundian.

Monstrelet, listing the smaller towns and fortresses in the area that had opened their gates to the king, gave as his opinion that if Charles had gone to some of the cities of Picardy, in the north—St. Quentin, Corbie, Amiens, and Abbeville, among others—they too would have received him; "they desired nothing else in the world but to do obedience to him." These cities were close to Flanders, the duke of Burgundy's most valued territory, and Charles may have hesitated to approach them lest it endanger his diplomacy.[23]

Though the defection of so many towns around Paris gave Bedford alarm for the capital's safety, news that Richemont was carrying the war to the borders of Normandy now caused him to take most of his English troops to Rouen. The remaining mainly Burgundian garrison was entrusted to Louis of Luxembourg, chancellor of France for the English king. Calling together the officials of Parlement and of the city of Paris and the abbots and priors of local monasteries, Louis administered an oath of obedience to Henry VI, "the king of France and England, according to the peace treaty [of Troyes]."[24]

That very day (August 26) Joan and Alençon arrived in St. Denis, just north of Paris, with a vanguard of troops, causing panic in the capital.

The inhabitants of the nearby villages had already flocked into the city with their animals and their grain, harvested before it was ripe. No one dared leave to harvest grapes or other produce, reported the Bourgeois of Paris, and prices soared. Defensive preparations were rushed, more guns emplaced at the city gates and on the walls, barrels of stone ammunition hoisted, barricades raised, and the system of dry and wet moats repaired.[25]

While Joan and Alençon paused at St. Denis, Charles pursued his own offensive on the diplomatic front, and on August 28 concluded a four-month armistice covering the Seine valley from Nogent to the Channel and the Burgundian-held towns of Picardy. Seine towns with bridges were excluded, so that the army would be able to fight its way south if necessary, and so was Paris itself, which the duke of Burgundy reserved the right to defend. The English were invited to join the cease-fire later if they wished.

In this new, broad armistice Charles conceded Burgundian possession of the Picard towns that Monstrelet thought ready to come over to him. What he got in return, the prospect of a general peace conference at Auxerre the following April, hardly seemed much of a bargain, and he was in no hurry to notify Joan and Alençon of his act.[26] Yet the Compiègne armistice drew the duke of Burgundy a step further away from the English and did not prevent an attempt to win Paris. The king moved south to Senlis, forty kilometers north of the capital, where the Alençon chronicler says that Alençon called to beg him to join Joan and the vanguard at St. Denis (other chroniclers say that he had already done so at the end of August).[27] On September 7 the royal army arrived before the city walls, near the Marché aux Porceaux (Swine Market), outside the Porte St. Honoré, on the northwest side of the city. "The Maid and all the company were greatly rejoiced," said the Alençon chronicler, "and there was not a single person, of whatever rank, who did not say, 'She will put the king in Paris, if it is left to her.' "[28]

Yet Charles placed little stock in an assault on the populous and powerfully fortified capital. Clement de Fauquembergue, scribe of the Paris Parlement, reported that Charles hoped to gain the city "by popular tumult . . . rather than by power of force." On September 8, as the attack was begun, Armagnac partisans inside the city tried to create such an effect by "crying that all was lost, and that the enemy had entered Paris and everyone should flee and save himself."[29] Simultaneously,

Assault on Paris; Joan directs the filling of the moat with fascines

Alençon made an appeal to the city government in a letter to the provost of Paris, the provost of the merchants, and the aldermen, greeting them, according to the Bourgeois of Paris, "with fine language intended to stir the people up against each other and against them." But the city council replied telling the Armagnacs "not to waste their paper on this kind of thing; no one took any account of it."[30]

Despite the efforts of the king's partisans, public opinion in Paris proved unready for an Armagnac coup. According to Clement de Fauquembergue, the city had "ample supplies . . . provided a long time before, and the inhabitants and the garrison were united in resistance to the assault." Unlike the towns that had surrendered during the summer, Paris apparently had no confidence in a royal amnesty. In Fauquembergue's words, the citizens were convinced that "it was [the king's] intention to reduce to a plowed field the city of Paris, the town of a most Christian people—a hard thing to believe."[31]

The fact that the assault was made on the day of the Nativity of the Virgin brought Joan sharp criticism at her trial. She in effect credited the choice of date to "certain nobles," meaning Alençon, Gaucourt, and the other captains.[32] (The criticism had a sense other than superstition—the Paris citizens were in church when the attack began, and it was considered a breach of fair play.)

The Swine Market was on a hill, behind which the French posted cannons and culverins as an ambush in case the defenders of the city sent out a sallying force from the Porte St. Denis to the east. The English part of the garrison paraded on the walls, carrying a white banner and one with a great red cross of St. George. According to the Bourgeois of Paris, the professional troops in the garrison numbered only "forty or fifty men-at-arms," mostly English. Doubtless the Bourgeois minimized the number out of irritation at the city's protectors, but it is clear that not only Bedford but Philip had withdrawn troops, leaving the defense of Paris almost entirely in the hands of the city's own communal militia. The attackers, "a good twelve thousand or more," according to the Bourgeois, assembled just before noon, hauling up carts laden with fascines to fill the moats.[33]

The assault began, the attackers shouting abuse at the defenders as they fought. The Bourgeois reported that Joan stood on the bank above the moat and cried to the Parisians, "Surrender to us at once, in Jesus's name! [At Rouen Joan insisted that she had not invoked Jesus, but had said, "Surrender to the king of France."] If you don't surrender before nightfall we shall enter by force whether you like it or not, and you will all be put to death without mercy." According to the Bourgeois, a crossbowman replied, "Shall we, you say, whore, tart!" and shot her through the leg; another bolt wounded her standard-bearer in the foot, and when he raised his visor to remove the bolt, a third shot hit him between the eyes and killed him.[34]

The chroniclers tell the story less melodramatically; under fire of the culverins, cannons, and arrows, Joan crossed the dry moat and reached the "donkey's back," the ridge that separated it from the wet moat. Testing the water with her lance, she found that it was too deep to cross. The heavy crossbow and artillery fire from the walls kept the attackers from bringing up their fascines and scaling ladders. As Joan rallied the assailants, a bolt from a crossbow pierced her thigh, but she refused to leave, only taking shelter behind the "donkey's back," until as darkness fell Gaucourt and others carried her protesting out of the moat. As they set her on her horse and took her back to her lodgings in the village of La Chapelle, she was still insisting, "The place would have been taken."[35]

The Bourgeois happily estimated Armagnac casualties at 1,500—the number, he said, certified by the herald who came to get a safe-conduct to recover the dead—out of which at least 500 were killed or mortally wounded. The Armagnacs had gained nothing but "sorrow, shame, and disgrace . . . but a fool will never believe anything till he's tried it." The trouble was their reliance on "the words of a creature in the form of a woman . . . what it was, God only knows." Joan, he asserted, had promised the Armagnacs "that they would certainly win Paris by assault . . . that they would all be made rich with the city's goods and anyone who resisted would be put to the sword or burned in his house."[36] Monstrelet also testified to Paris public opinion's conviction of the dangers of switching allegiance: the Parisians agreed after the day's fighting "more than ever" to resist with all their power, to the death, persuaded that Charles meant "to destroy them all."[37]

The following day, in spite of her wound, Joan rose early and summoned Alençon, ready to resume the attack and insisting that she would never leave until the city was taken. Alençon and some of the other captains were eager to follow her, but there was a dissenting faction. While the army's leaders debated whether to attack or retreat, a troop of fifty or sixty knights previously loyal to the Burgundian cause, under the leadership of the Sire de Montmorency, rode out from Paris to join Joan's company.* Their arrival tipped the decision in Joan's favor. But as the army was preparing to return to the city walls, René of Anjou and the count of Clermont rode up, sent by the king to summon Joan back to St. Denis. Joan and the rest of the company obeyed, but with the secret resolution that after visiting the king they would return on their own to attack Paris from a point farther west, crossing the Seine by a temporary bridge which Alençon had had constructed. The following day they rode to the bridge, only to find that the king, learning of Joan's insubordination, had quietly foiled her plan. Rather than summoning her and arguing, he had had the bridge dismantled during the night.[38]

The failure of the assault had convinced Charles that Paris was not yet ripe for plucking. Unlike the other towns, the capital remained obstinately Burgundian, and even if the royal army penetrated its walls the threat loomed of a bloody struggle within. Charles decided to with-

---

*Some chroniclers say that Montmorency had already joined the king's party and fought at Joan's side in the battle on September 8.

draw the army to the Loire, leaving governors and garrisons in the liberated towns to await a more propitious time for recovering the capital.

Before Joan left St. Denis, she placed before the image of the Virgin and the relics, on the altar of the basilica where the French kings were traditionally buried, "her suit of white armor . . . together with a sword" that she had won before Paris, "out of devotion, according to the custom of soldiers when they were wounded. And since she was wounded before Paris, she offered them to St. Denis, that being the battle cry of France."[39]

A few days after the battle, Bedford returned to victorious Paris. He sent troops to St. Denis, which the Armagnacs had left "without paying their lodging," according to the Bourgeois, having promised to compensate the townspeople with loot from Paris. To their losses, Bedford and the Paris officials added heavy fines for their surrender to Charles, and the Anglo-Burgundian troops pillaged the town, making off with Joan's armor.[40]

Joan, "with very great regret," accompanied the king back to the Loire. The Alençon chronicler, angry at Charles for ending the campaign, concluded gloomily, "And thus was broken the will of the Maid and of the king's army."[41] That was gross exaggeration, though the enormous expenses of the past year did indeed place constraints on military activity for the immediate future.

Stubborn Paris remained untaken and unpersuaded, but it was now virtually an island in an area where the countryside and walled towns were mostly Charles's. Despite the armistice, small-scale fighting simmered all around the capital as royal garrisons and Armagnac bands harassed and pillaged. "The borders of the Île de France and the region of Beauvais remained in great tribulation," admitted Monstrelet.[42]

Final victory had not been achieved, but the gains made were irreversible.

9. Winter; the Last Campaign

THE ARRIVAL OF THE KING IN GIEN on September 21 signaled the disbanding of the army that had gathered for the march to Reims. Alençon, Joan's close companion since the beginning of the Loire campaign, and whom she "loved greatly, and for whom she would do what she would have done for no other," went off to his estates at Beaumont, north of Le Mans. Soon after, he gathered a force to harass Normandy. According to the Alençon chronicler, he asked permission for Joan to join him, knowing that "her presence would bring many into his company who would not move if she were not with them." The royal council refused, and Joan and Alençon never again fought side by side.[1]

Charles's project of peace with Burgundy was meantime threatened by one of the very successes of the march on Paris. A supplementary agreement to the armistice of August 28 had provided for the return to Burgundy of the strongly fortified town of Compiègne, at the confluence of the Oise and the Aisne, strategically located between Paris and Burgundian Picardy. Compiègne declined to be returned.

The governor installed by Charles after the Paris campaign, Guillaume de Flavy, was prevented from surrendering the town by the opposition of its inhabitants, who feared Burgundian reprisals for their defection to Charles. Charles sent chancellor Regnault of Chartres and other royal councillors to persuade the citizens that the surrender was necessary in order "to withdraw [the duke] from the English alliance." The inhabitants replied that they were "very humble subjects of the king, wanted to obey him and to serve him with body and goods"; but as for committing themselves to the duke of Burgundy, they dared not "because of the great hate that the duke had conceived against them." They begged the king to forgive their disobedience, but none of the chancellor's adjurations could change their minds, determined as they were "rather to lose their own persons and their wives and children than to expose them to the mercy of the duke."[2]

Despite the awkward contretemps, the king still hoped, according to the *Journal du Siège,* that Philip would yield Paris. But when the duke visited Paris (September 30) with a large escort, he used the threat of a separate peace to win concessions from the English. Backed by the University, Parlement, and the citizens, he extracted from a reluctant Bedford all authority over the city, with the title of governor of Paris and lieutenant general of Anglo-Burgundian France, including the government of several towns in the neighborhood of Paris, in Champagne, and in the north. Bedford returned to Normandy.[3] Thus was formalized the shift in power which had occurred in the course of Charles VII's post-coronation campaign, with the duke of Burgundy gaining control of the Paris region and Champagne, while the English drew back to Normandy and Aquitaine.

The armistice was now extended to include Paris, a concession by Charles that confirmed Philip's new power. Philip was able to depart for Flanders (October 17) to prepare for his marriage to Isabella of Portugal, taking with him his Picard escort, "about six thousand of them, as thieving a set of men as ever entered Paris since the miserable war began," said the Bourgeois. "As soon as they had passed the gates, they robbed or beat every man they met."

The Bourgeois, in fact, was becoming disillusioned with both the Burgundians and the English. Before he left, the duke of Burgundy issued a proclamation bidding the Parisians to defend their city in case of an Armagnac attack. "Thus he left Paris without a garrison! Imagine, that was the best he could do for the city," wrote the outraged Bourgeois.

Despite the armistice, the neighboring villages were forced to pay protection money to the Armagnacs, and no one dared set foot outside the suburbs.[4]

A change in relationships was also taking place in the French camp. The state of Charles's finances sharply restricted the scale of military activity for the immediate future, with a consequent reduction in Joan's role. Charles, now master in his own house, undoubtedly appreciated all she had done, but may have shared the annoyance some of his councillors felt over Joan's independence. The combination of these circumstances, added to the failure of the assault on Paris, robbed her of a little of her magic as the court settled down in Bourges. There she lodged for three weeks with Marguerite La Touroulde, wife of the king's receiver general, "sleeping, eating, and drinking" at Marguerite's house. The two women, who slept together almost every night (a normal medieval custom) and visited the public baths together, talked freely. At the Rehabilitation Marguerite said that she had seen "nothing sinister" in Joan, had found her pious and good, "very simple and ignorant and [knowing] nothing whatever except about war."

At Bourges, as previously at Loches, Joan found herself the object of a veneration that embarrassed her. If her stock had fallen with the king and his council, it had risen with the common people. Women brought rosaries and other holy objects to Marguerite's house for Joan to touch. She treated them as she had the duke of Lorraine when he had asked her for a cure; she laughed and said to Marguerite, "Touch them yourself —your touch will do as much good as mine."[5]

After a sojourn at Bourges, the court made a series of peregrinations, during which Joan had an encounter with another visionary, a woman called Catherine of La Rochelle. They met, Joan said, "at Jargeau and at Montfaucon-en-Berry." Catherine, a married woman with children, was a protégée of Brother Richard, along with a Breton mystic named Pieronne and another woman whose name we do not know. Catherine claimed to have had visions of a "white lady, dressed in cloth of gold, who told her to go through the good towns, and that the king would give her heralds and trumpets to proclaim that whoever had gold, silver, or treasure should at once bring it forth, and that she would know those who did not and those who had hidden it, and would know where to find the treasure, and it would serve to pay Joan's men-at-arms." Catherine also "wished to go to the duke of Burgundy to make peace." Joan bluntly told Catherine to go home to her husband and look after her house and children; as for diplomacy, "it was her opinion that they would find no peace save at the lance's point." To be sure that her instincts about Catherine were correct, however, she consulted St. Catherine and St. Margaret, who told her that "this Catherine was mad and a liar."

Joan put Catherine to a test. Catherine said that the white lady appeared to her every night. Joan slept with her, kept awake until midnight, but finally fell asleep. The next morning Catherine said that the lady had appeared. Vexed, Joan took a nap, and the following night again shared Catherine's bed, and this time remained awake all night. From time to time she asked, "Will she come soon?" Catherine answered, "Yes, soon," but no one came. Joan told the king that Catherine was "a fool and a liar," and quarreled with Brother Richard, who felt that Catherine could be useful.[6]

In October the royal council decided on a local military operation. La Charité, a town on the Loire fifty kilometers east of Bourges, had long been held by a Burgundian captain named Perrinet Gressart, who had become a virtually independent power in the neighborhood. A campaign against the town could be undertaken without technically violating the truce, and would clear the Loire of a Burgundian stronghold and eliminate a source of harassment.

A piece of advice which Catherine of La Rochelle gave Joan, and which she might well have listened to, was to not go to La Charité—"it was too cold."[7] Joan herself said that she wanted instead to go "into France" (the Île de France, this time), but the other captains said they must first go to La Charité.[8]

The initial attack in the brief campaign was launched not against La Charité but against the town of St.-Pierre-le-Moûtier, on the Loire forty-seven kilometers to the south, commanded by a relative by marriage of Perrinet Gressart's. The royal army assembled in Bourges and, led by Joan and Charles d'Albret, marched east late in October. A first assault was unsuccessful, because, Jean d'Aulon said, of "the great number of men-at-arms in the town, its great strength, and the great resistance its defenders put up, forcing the French to fall back." D'Aulon, who had been disabled by an arrow wound in the foot, saw that Joan was stubbornly remaining behind with a handful of men. Mounting, he galloped to her side to urge her to retreat with the others. Joan took off her helmet and replied with one of her enigmatic outbursts, saying that she was not

LETTRE DE JEHANNE AUX HABITANTS DE RIOM — 9 NOVEMBRE 1429

Letter from Joan to the Inhabitants of Riom—November 9, 1429,
facsimile from *Les Lettres de Jeanne d'Arc et la pretendue abjuration
de Saint Ouen* by Comte C. de Maleissye.

alone, but she had 50,000 men with her, and would not leave until she
had taken the town. Literal-minded d'Aulon could see only "four or five
men" with her, and urged her again to come away. Instead Joan directed
that fascines be thrown into the moat, an order d'Aulon hastened to help
execute, and to his amazement the town was taken; the defending garrison surrendered.[9]

La Charité presented a more difficult undertaking. In search of supplies, Joan and Charles d'Albret went south to Moulins, whence they
sent letters still farther south to Riom, asking for gunpowder, saltpeter,
sulfur, arrows, crossbows, and other munitions. Joan's letter, dated November 9, 1429, survives and bears her own signature. Evidently she had
learned to write, or at least to sign her name.[10]*

Joan had already appealed to Clermont-Ferrand, south of Riom,
which sent saltpeter, sulfur, and arrows, as well as gifts for Joan—a
sword, two daggers, and armor.[11] Orleans sent men-at-arms and gunners,
with money and clothing.[12]

*When scholar Jules Quicherat first saw the letter, in the municipal archives of Riom
in the 1830s, the wax of its seal bore a fingerprint and a black hair, possibly Joan's (the
hair has since disappeared).

Georges de la Tremoille's castle at Sully-sur-Loire, where Joan stayed with the king before starting on her last campaign

:pite the towns' efforts, the siege could only be maintained for a
1. The Alençon chronicler blamed the failure on the king, who "did
not raise funds to send [Joan] either supplies or money to support her
company."[13] According to Joan, there was at least one assault,[14] while
Jean Chartier's chronicle reported that the town was bombarded, but
that when the siege was raised the French abandoned "the greater part
of their artillery."[15]

Reluctantly Joan returned to court. In December the king conferred
letters of nobility on her and her whole family, transmittable to their
heirs in both the male and female lines. The family's name became "du
Lys" (after the fleur-de-lis of France). A coat of arms was designed
consisting of an azure shield bearing two golden fleurs-de-lis, between
them a sword supporting a crown. At her trial, Joan sought to minimize
her honors and rewards, which brought charges of pride, vanity, and
greed, and insisted that she had never used the coat of arms, implying
that it had been given not to her but to her brothers "without her
asking." The arms, however, were indeed awarded to her; the royal grant
survives in the Bibliothèque Nationale.[16]

As for more concrete tokens of gratitude, Joan said that they were few;
she had asked for nothing from the king except for her military needs
—arms, horses, money to pay the men of her household.[17]

In January Joan was back in Orleans, where the townspeople gave her
a feast, with capons, partridges, pheasants, rabbits, and wine; one of her
brothers received a doublet. She leased a house in the Rue des Petits
Souliers, near the inn whose roof had been pierced by a cannonball,
probably meaning to have her mother live there.[18]

The renewal of hostilities was signaled by news that arrived in February. In order to re-enlist the duke of Burgundy in the war, Bedford had
bestowed a large concession—possession of the county of Champagne.[19]
To make good the title to his new territory, the duke undertook to
recover the towns that had gone over to Charles in the summer of 1429.

The following month, Joan accompanied the king to La Tremoille's
castle at Sully-sur-Loire. From there she wrote the inhabitants of Reims
two letters. The first (March 16) sought to reassure them about their
fears of capture by the Burgundians in the new offensive. She promised
to try to intercept any besieging army, but if she could not, the Rémois
should close their gates, and she would "make [the Burgundians] put on
their spurs so quickly that they won't know where to go, and they will

soon be destroyed." She had some other news that would make the citizens joyful, but was afraid that her letter might be intercepted.[20] The good news may have been a hoped-for coup in Paris.

The second letter (March 28) replied to a message from Reims telling her of a plot by a canon and a chaplain of the cathedral to deliver the city to the Burgundians. The town and church officials hastened to deny their complicity, and Joan assured them that the king was pleased with them, and if they needed help, he would send it.[21]

A letter of a totally different character, written at Sully on March 23, was sent via the German emperor Sigismund and addressed to the followers of the Bohemian reformer John Hus, burned at the stake as a heretic in 1415. Accusing the Hussites of "profaning the sacraments of the Church, destroying the articles of faith, overturning the temples, breaking and burning holy images," it threatened them: "I would have long since visited you with my avenging arm if I were not occupied with the English war. But if I do not soon learn that you have amended your ways and returned to the bosom of the Church, perhaps I will leave the English and turn against you to exterminate this frightful superstition with the sword and end either your heresy or your lives. If you return to the light, if you enter the bosom of the Catholic faith, send me your ambassadors. But if you persist in your resistance . . . expect to see me, with the strongest human and divine power, to pay you in your own coin."[22]

The letter, in Latin, was certainly not written by Joan, and she may have had little to do with its composition, which was probably that of her confessor Pasquerel. Yet the sentiments were not out of keeping with her feelings about heresy. She had previously written both the English and the duke of Burgundy suggesting they join in crusades against the infidels, who in the eyes of the Church included the heretic Hussites. Joan entertained no notions of changing or reforming the Church, its sacraments, articles of faith, or any other element; and she regarded those who did as dangerous.

While Joan was traveling with the court and fighting at La Charité, Paris had suffered a hard winter; the effects of the king's post-coronation campaign continued to be felt in the harassment of the surrounding areas by Armagnac bands. The Bourgeois wrote that they had "committed more crimes around Paris than ever Roman tyrants, forest brigands, or murderers forced any Christians to suffer." Even some citizens, made desperate by deprivation, had turned brigand, he reported. Late in December an expedition had been sent out to arrest them, and on January 2 twelve of them were hanged. A week later ten were beheaded at the Halles. An eleventh was "a very handsome young man about twenty-four years old—he was stripped and ready to be blindfolded when a young girl born in the Halles district boldly came forward to ask for him, and managed to persuade them to take him back to the Chatelet; and then they were married."[23]

On March 21, an Armagnac raid "did much harm," and when a group of Burgundians and Parisian citizens rode out to counterattack, they were all captured and held for ransom. On March 23, the Armagnacs grew bolder and assaulted St. Denis at night, scaled the walls, killed the watchmen and many of the Picard garrison, plundered the town, and got away with horses and "very great loot."[24]

Joan's hoped-for coup was attempted shortly after this. "Some of Paris's principal men," the Bourgeois wrote, members of Parlement, town officials, merchants, and guild members, were implicated in a conspiracy "to admit the Armagnacs into Paris, at no matter what cost." A Carmelite monk acted as courier between the Parisian conspirators and the Armagnacs outside the city. But the plot was discovered and the Carmelite seized and tortured. He implicated his co-conspirators, and during the week before Palm Sunday more than 150 were arrested. Six were beheaded in the Halles on the eve of Palm Sunday, others were drowned, died under torture, or fled. The Armagnacs once more appeared at the gates of Paris, but without help from within were unable to enter.[25]

At the end of March or the beginning of April, apparently in anticipation of the coup, Joan had left Sully and ridden north to Melun, south of Paris, at that moment besieged by Armagnac forces. The Alençon chronicler said that she went "without the king's knowledge, and without taking leave," pretending that she was going for an outing;[26] in reality, her expedition seems to have had the king's blessing, since she was supplied with money ("ten or twelve thousand crowns") and several horses and was accompanied by a little troop—Jean d'Aulon, her brother Pierre, and "two or three lances."[27] Later she was joined by a mercenary captain named Barthelemy Baretta with his company of about 200 men, a Scots captain named Kennedy, Regnault of Chartres, the count of Vendome, and "several other captains and men-at-arms."[28]

Shortly after Joan's arrival, Melun expelled its Burgundian garrison and opened its gates to the Armagnacs. At this point Joan began to have premonitions of disaster, related to her forebodings of the previous summer. "In the moat of Melun," she said, her voices told her that she would be captured "before the feast of St. John [June 24], and that it had to be so, and that she should not be cast down, but take it all in good part, and God would help her." After that, she said, her voices repeated the prediction almost every day; she begged them that when she should be taken prisoner she might die quickly, without having to undergo long imprisonment; but they told her she should be resigned, "it must happen so."

The voices did not tell her when she would be taken, Joan said. "If she had known it, she would not have gone," reported the record of her trial, "and she had several times asked them when, but they would not tell her." Subsequently she "handed over most of the conduct of the war to the captains," but did not tell them about her revelation that she would be captured.[29]

From Melun, Joan went on to Lagny, in the king's obedience since the previous July, where she heard reports of a Burgundian band pillaging the neighborhood. Joan and the other captains set out in pursuit and brought the Burgundians to bay. The enemy archers dismounted, English-fashion, and planted their iron-tipped stakes; the French attacked twice, according to Monstrelet, but were driven back; then reinforcements arrived from Lagny and other nearby towns, equipped with culverins, crossbows, and "other habiliments of war," and the French, although suffering considerable losses in men and horses, surrounded the Burgundians and "put most of them to the sword."[30]

Among the prisoners was a Burgundian captain, notorious to the Armagnacs, named Franquet d'Arras. Joan planned to exchange him for one of the conspirators in the failed plot of March in Paris. When it was discovered that the conspirator, known as the "lord of the Hotel de l'Ours," had been executed, the bailiff of Senlis demanded that Franquet be turned over to him and the magistrates of Lagny for trial, with a foregone conclusion. Joan told the bailiff, "Since my man whom I wanted is dead, do with this man as you ought to by justice." Franquet's trial lasted two weeks, during which confessions were extracted of murder, robbery, and treason.[31] Then he was executed. Joan was widely criticized for condoning the execution of a ransomable (noble) prisoner of war,

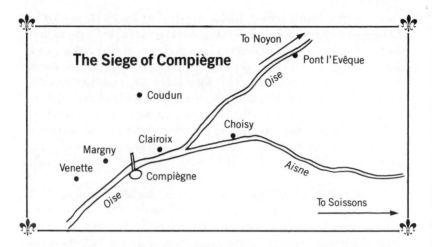

The Siege of Compiègne

who "was a man of valiant conduct," according to Burgundian chronicler Monstrelet.[32] Some modern writers have even seen in Joan's decision a deterioration of character, or on the other hand a victory of bourgeois morality over the feudal code. The truth is probably simply that Franquet had made himself a more than ordinarily hated *routier*. There may also be some political meaning—the swing of popular opinion against the Burgundians.

A curious incident at Lagny demonstrated Joan's growing cult. A three-day-old infant, given up for dead, was brought to her at the church of Notre-Dame. As Joan described it, the child was "as black as her tunic." The girls of the town (the *pucelles*) asked her to join in praying to God and the Virgin. Following their combined prayers, the baby "yawned three times," and began to regain its natural color. It was quickly baptized, and though it immediately died, the incident was trumpeted as a miracle.[33]

From Lagny, Joan went north to Senlis, where early in May she learned that Anglo-Burgundian forces were converging on Compiègne under the personal command of the duke of Burgundy. On May 6 Philip arrived at Burgundian-occupied Noyon, twenty-four kilometers north of Compiègne, and the following day launched an attack on a fortified bridge just east of Compiègne at Choisy-au-Bac. Joan arrived in Compiègne on May 14 and next day rode out with Xaintrailles and three other captains to attack Pont l'Evêque, whose capture would cut the

Joan's capture at Compiègne.

Burgundians off from their base at Noyon. The attack seemed to be making headway when reinforcements arrived from Noyon and drove off the French, who retreated to Compiègne to find that Choisy had fallen to the Burgundians.[34]

On May 18 Joan and the army, accompanied by Regnault of Chartres and the count of Vendome, rode to Soissons, thirty-eight kilometers to the east, the site of the nearest bridge over the Aisne, intending to cross and attack the Burgundians at Choisy from the rear. They arrived to find the gates closed to them. Soissons had gone over to Charles shortly after the coronation; but Philip had now bought its captain, a Picard named Guiscard Bournel, for 4,000 golden saluts.*[35] Joan is reported to have said that if she had Bournel in her hands she would "have him cut in four pieces."[36]

At this moment the chronic shortage of money forced a difficult decision. Compiègne was already fully garrisoned, and Joan's army was becoming a problem for the countryside to support. It was decided to disband it. Joan parted from chancellor Regnault of Chartres for the last time. Instead of returning to Compiègne, she rode southwest to Crépy;

*A salut is a gold coin worth about the same as a crown (écu).

there she learned that the duke of Burgundy and the earl of Arundel were already encamped opposite Compiègne with a large force. She left Crépy during the night with a company of 400 men. Warned that their numbers were small against the Anglo-Burgundian army, she said, according to the Alençon chronicler's hearsay report, *"Par mon martin,* there are enough of us; I'm going to see my good friends of Compiègne."[37] On May 23, by her own account, she reached the town "at a secret hour in the morning," and entered without the enemy's being aware of her arrival.[38]

Compiègne lay on the southern bank of the Oise, with the forest of Compiègne at its back and the Oise and the Aisne protecting it to the north and west. The Anglo-Burgundian troops were camped on the northern bank. Monstrelet, who was with the Burgundian army, described the disposition of the troops: the bridge that connected Compiègne with the village of Margny on the opposite bank was commanded at its northern end by a Burgundian captain named Baude de Noyelles. Upriver, John of Luxembourg, a powerful Burgundian lord, and brother of chancellor Louis of Luxembourg, the official who had governed Paris at the time of Joan's assault, was encamped at the village of Claroix. Downriver, an English company under Sir John Montgomery occupied the village of Venette. A few miles to the rear, the duke of Burgundy held the fortress of Coudon.[39]

At five o'clock on the afternoon of May 23, Joan led a party of five or six hundred men out of the bridge gate for a surprise attack on Baude de Noyelles and his company at the bridgehead on the opposite bank, with the object of freeing the bridge.[40] The commander of the garrison of Compiègne, Guillaume de Flavy, had placed culveriners, archers, and crossbowmen on the walls to cover their retreat.[41]

The attack might have succeeded; twice, Joan said, she drove Baude de Noyelles's men back to his camp, and a third time "as far as halfway there."[42] But the situation was different from that at Orleans when Joan had led the storming of St. Loup, or the attack on the Tourelles; the Anglo-Burgundian forces were not sealed up in isolated fortresses and cut off from each other by the river. John of Luxembourg, riding toward the bridge with a party of knights, saw the danger and gave the alarm, summoning Burgundians downriver from Clairoix, who drove the French attackers back, while the English riding up from Venette cut off the rearmost, among whom was Joan. She was driven off the causeway approach to the bridge and into the fields, and moments later the drawbridge was hastily raised to prevent her pursuers from entering the town. Joan was dragged from her horse by a Burgundian archer, who seized her by the panels of her cloth-of-gold *hucque,* and handed her over as prisoner to the archer's Burgundian lord, Lyonnel de Wandonne, known as the Bastard of Wandonne. With her were taken Jean d'Aulon and his brother Poton and Joan's brothers Pierre and Jean.[43]

Later, in view of Joan's several attempts to escape, there was controversy over whether she gave her *parole,* her word of honor, to her captor. Monstrelet said that she "surrendered and gave her faith [as a prisoner]" to Wandonne.[44] Georges Chastellain, not present, whose information was taken mostly from Monstrelet, reported that Joan asked Wandonne if he was a nobleman, then "gave him her faith."[45] The Alençon chronicler (also hearsay) wrote that Joan refused to give her word of honor, saying, "I have sworn and given my faith to someone other than you and I will keep my oath."[46] Joan herself stoutly denied giving her *parole:* "Never did I give my faith to any man."[47]

The charge, made by early chroniclers, that Joan was betrayed by Guillaume de Flavy, is long since discredited. Flavy had resisted the Anglo-Burgundians and continued to resist them. The drawbridge had to be raised to save the town, and an attempt to rescue Joan would have been risky. Nevertheless, a question remains: Would Alençon or Dunois have been thus abandoned? Perhaps so, but Flavy's action may reflect a loss of prestige by Joan.

If Joan had indeed lost some of her power with the French, she had lost little of it with the Burgundians and English, who carried her off "more joyous than if they had seized five hundred men-at-arms," wrote Monstrelet, "for they feared no captain or leader as much as they had up to the present day feared the Maid."

When the duke of Burgundy came to Margny, he found crowds of English and Burgundians gathered in the fields by the river rejoicing over their prize. He visited Joan, but Monstrelet, present at the interview, reported only that "he said some words to her which I can't remember."[48]

That evening, the duke triumphantly dictated a letter to the inhabitants of St. Quentin telling them the news which he hoped would bring them "joy, comfort, and consolation," and which would expose the "error and foolish credulity of all those who have been favorably inclined toward the deeds of this woman."[49]

Joan was turned over to the Bastard of Wandonne's lord, John of Luxembourg, who took her to his camp at Claroix, and a few days later to the castle of Beaulieu, near Noyon, which was under Wandonne's command.

Thus began an imprisonment which lasted until her death a year later.

⚜
10. Captivity

THE NEWS OF JOAN'S CAPTURE reached Paris on May 25, 1430. The following day the University of Paris, in the name of the Inquisitor of France, wrote the duke of Burgundy demanding that Joan be brought before the University and the Inquisition to answer for "the many crimes akin to heresy" of which she was suspected.[1] The promptness of the reaction to Joan's capture was occasioned by the fear, expressed in a subsequent letter to John of Luxembourg, that "some of the enemies [of the king of England]" might free her "by extraordinary means and, even worse, by money or ransom."[2]

As a prisoner of war, Joan was theoretically subject to ransom and exchange, but despite the University's expressed fear, neither side seriously considered the possibility. Joan was no ordinary prisoner. Jacques Gelu, archbishop of Embrun in the Dauphiné, wrote Charles urging him to save Joan and pay whatever price was asked, but no offer for her ransom was ever recorded.[3] The only mention of any negotiations for Joan occurs in a letter from an Italian merchant in Bruges to Venice in December 1430 (published in the *Morosini Chronicle*): "Rumors were heard that the Maid was in the hands of the duke of Burgundy, and many people said that the English would buy her, and that at this news, the

dauphin sent [the Burgundians] an embassy to tell them that on no
condition in the world should they consent to such a business, or he
would subject to similar treatment those of their party who are in his
hands."[4] However, no other source confirms that such an embassy took
place. Were Charles and his councillors convinced that an offer of ransom would be useless? Was there a feeling that Joan had lost some of her
value? Certainly, her dramatic rise to favor had stirred resentment at
what was perceived as her willfulness and pride.

Chancellor Regnault of Chartres had even found a substitute for her.
In a letter reporting her capture to the people of Reims he told of a young
shepherd who had recently come to the king from the mountains of
Gevaudan in south-central France and who, like Joan, had been commanded by God to "go with the king's people, and the English and
Burgundians would be discomfited." The shepherd, Guillaume, promised "neither more nor less than Joan had done." According to Regnault's report, Guillaume proved not above criticizing his predecessor:
God had allowed Joan to be captured because of her pride, and because
of the rich clothing she had worn, and because "she had not done what
God commanded her, but her own will," an opinion in which Regnault
concurred: Joan "would not listen to advice, but did everything at her
own pleasure."[5] As a sign of his mission, Guillaume bore the stigmata;
"his hands, feet, and side . . . were all stained with blood, like St.
Francis," reported the Bourgeois of Paris.[6]

In contrast to the hostility and indifference shown by the court was
the concern expressed on the popular level. Masses were said for Joan
at Orleans, Blois, and Tours; at Tours the canons of the cathedral and
the clergy led a procession, walking barefoot through the streets.[7]

As for the attitude of her captors, one of the Rehabilitation witnesses,
a citizen of Rouen, expressed a widely held popular opinion in comment-
ing that "such a trial would never have been brought against Joan except
for the fact that she was against the English and in the army"[8]—that is,
she was brought to trial for heresy only because she had fought against
the English.

A distinction must be made between the attitude of the English and
that of the University and Church. The English not only wanted to
discredit Joan but were determined that she should die.

That the English feared her, everyone at the Rehabilitation agreed: "as
much as a large army," "more than all the rest of the French army,"

"more than a hundred soldiers." A Benedictine monk of Rouen testifying at the Rehabilitation explained the feeling on the basis of English superstitiousness: the English judged Joan's deeds in the war to be supernatural, but then everyone knew the English were superstitious; it was proverbial.[9] (Humanist pope Pius II thought that the French were superstitious, which suggests that superstition, like venereal disease and sexual deviation, is always the attribute of another nationality.) The English were not alone in believing in Joan's supernatural powers. She claimed them herself, and most of her comrades-in-arms believed in them. The disagreement was over the source of the power.

Superstition in the Middle Ages, as today, meant irrational belief; yet belief in the supernatural, quite apart from orthodox religion, was almost universal. Belief in witches was part of Church doctrine. To the English and the Burgundians, Joan was a frightening supernatural force, a "creature in the form of a woman . . . what it was, God only knows." At the same time, she was an object of contempt: a woman, a "cow wench," a presumptuous female peasant who had pushed her way into the ranks of the nobility, a person of low morals. (How could a woman live with soldiers and be otherwise?)

The English feared her, felt angrily vindictive, and hoped to attack Charles VII's credibility through her. But Joan could be tried only as a heretic or a witch. Had she simply been a female Du Guesclin, no one could have touched her. She was tried because she fought against the English and said that she was sent by God. The English sincerely believed that she was, on the contrary, in league with the devil.

Converging with the English interest in Joan was the differently grounded interest of the University of Paris.[10] Since its founding in the twelfth century a powerful element both in the Church and in European intellectual life, the University was by Joan of Arc's time an influential political force. In the dispute between Orleanists-Armagnacs and Burgundians, the University sided with the Burgundians, the party of reform, a posture that accorded with its leadership of the conciliar movement, the attempt to introduce constitutional government into the Church. Its support of the double monarchy as a solution to the war accorded with its consistent pacifism, grounded in a belief that peace was an absolute good both for secular reasons and for the unity of the Christian faith.[11]

Much of the University's power lay in its reputation as a theological authority, which had led to its assuming most of the functions of the Inquisition in northern France. In its heresy hunting, it had shown itself milder than the Inquisition, but it shared the Inquisition's conviction that if possible the souls of heretics must be saved from hell fire, and that those who refused to recant must be executed to prevent the spread of their ideas, and to save other souls.

Like other medieval churchmen—the educated elite—many of the University masters served as functionaries in the governmental bureaucracy. Most of the Armagnac masters had fled Paris at the time of the Burgundian revolution of 1418. The remaining faculty furnished a source of office holders to Anglo-Burgundian France. These positions and the benefices granted them by the Anglo-Burgundians supplied their livelihood.

But quite apart from any question of self-interest, the University could hardly fail to be hostile to Joan. Jacques Gelu, the Armagnac churchman who was consulted about Joan at the time of the Poitiers inquiry, had premised the theory of Joan's divine mission on the statement that Charles was the just and rightful king. Most of the Paris masters, on the contrary, believed Henry to be the just and rightful king. Charles had been legally disinherited; he was judged to be an accomplice in assassination; he was the leader of a corrupt faction that obstinately prolonged a wasteful war. As guardians of religion against heresy, the University masters asked themselves the question: How could Joan have been sent by God to serve such a king in a war against the English and Burgundians, good Catholic people? If Joan was not inspired by God, she was probably inspired by the devil, was possibly a witch, and in all her pretensions was a kind of walking insult to churchmen on the Anglo-Burgundian side.

The prime mover in the University's campaign to obtain Joan from John of Luxembourg was Pierre Cauchon, bishop of Beauvais, who claimed the right to preside at her trial, since she had been captured in his diocese. Cauchon was a University master (at one time rector), a leader of the Burgundian faction in Paris, who had committed himself more than most to the success of the English dynastic cause, serving as a councillor and diplomat for the English and helping to negotiate the treaty of Troyes. The events of 1429 had affected him personally, driving him first from Reims and then from Beauvais, and threatening his career.[12]

Cauchon has been the target of centuries of invective. By the time of the Rehabilitation he was dead, and witnesses who were themselves involved in the outcome of Joan's trial awarded him the brunt of the blame. Most later writers have accepted their testimony. Shaw is the only commentator of stature to defend Cauchon, claiming that he was "far more disciplined and conscientious both as priest and lawyer than any [1920] English judge ever dreams of being in a political case in which his party and class prejudices are involved." In modern times, in a country under the strain of civil and foreign war, his scruples "would seem ridiculous and ungentlemanly."[13]

Shaw probably erred on the side of revisionism. Cauchon's eagerness to try Joan certainly suggests self-interest. An ambitious, energetic, capable man, he saw Joan as a personal nemesis. On the other hand, it seems quite credible that he felt that he was acting in the interests of truth and justice.

On July 14, Cauchon arrived from Paris at the Burgundian camp before Compiègne to present letters from the University demanding that "the woman who is commonly called Joan the Maid, prisoner, be sent to the king [of England] to be delivered over to the Church to be tried, because she is suspected and accused of having committed many crimes, sorceries, idolatry, invocations, and other several matters touching our faith and against that faith." On behalf of the king of England, he offered 6,000 pounds to the soldiers who had captured Joan, a pension of 200 to 300 pounds to the Bastard of Wandonne, and a ransom of 10,000 pounds to John of Luxembourg.[14]

But John of Luxembourg was in no hurry to conclude an agreement, and the money had first to be raised.

Joan had spent two weeks in her prison at Beaulieu. If we are to believe the Alençon chronicler's hearsay account, her spirits were good. When her own squire Jean d'Aulon, who "served her in prison," told her that he feared that Compiègne would be forced to surrender, she reassured him, saying that the places the king had recovered through her would be "diligently defended by him and never retaken by his enemies."[15]

At Beaulieu Joan made an attempt to escape. Prying apart the planks of the floor of her cell, she squeezed through, reached the ground floor, and was on the point of turning the key to lock her guards in the tower when the porter surprised her.[16]

Her escape attempt caused her captors to move her farther from

Only remaining tower of the castle of Beaurevoir, where Joan was imprisoned in July–August, 1430

possible rescue, to John of Luxembourg's castle of Beaurevoir, north of St. Quentin. Here she remained for "about four months," until the end of October or beginning of November, according to her own testimony,[17] although other evidence seems to indicate that she left Beaurevoir in September.[18]

Of the castle where Joan was imprisoned, the ruin of a single watchtower survives today, standing alone on a mound in the middle of the fields, on the southern edge of the village of Beaurevoir. At the time of Joan's confinement, the castle was an imposing structure, surrounded by a system of very deep dry moats. Curtain walls punctuated by towers enclosed a residence and a square keep, in one tower of which Joan was lodged. The castle, which had served as prison to Poton de Xaintrailles in 1423–1424, had just been largely rebuilt.[19]

A redoubtable captain who had lost an eye and suffered disfigurement in the civil war, John of Luxembourg was a fiercely loyal follower of the duke of Burgundy. The women of the house, however—his elderly aunt, Jeanne of Luxembourg; his wife, Jeanne of Bethune; his stepdaughter, Jeanne of Bar—were less partisan. According to Joan's testimony at her trial, Jeanne of Luxembourg asked her nephew not to hand Joan ǫ to the English.[20] Whether or not the aunt's plea had any effect, ꞏ shortly left Beaurevoir for Avignon, where she died a few weeks later.

The ladies offered Joan a woman's dress, or cloth to make one, and urged her to wear it, but Joan answered that she did not have God's permission, and that it was "not yet time" to do so. At her trial she said that "if she had to [wear a woman's dress] she would sooner have done it at the request of those ladies than any others in the kingdom of France, except the queen."[21]

Another attitude toward Joan as a captive is revealed by the testimony of a Burgundian knight named Haimond de Macy who visited her at Beaurevoir, and who by his own testimony at the Rehabilitation "tried several times, playing with her, to touch her breasts, trying to put his hand into her bosom, which she would not allow him to do, but repulsed him with all her might." The knight was impressed by her modesty "both in speech and behavior," and surprised that she resisted him.[22]

Little more is known about Joan's imprisonment at Beaurevoir. Two men from Tournai who had been at the coronation visited her and agreed to carry a letter from her to their town asking for twenty or thirty crowns "for expenses," implying that she had a need of money and a way of spending it. (The money did not reach her until after she had left Beaurevoir.)[23]

Joan had been at Beaurevoir for some weeks when she made her second escape attempt. She "commended herself to God and Our Lady" and leaped "from the top of a high tower," an estimated sixty or seventy feet, landing in the dry moat. The Burgundian guards found her stunned and thought at first that she was dead; but miraculously there were not even broken bones, and although for two or three days she was unable to eat or drink, she soon recovered—comforted, she said, by St. Catherine.

Her leap may have been half-suicidal. Joan herself seemed uncertain. She had become depressed both about the progress of the war and her own fate. However she insisted that she "did not do it out of despair," but "to escape and avoid being handed over to the English," and to help the people of Compiègne.[24]

At about the time of Joan's leap from the tower at Beaurevoir, the Breton visionary who along with Catherine of La Rochelle had been one of Brother Richard's protégées was being tried by a Church court in Paris. Pieronne and the third mystic of the Franciscan's little troop had

been captured by the Anglo-Burgundians in Corbeil in March. Possibly
they had accompanied Joan on her journey northward from Sully. Questioned by Church officials, Pieronne injured her own cause by defending
Joan's, maintaining, in the Bourgeois of Paris's words, that "the lady
Joan, who fought alongside the Armagnacs, was good and that what she
did was well done and according to God's will." Pieronne claimed that
"God often appeared to her in human form and talked to her as one
friend does to another," and that she had last seen him wearing a long
white robe with a red tunic underneath ("which is blasphemous," observed the Bourgeois). She refused to recant, and on September 3, 1430,
was burned in the square in front of Notre-Dame. Her companion, said
the Bourgeois, was set free "for the time being," and we do not know
what happened to her.[25]

Whether because of her attempted suicide/escape or the progress of
Cauchon's negotiations, Joan was soon moved still farther from the war
zone, to Arras, where she was confined in a residence belonging to the
duke of Burgundy. Here someone apparently tried to help her escape by
smuggling in a file, but it was discovered.[26]

Meanwhile Cauchon continued to act as an intermediary, visiting
Beaurevoir (we do not know whether he actually saw Joan), Calais (to
confer with the English), and Flanders (to talk to Philip of Burgundy).
A document later signed by him (January 31, 1431) acknowledged the
receipt of 765 pounds for expenses from the receiver general of Normandy for "seven score and thirteen days spent in the service of the
[English] king."[27]

In September 1430, while Joan was still at Beaurevoir, the people of
Normandy were assessed an "aid" (tax) of 120,000 pounds for the con-
tinuation of the war. Of the sum, 10,000 pounds were earmarked "for
the purchase of Joan the Maid, who is said to be a sorceress, a military
person leading the dauphin's armies."[28]

On November 21 the general congregation of the masters of the University wrote to Henry VI, congratulating him on having Joan in his
power and asking that she be turned over to Cauchon and the Inquisition, "so that she might be brought to justice and the great evils and
scandals she had caused be repaired."[29] On the same date, the University
wrote Cauchon rebuking him for his dilatoriness in bringing Joan to
justice (not everyone thought Cauchon's zeal excessive).[30]

Paris was the site originally proposed for Joan's trial. It was the natural location—the capital, the home of the University, the headquarters of the Inquisitor General of France. But Paris was no longer safe; Joan's victories and the post-coronation campaign had left it surrounded by territory recovered by the king. Rouen, in the heart of Normandy, the administrative center of English-occupied France, was heavily garrisoned with English troops. There Joan could be tried in security under the eyes of Bedford, Cardinal Henry Beaufort, the earl of Warwick, and the English great council.

Early in November, Joan was moved again, this time all the way to Le Crotoy on the English Channel, to a castle built almost a century before by Edward III to guard the mouth of the Somme, and surrounded on all sides by the ocean.

On December 20, she was transferred across the estuary to St.-Valery-sur-Somme, the port from which Duke William of Normandy had sailed in 1066. Thence a detachment of English soldiers took her to the castle of Eu, near Dieppe, and finally to Rouen.

11. The Trial: Preliminaries, Preparatory Interrogation

IN ROUEN, Joan was imprisoned in the castle of Bouvreuil, built by King Philip Augustus in the thirteenth century, another monument to the long struggle between the English and French kings.

Although little is known about the physical conditions of Joan's captivity up to this point, except that her attempts to escape indicate that she was not fettered, the Rehabilitation witnesses provided a good deal of information about her prison at Rouen. The room in which she was confined "looked out to the fields"; it was apparently in a tower on the north side of the castle, directly west of the only part of the building that stands today, the great round tower of the keep.[1] The room was reached by climbing up eight steps from the castle courtyard, and it was "very dark."[2] The oval courtyard of the castle was lined with buildings constructed against the walls: the great hall, where governmental functions took place; kitchens and servants' quarters; the apartments of Regent Bedford, at the moment occupied by the earl of Warwick, who was captain of the castle; and opposite Joan's tower, the king's residence, where the young Henry VI (now eight years old) had been living since June of the previous year. In the middle of the courtyard stood a chapel, linked with the king's apartment by a gallery.[3]

152

Donjon of the castle of Rouen. Here Joan was shown the instruments of torture on May 9, 1430.

The English took special precautions to prevent escape. The lock to Joan's door had three keys, one kept by the Sub-Inquisitor, one by the promoter (a kind of prosecutor) Jean d'Estivet, the third by Cardinal Henry Beaufort or his chaplain.[4] Except for interrogations, Joan was never permitted to leave the room. She slept with her legs shackled to a large log or block of wood, five or six feet long.[5] For an even closer confinement, an iron cage had been constructed, but whether it was ever used is unknown. A priest named Jean Massieu, who served as court usher and escorted Joan to and from interrogations, said that a blacksmith had told him he had made a cage in which the prisoner was held in a standing position, secured at the neck, hands, and feet, and that Joan was kept in it "from the moment when she was brought to Rouen until the opening of her trial."[6] The usher himself never saw it, but a mason who got permission to visit Joan said that the cage had been weighed at his house (perhaps to assess its cost), but he had never seen her in it, nor had any other Rehabilitation witness.[7]

Her guards were five English soldiers, three of whom stayed in her room at night while two remained outside the door. They were "men of the lowest sort," the usher testified, "such as would be called in French *houcepailliers* [ruffians]."[8] The names of most of the guards are known; they were commanded by John Gray, a gentleman in the service of the duke of Bedford, with the assistance of two other gentlemen. Joan often talked to the guards, chiefly about her hope of being rescued or released. Whether they were as bad as Massieu painted them, they contrived to add to the miseries of chains and confinement. One of the court notaries reported that he had heard it said in Rouen that they tormented her by sometimes telling her she would be killed, sometimes that she would be freed.[9] Like Haimond de Macy at Beaurevoir, they made sexual overtures to her; one of the reasons she advanced for continuing to wear male dress was that they had tried to rape her.[10] Female prisoners must often have been subjected to such treatment, although Joan's virginity and the fact that she was a political enemy may have given additional motivation.

Probably not long after her arrival in Rouen, Joan underwent another examination for virginity, this time under the direction of the duchess of Bedford, sister of the duke of Burgundy.[11] We are told that Joan invited the examination herself. When asked why she called herself *Pucelle,* she answered, "I can assure you that I am such, and if you don't believe me, have me examined by women."[12] (An improbable story was told by one of the notaries: he had heard that the duke of Bedford spied on the proceedings from the neighboring room.)[13] The examination once more proved her a virgin, though the secretary of a University of Paris master said he had heard that she had "a slight injury from riding horseback."[14] Afterward the duchess gave strict instructions that the guards were to stop their sexual advances.[15] Nevertheless, during the trial Joan complained bitterly to Cauchon and Warwick that the soldiers continued to harass her, despite her "tightly laced hose." Once she screamed and Warwick came to her aid, and if he had not, Joan said, the guards would have raped her.[16]

The examination itself brought further harassment. A tailor sent afterward by the duchess of Bedford to measure Joan for a woman's clothes "touched her lightly on the breast," and Joan slapped him.[17]

Nothing was ever said in the trial records about this examination or the proof that Joan was a virgin; but the court's knowledge of it was signaled by the omission of any assertion to the contrary.

During the month of January, preliminary arrangements for the trial took place. In December Cauchon had obtained a concession from the cathedral chapter of Rouen to allow him to try Joan "as if he was in his own diocese of Beauvais," and early in January Joan was formally consigned to him by the English for trial, although she remained in her castle cell under English guard.[18]

For the trial, Cauchon invoked the Inquisition.[19] Organized by Pope Gregory IX to combat the Albigensian heresy in Italy and France in the thirteenth century, the Inquisition was staffed by members of the Dominican order. Trial involved the local bishop and a certain number of "assessors"—assistants—who were present as consultants, a kind of jury, but with only advisory power.

The procedures of this ecclesiastical tribunal were quite different from those of lay courts. The Inquisitor regarded himself as not only a judge but a sort of father confessor whose task it was to search out the secret thoughts and opinions of the accused rather than to question witnesses about his deeds. He united in himself the roles of prosecutor and judge, and in the all-important purpose of saving the souls of the accused and protecting other souls from contamination annulled many of the rules that governed ordinary courts. All that was needed to bring suit was a public rumor of misdoing, a *diffamatio*. In accordance with the procedures of canon law courts, based on those of Roman law courts, defendants had to testify against themselves, had no opportunity of challenging prosecution witnesses, and were denied counsel and often appeal. There was a large presumption of guilt. Spies were often planted in prison to trap suspects into admissions. Above all, in a crime such as heresy, which involved thoughts rather than acts, confession was of such importance that every effort, including torture, was made to obtain it.

Special conditions also surrounded the punishment decreed by the Inquisition. Church courts could not pronounce the death sentence. Punishment for confessed and repentant heretics was limited to "salutary penances"—scourging, pilgrimages, the wearing of a yellow cross sewn on clothing (the "cross of infamy"), fines, and in severe cases life imprisonment. When the accused did not repent, he was turned over to secular justice, with burning at the stake the usual penalty for heresy and witchcraft, rather than hanging or decapitation, the methods of execution for other capital crimes. The rationale was apparently fear that the victim might magically escape, and a desire to destroy the body so that relics might not be saved.

Cauchon called on the Sub-Inquisitor for Rouen, Jean Le Maitre, to share the role of judge. Le Maitre proved reluctant to respond. He protested that his jurisdiction was Rouen, whereas Cauchon was trying Joan as bishop of Beauvais.[20] Cauchon wrote to the Inquisitor General in Paris, who gave his authorization for Le Maitre to serve.[21] The Sub-Inquisitor was evidently no such enthusiastic partisan of the English as Cauchon. Several of the assessors testified that it "very much displeased him" to participate in the trial; he felt threatened by English pressure. The usher Jean Massieu said that Le Maitre had "several times excused himself from taking part in the trial, and did his best not to be present, but he was told by some of his acquaintances that unless he took part, he would be in danger of death; and he did this compelled by the English." Le Maitre remarked to Massieu on more than one occasion, "I see that unless this matter is carried out as the English wish, death is imminent."[22] Cauchon summoned Le Maitre on February 20, and the Vice Inquisitor briefly appeared, only to absent himself again until mid-March. For the intervening period, Cauchon was the sole judge. After that Le Maitre attended sessions at intervals but took no part in the interrogations.

Already on January 9 Cauchon had named his promoter, Jean d'Estivet, who had occupied that office in the ecclesiastical court of Beauvais. Three notaries were appointed: Guillaume Manchon, Guillaume Colles, also known as Boisguillaume, and Nicolas Taquel, all attached to the ecclesiastical court of Rouen. The assessors, or assistants, numbered about sixty and were drawn from the faculty of the University, from the Dominican order, from among the cathedral canons of Rouen, and from the ranks of priors, abbots, and Church legists. Eight were English, the rest French. About forty regularly attended the trial sessions. Many were young, in their late twenties or early thirties, a few not much older than Joan. Many were on the threshold of distinguished careers, as bishops, as cardinals, in the papal court of Rome, in Church councils, or in the service of princes. Some later served Charles VII.

Witnesses at the Rehabilitation agreed that some of the assessors came of their own free will, some to win English favor, some because they dared not refuse. A few who were opposed to the trial were bold enough to raise objections. One, Nicolas de Houppeville, a middle-aged University of Paris master, testified at the Rehabilitation that he had told

Cauchon that the bishop had no right to serve as judge; it was not proper for him, as a member of the opposition party, to try Joan, since she had already been examined by the clergy of Poitiers and the archbishop of Reims, Cauchon's own superior. Cauchon was indignant, and summoned Houppeville to appear before him. Houppeville complied, but proved no more amenable: he told the bishop that he was not Houppeville's superior and had no right to judge him, any more than Joan. He was subject to the ecclesiastical court of Rouen. When Houppeville insisted on stating his case before that court, he was taken to the castle and thrown in prison. He asked why, and was told that it was "at the request of the bishop of Beauvais." Later he was threatened with exile, but was rescued by the intervention of friends.[23]

Several of the assessors complained about what was a flagrant irregularity of the procedure, the fact that Joan was kept in a military rather than an ecclesiastical prison; but the English were adamant about keeping her in their hands. One of the assessors, an Augustinian monk named Jean Lefèvre, testified at the Rehabilitation that he complained that she should not be in the hands of laymen, and especially Englishmen, since she had been handed over to the Church. Many agreed with him, but he argued to no effect.[24] Even some who were not particularly sympathetic to Joan felt this, but Thomas de Courcelles, the University theologian who later translated the trial record into Latin, said that he could not remember whether the question ever arose during deliberations.[25]

Another irregularity was that the English paid the expenses of the trial —not only Joan's ransom and Cauchon's expenses in negotiating it, but the expenses of the court and the stipends of its officers and members.

Cauchon had no misgivings. He gathered a group of assessors "in a certain house near the castle" and told them that they must serve the king Henry, and that they were going to conduct "a beautiful trial [*unum pulchrum processum*]" against Joan.[26]

The first task of the court was to collect evidence against Joan, not only of heresy and sorcery but of any kind of misbehavior that could be uncovered. Cauchon went about it with the energy of an ambitious prosecutor exploiting an important case, dispatching agents in many directions to investigate Joan's past.

The only part of this pretrial investigation about which we have concrete information was the inquiry made in Domremy and its neighborhood, where three different agencies seem to have been at work. One,

attested to at the Rehabilitation by a priest of Domremy, was a group
of Franciscan monks.[27] A second was a royal commission consisting of
two officials, Nicolas Bailly and Gerard Petit, from Andelot, near
Domremy, and their deputies, who questioned Joan's former neighbors
(as Bailly also testified at the Rehabilitation).[28] A third, identified only
as "a notable man from Lorraine," investigated Joan in Domremy and
"five or six neighboring parishes," and arrived in Rouen to report his
findings (where a Rehabilitation witness, a merchant of Rouen who had
originally come from a village not far from Domremy, encountered
him).[29] The Lorrainer and Bailly and Petit all reported favorably. The
Lorrainer, in fact, said that "he had found nothing in Joan which he
would not wish to find in his own sister." Their reports all met with angry
receptions. Cauchon accused the Lorrainer of being "a traitor and a bad
man," said that he had not done what he was instructed to do, and
refused to pay him. When Bailly and Petit submitted their findings to
Jean de Torcenay, bailiff of Chaumont, he was equally displeased, and
reviled them as "false Armagnacs."

The minutes of the trial make clear that Joan's activities were
thoroughly researched at Orleans, Troyes, Reims, Senlis, St. Denis,
Lagny, Compiègne, and other places, and during her imprisonment at
Beaulieu, Beaurevoir, and Arras. None of the findings were entered in
the record, but they are indicated in the accusations and in Joan's interrogation. Some of the reports were concerned with large issues—Joan's
claim that she was sent by God, her alleged pride, ostentation, and
presumption—others with an array of trivia—rumors that she had found
lost objects by sorcery, the inscriptions on her rings, the marks on her
sword.

On January 13 Cauchon read the findings of the inquiries at a conference at his house, concluding that Joan had a commonly known bad
reputation, a *diffamatio,* the necessary precondition for the trial.[30]

Joan's trial came at the end of an age of political witchcraft trials.[31]
Early in the fourteenth century the charge of witchcraft was invoked
eight times within a few years in suspected attempts on the lives of
French kings. Pope John XXII (d. 1334) prosecuted several political
enemies on charges of sorcery and sent the bishop of Cahors to the stake
for using image magic against him. A number of politically motivated
trials for witchcraft and diabolism occurred in England, notably that of

twenty persons in 1324 accused of trying to kill Edward II and his favorites by magic.

The era following Joan's trial, on the other hand, witnessed the proliferation of an entirely different kind of witch trial, in which the accused were unknowns, mostly poor, mostly women, people on the fringes of society, who were burned in the "vast holocaust" of the later fifteenth and the sixteenth centuries.

Despite its numerous antecedents, Joan's has sometimes been called the first great witchcraft trial, and a witchcraft trial was undoubtedly what Cauchon believed he was conducting. It was as such that the proceedings began. The distinction between witchcraft and heresy was a fine one, since witchcraft was regarded as a form of devil worship and therefore heresy. In some areas (notably in Switzerland) the word for witchcraft was the same as that for heresy.

While the preliminary inquiries proceeded, Joan was subjected to the Inquisition's tactic of the prison informer. One witness at the Rehabilitation said there were two informers, the promoter Estivet having also visited Joan in disguise.[32] The principal spy was Nicolas Loiseleur, a canon of Rouen cathedral and a close associate of Cauchon. He wore a layman's clothes (he was *in habitu brevi*) when he first entered Joan's cell pretending to be from Lorraine and of Armagnac sympathy; but evidently he later revealed that he was a priest, because he was made Joan's confessor.[33] The notary Boisguillaume said that Loiseleur acted as an agent provocateur, encouraging Joan to defy the court and resist attempts to induce her to modify her statements, that Loiseleur told her that she must not trust the judges "for if you do, you will be destroyed."[34] It seems more likely that he was trying to extract information and a confession. On one occasion, according to notary Guillaume Manchon, he, another notary, Cauchon, and Warwick were hidden next door where they could listen while Loiseleur questioned her. The bishop and Warwick told the notaries to write everything down, but Manchon replied that it was not right to begin the trial in this way, and that they would be glad to record testimony if it was elicited in the proper judicial form.[35]

Medieval justice was typically summary—not necessarily inequitable, but swift: a quick hearing and either punishment (often death, seldom imprisonment) or acquittal. By contrast, Joan's trial was extraordinarily exhaustive, lasting no less than three months. The first part consisted of the "preparatory interrogation," occupying fifteen court sessions over a period of nearly a month.

Cauchon did not himself usually ask the questions. The interrogators are only occasionally identified in the record, but seem to have been most frequently University of Paris master Jean Beaupère and Jean La Fontaine, a priest of the diocese of Bayeux, in Normandy, who was Cauchon's "commissioner" (deputy or lieutenant).

The subjects on which Joan was questioned were introduced in a more or less chronological order, but at intervals the interrogators suddenly changed topics or returned to an earlier question, seeking to catch her off guard. The interrogations began in the morning, lasted up to three or four hours, and were sometimes continued after the noon meal. "The doctors themselves became weary," said one Rehabilitation witness.[36]

The questions were sometimes simple and straightforward, but often they were difficult—"convoluted and captious," one assessor characterized them.[37] Joan's answers were unfailingly prompt, and sometimes astonished the assessors by their quickness, logic, and wit: "Even a wise and subtle man of learning, questioned by so many masters and in such company as was Joan, would have been perplexed and overwhelmed,"[38] especially one who knew nothing of the law and of judicial procedure.

Her memory in particular impressed the court; sometimes she corrected the notaries about what she had said, and proved to be right.[39] "I have already answered that," or "I refer to the notary," she asserted, or "On such and such a day I was asked that," or "I was asked that eight days ago."[40] On one such occasion, the notary Boisguillaume insisted that Joan had not already been asked a certain question, the minutes were consulted, and Joan was vindicated. She turned to Boisguillaume and cheerfully told him that if he made another mistake she would pull his ears.[41]

Sometimes the assessors praised her: "You speak well, Joan."[42] One theologian said, "She answered well, notwithstanding the fragility of women";[43] another voiced the obverse of the same proposition: "She was very subtle, with the subtlety of a woman."[44] Notary Guillaume Manchon declared that she could not have defended herself against so many learned men unless she was inspired.[45]

The notaries—at first Manchon and Boisguillaume, later Nicolas Taquel—recorded the proceedings in French, collating their notes after each session and producing official minutes, which they signed. These notes were not in the dialogue form of modern court reporting but in the third person, with only an occasional direct quotation.*

Disputes sometimes arose about exactly what Joan had said, and Manchon wrote "*Nota* (Note)" at the head of any reply that was questioned, so that Joan could be interrogated again and the conflict resolved.[46] Sometimes during the first week of trial, he complained, the judges rephrased answers or translated them into Latin, "or otherwise changed my understanding of the meaning."[47] He was also annoyed, at the first session, to find that he and Boisguillaume were not the only people present who were taking notes. "Some secretaries of the king of England, two or three of them . . . wrote down as they pleased Joan's sayings and depositions, omitting her explanations and anything which worked in her favor." He threatened to resign his post unless this practice was discontinued, and he won his point.[48] A young man, Jean Monnet, employed by University of Paris master Jean Beaupère, also took notes, he explained at the Rehabilitation, "not as a notary, but as Master Beaupère's clerk and servant";[49] Manchon said that there were great differences in what they recorded, and that there was "great contention" between them about it.[50]

But Manchon's major complaint was that during the first week of the trial Cauchon installed two other notaries in the embrasure of a window behind a serge curtain—Manchon believed that Nicolas Loiseleur, the informer, was with them—and they wrote down the testimony, "omitting Joan's excuses."[51] Why Cauchon resorted to the stratagem is unknown. The notes written behind the curtain disappeared, and there is no question of the authenticity of the official report written and signed by Manchon and Boisguillaume. Evidently Cauchon wanted an independent record of his own, we can only speculate why.

First Session, Wednesday, February 21, 1431

The first interrogation was held in the castle chapel. Joan was brought in by usher Jean Massieu. Cauchon opened the proceedings by explaining to her that he was her judge, since she had been captured in his diocese, and that there was common report of "a number of her deeds which were contrary to our faith," and therefore she had been handed over to him to try for heresy.[52]

*Quotations in the account that follows are given as they appear in the trial record.

Joan was asked to swear on the Holy Gospels to tell the truth "about everything she should be asked." At once the proceedings struck a snag. She replied, "I don't know what you might question me about. Perhaps you may ask me such things as I will not tell you." Cauchon asked, "Will you swear to tell the truth about whatever is asked you concerning the faith and everything else that you know?" Joan answered that she would gladly swear to tell the truth about her father and mother, and about everything that she had done since she had left home, but as for her revelations from God, she had never told anyone about them except her king. "Even if they cut her head off, she would not reveal them," the trial record reported, "for her visions, or her secret counsel, told her to reveal them to no one." In about a week, however, she added, she might have further instructions about whether she should reveal them.

Cauchon several times repeated his demand that she take the oath "to tell the truth about matters concerning the faith." Finally Joan knelt, put her hands on the missal, and swore that she would tell the truth about everything asked her concerning the faith, but that she would say nothing about her revelations.*[53]

This contretemps over the oath had serious implications, as became clear with its recurrence at the beginning of many subsequent sessions. A leading modern French jurist has pointed out that Joan was what lawyers call a "bad client," one whose attitude harmed her case. Her most quoted replies, the evasions, refusals to answer, responses in the form of questions, answers that derided the interrogator and pointed up the clumsiness of his questions, while delighting later readers and playgoers, were the kind that defense attorneys shudder to hear. But his conclusion that Joan's replies may have been doctored by the notaries to make her look bad to the legal profession seems improbable.[54] Joan's speech and behavior as reported by Rehabilitation witnesses have the same qualities—colorful, cryptic, sharp-tongued, frank, impudent. At the friendly Poitiers inquiry she was distinctly more cooperative than at Rouen, where her hostility toward her interrogators, particularly Cauchon, was evident; but even at Poitiers she treated her questioners, learned theologians and prominent churchmen that they were, with scant reverence. Andrew Lang explained her attitude by saying that

---

*According to the Orleans manuscript. The Latin record of Thomas de Courcelles states that she took an oath without reservations, implying that she later broke that oath.

Joan's direct experience of revelation made her feel that "the Doctors were pedants, their heavenly science was foolishness," a Victorian Protestant interpretation.[55] Although Joan believed unswervingly in her own revelations, she had no such convictions about revelation in general, and no negative feelings toward the Church as she experienced it at the grassroots level. Significantly, too, she had little respect for other people's alleged direct experience of God, such as Catherine of La Rochelle's. To her, religion meant mass, confession, and the parish priest; the need for theology was outside her comprehension. The questions put by the learned theologians, friend or enemy, annoyed and harassed her. She neither understood nor saw the need for them, but only wished they would stop.

Once Joan had taken the limited form of the oath, she was questioned about her birth, her parents, godparents, baptism, and religious education. The interrogation proceeded smoothly enough until she mentioned her mother's teaching her the Pater Noster, Ave Maria, and Credo. Cauchon commanded her to say the first two, and Joan refused unless Cauchon would hear her in confession. This Cauchon would not do because he wished to treat her as if she had been excommunicated, even though no such sentence had been pronounced. He offered to let her say her Pater Noster to "one or two notable French-speaking men," but Joan, evidently seeking to force the court to accept her as a communicant, said that she would not perform for them either unless they heard her confession.[56]

The session proceeded in an atmosphere of "the greatest tumult." Almost every word Joan spoke was interrupted. At one point six assessors, as well as Cauchon, were questioning her; when one put a question, another interrupted her answer. Several times Joan said, *"Beaux seigneurs,* one at a time!"[57]

Cauchon finally closed the session by warning Joan not to try to escape, but again Joan balked; she declared that she had given her word of honor to no man. She complained about the fetters on her legs; Cauchon said that he had ordered them because of her several attempts to escape. Joan replied that escape was the right of any prisoner, and she would escape if she could. The bishop then ordered John Gray and his assistants to take an oath to guard her strictly and not to allow anyone to speak to her without express permission.[58]

Second Session, Thursday, February 22

The following day the court was moved to a small room off the great hall of the castle; here it met for the subsequent four sessions. On her way to the room, Joan passed the chapel, and the usher Massieu allowed her to pause for a moment and pray. He was bitterly rebuked and even threatened for this by promoter Estivet, who called Joan "an excommunicated whore," and thereafter stood in front of the chapel door to prevent her from praying.[59]

Jean Le Maitre, the reluctant Sub-Inquisitor, was present at the second session, but made excuses about his competence to share the judge's bench. Despite his doubts, and "so that the trial should not be null and void, in answer to his conscience," he would take part.[60] He did not, however, attend another session until March 13, when Cauchon again put pressure on him to appear.

Again the proceedings began with a wrangle about the oath; Joan said she had sworn the previous day, and that should be enough: "You are burdening me too much." Finally she agreed to take the oath in the same form as the day before. But when Jean Beaupère began the questioning, she told him, "You may ask me such things that I will tell you the truth about some and about others I will not." And she added a threat, which must have done little to mollify the court: "If you were well informed about me, you would wish that I were out of your hands. I have done nothing except by revelation."[61]

The questions soon touched on sensitive territory: Joan's first revelations, her assumption of male dress, and the sign she had shown the king at Chinon. She answered most of the questions freely; but when it came to the matter of male clothing, she at first refused to say who had originally suggested that she wear it, then replied that she would not put the burden of that decision on any particular person. When she was asked about her meeting with the king, she gave a response that was to be repeated many times during the trial: *"Passez outre* (Go on to the next question)."* When the voice pointed the king out to her, was there any light? *"Passez outre."* Did she see an angel above the king? "Forgive me, but *passez outre."* She added that before the king put her to work, she showed him "many beautiful apparitions and revelations." What were they? "I will not tell you. You shall not have an answer now; but send to the king, and he will tell you." She was asked about the assault on Paris; was it a good thing to attack on a feast day? *"Passez outre."*[62]

Third Session, Saturday, February 24

The session again opened with a lengthy argument between Joan and Cauchon about the administration of the oath. Joan protested that she might be forced to perjure herself (not in the sense of lying, but of breaking a previous vow) by speaking about matters, especially her revelations, that she had sworn not to discuss. Turning to Cauchon, she said, "I say to you that you should beware of saying that you are my judge, for you are assuming a great responsibility, and you burden me too much." Cauchon warned her that by refusing to take the oath, she was rendering herself suspect. The discussion ended with Joan's taking a limited oath, as before.[63]

Beaupère began by asking her when she had last heard her voice. "I heard it yesterday and today," she replied. She had heard it three times —in the morning, at vespers, and in the evening—and on some days she heard it more often than that. What was she doing when the voice came to her? She was asleep, and the voice wakened her. Did it waken her by touching her arm? It wakened her without touching her. Was it in her room? She did not know, but it was in the castle. Did she thank the voice and kneel? She thanked it seated on her bed and clasped her hands and asked for help and advice. The voice then told her that she must answer boldly, that she must seek advice from our Lord and He would help her.

Here Joan turned once more to the bishop with a warning: "You say that you are my judge; beware of what you do, for truly I have been sent by God, and you are placing yourself in great danger."[64]

Beaupère continued: Did the voice ever change its advice? She replied that she had never found in it two contradictory words. Did it tell her not to answer everything she was asked? "I will not answer you on that matter. And I have revelations concerning the king which I will not tell you." Had the voice forbidden her to talk about her revelations? "I have not been advised about that. Give me a fortnight's delay and I will answer you."

Was the voice an angel directly from God, or a saint? "The voice

comes from God; and I will not tell you everything I know, for I am
greatly afraid of displeasing my voices* when I answer you." How could
she displease God if she told the truth? "The voices instruct me to tell
some things to the king and not to you."⁶⁵

Beaupère asked Joan whether she could make the voice carry messages
to the king. Joan was dubious. Perhaps, if it were the will of God; she
would be very happy if it would. Why was the voice able to speak to the
king when Joan was present but not able to speak to him now? She
answered that perhaps it was not God's will. Without the grace of God,
she could do nothing.

She was then asked whether in the last few days when she heard the
voices, light accompanied them. She answered, "The light comes before
the voices." Did she see anything else? "I will not tell you everything;
I do not have permission, nor does my oath touch that. But the voice
is good and worthy; other than that I am not bound to answer."

Beaupère tried to press her further: Could the voice see, did it have
eyes? Joan replied with an aphorism: There was "a children's saying that
men are sometimes hanged for telling the truth."⁶⁶

Beaupère then asked the question that provoked Joan's most remembered reply: Was she in the grace of God? One of the assessors, Jean
Lefèvre, protested, for the question was unanswerable. If she said yes, she
was presumptuous, if no, she admitted to sin. The interrogator ordered
him to be quiet, and without hesitation Joan replied: "If I am not, may
God put me there; if I am, may God keep me there. I would be the most
miserable person in the world if I knew I were not in the grace of God."⁶⁷
Paraphrased from a popular prayer,† the words so neatly avoided the
trap Beaupère had set that the court was "stupefied" (according to
notary Boisguillaume).⁶⁸

The questioning shifted to Joan's childhood and the political allegiance of her native village. Had her voice told her when she was young
to hate Burgundians? Joan replied that after she understood that her
voices were for the king of France, she did not like the Burgundians. Had
the voice revealed to her that the English would come to France? The
English were already in France when her voices began to come to her.

*Both Joan and Beaupère alternated between singular and plural.
†The prayer recorded in three extant fifteenth-century manuscripts reads in one version:
"We pray for those who are in a state of grace, that God may keep them there until the
end, and for those who are in mortal sin, that God may rescue them from it quickly."

As a child, did she have a great desire to defeat the Burgundians? She had a great wish and desire that her king should have his kingdom. (Again, a nice answer.)[69]

She was now interrogated about the Ladies' Tree and the customs that surrounded it, and about the Bois Chenu. She said that her brother had told her that people said she had her first revelations at the Ladies' Tree, but it was not true. As for the Bois Chenu, at the time she came to the king, people asked her whether in her country there was a wood called the Bois Chenu, because there was a prophecy that a maiden would come from there who would do wonderful things. But she put no faith in it.[70]

The issue of her male clothing was raised again. Did she want a woman's dress? "Give me one, and I will accept it and go [that is, leave prison]; otherwise I will not accept it. I am content with this one, since it pleases God that I wear it."[71]

This offer by the court was the first of many; Joan's response was always in the same vein. It is difficult to comprehend the weight given to the matter, which became increasingly the issue on which Joan's fate hung. Why was it so important to the judges? At Poitiers the question had been deliberated, and the clerics had decided that, under the circumstances, her style of dress was permissible; Jean Gerson had also considered the matter and had come to the same conclusion. But at Rouen Joan's male clothing became the symbol, both to the judges and to Joan herself, of her resistance to the court.

Fourth Session, Tuesday, February 27

The questioning about Joan's voices continued; Joan said that she had leave from our Lord to say that they were those of St. Catherine and St. Margaret, "and their heads are crowned with beautiful crowns, very opulently and richly. If you doubt it, send to Poitiers, where I was questioned before." She knew them by their greetings, and because they told her their names. As for how they were dressed, or their age, she was not permitted to say. The first voice that had come to her, however, was that of St. Michael, "and he was not alone, but was accompanied by angels from heaven. . . . I saw them with the eyes of my body, as well as I see you; and when they left, I wept, and wished they would take me away with them." As for the form in which St. Michael appeared, or what he told her the first time, "You will have no other answer."[72]

The matter of male clothing was raised again; had the voice ordered her to wear it? Joan temporized; the clothing was a small matter, and she had not assumed it by the counsel of any living man. "Everything that I have done is at our Lord's command, and if He ordered me to do otherwise, I would obey, since it would have been at His command." Had she done well to assume male dress? Everything that she had done at the Lord's command she believed had been done well.[73]

The subject of Joan's arrival at Chinon was introduced once more, and again she was asked if there was an angel over the king's head when she had seen him for the first time. "By the Blessed Mary! if there was, I don't know, I didn't see it."[74]

She testified about the discovery of the sword at St.-Catherine-de-Fierbois, and a discussion of her different swords ensued: she had always worn the sword of St.-Catherine-de-Fierbois up to the time of the assault on Paris—but it was not the sword she had left on the altar at St. Denis. What had happened to it? After Lagny, she had a sword she had taken from a Burgundian there (Franquet d'Arras?); it was a good sword for war, and for giving buffets and swipes. The interrogator asked her if she had ever been in the town of Coulange-la-Vineuse, near Auxerre; the preliminary inquiries had evidently uncovered a story later told by chroniclers, that in that town Joan had broken the sword of St.-Catherine-de-Fierbois in chasing a camp follower, thereby bringing bad luck to her cause. Joan said the town's name meant nothing to her.[75]

At the court's request, Joan described her standard. The interrogator was particularly interested in the words JHESUS MARIA that it bore, which seemed to connect her with Brother Richard's heretical belief in the power of the name of Jesus. The court thought that she attributed magical powers to her standard. Which did she prefer, her sword or her standard? She much preferred her standard, perhaps forty times as much, and she carried it herself during attacks, "in order to avoid killing anyone." She had never killed any man. Who had caused her to design such a standard? "I have told you often enough that I have done nothing except at God's command."[76]

The questioning passed to the fighting at Orleans, and then to the siege of Jargeau. Why had Joan refused to conclude a treaty with the commander of the English garrison? The implication was that Joan's bloodthirstiness had prevented a peaceful surrender and resulted in the slaughter of English prisoners. Joan replied that the English had been unwilling to accept either her terms or those of the other captains. Had her voices counseled her about this? She did not remember.[77]

The court record says nothing more than this, but a probably apocryphal detail comes from another source. The duchess of Bedford's physician, Jean Tiphaine, testified at the Rehabilitation that one of the assessors, Jacques de Touraine, was the interrogator, and that the question was actually whether Joan had ever been "in a place where Englishmen were killed." Joan's response, according to Tiphaine, was "In God's name, yes. How gently you speak! Why don't they leave France and go back to their own country?" A "great English lord" (whose name Tiphaine could not remember) present at the session was impressed with the answer and remarked, "Truly, she is a good woman. If only she were English!"[78]

Fifth Session, Thursday, March 1

The interrogation was conducted by Cauchon, and the session was characterized by the violent hostility between him and Joan. The argument about the oath recurred, with the same resolution as before. This time, after taking the limited oath, Joan said, "I will tell you the truth just as if I were before the Roman pope." Mention of the pope gave Cauchon an opening. When she spoke of our lord pope, which did she believe was the true pope? Joan answered with a disingenuous question: Were there two?[79]

Cauchon turned at once to Joan's reply to the count of Armagnac's letter asking about the three popes. Cauchon believed that her reply (that she would think about it and let the count know) showed her as arrogant and presumptuous. The letters, obtained by what means it is impossible to say, were introduced as evidence and entered into the record. Joan defended herself by saying that she had been on the point of mounting her horse when she dictated her answer; then she said that the messenger had been in a hurry. "If he had not gone away so hastily he would have been thrown into the water, though not through her" (evidently the soldiers threatened to drown him). Pressed by Cauchon, she said that as for consulting the "King of the world" about the matter, as she had promised in her letter, "she knew nothing about it." She did not know what to tell the count as to which pope the Lord wanted him to obey; as for herself, "she believed in the pope at Rome," and her message about giving the count a further answer referred to an entirely different matter; furthermore, she had never written or dictated anything about the three popes. The court remained unconvinced.[80]

Some of Joan's other letters—to the English king, to Bedford, and to the English captains—were also entered into the record, and Joan was asked why she put the words JESUS MARIA on her letters, with a cross. Joan replied that she sometimes put a cross on her letters and sometimes did not. The cross signified that the letter was not to be taken seriously, and the person to whom it was addressed was not to do as the letter instructed him.* She acknowledged that she had written the letters, but said that some of her words had been changed. She had told the English to surrender not to the Maid but to the king; she had not referred to herself as *chef de guerre;* and she had not said that she would drive the English out of France "body for body *(corps pour corps)*."[81]

The subject of the letters led Joan to a prediction. Before seven years had passed, the English would have a worse defeat than at Orleans; they would have lost everything they held in France. "I know it by the revelation that has been given me, and I know it as well as I know you are here." She could not tell the day or the hour. As for the year: "You will not learn this, but I hope that it will be before St. John's Day [June 24]." Joan had evidently told John Gray, who commanded her guards, that the English would be overthrown before St. Martin's Day (November 11). Asked about this statement, she said that many things would happen before that time, and the English might be brought low. How did she know? St. Catherine and St. Margaret had told her.[82]

Again the questioning turned to her revelations. Did the angel Gabriel appear to her with St. Michael? She did not remember. How were the saints dressed? Their heads were richly crowned, but she would say nothing of their other clothing. How did she know whether they were men or women? By their voices, and by what they revealed to her. What part of them did she see? The face. Did they have hair? She answered, *"Il est bon à savoir* [You'd better believe it]!" (Literally, "It is good to know.") Was their hair long? "I don't know." She did not know if they had any arms or other members. How could they speak if they had no

---

*French scholar Jean-Baptiste-Joseph Ayrolles suggested in *La vraie Jeanne d'Arc* (1890) that Joan was employing either a ruse, intending false information to fall into enemy hands, or a means of getting rid of importunate petitioners who asked her for recommendations.

other members? "I leave that to God." She said that the voice was beautiful, sweet and soft, and it spoke French. Did St. Margaret speak English? "Why should she speak English, when she is not on the English side?"[83]

Joan was questioned about her rings. One, which had been taken by her Burgundian captors, bore the words JESUS MARIA (again the court was attempting to connect her with Brother Richard's sect). It had been given her by her mother or father in Domremy. The other ring was given her by her brother; Cauchon himself had confiscated it. Joan first said, "You have it—give it back to me," then that he should give it to the Church.

Had Joan employed her rings in white magic? No, she had never cured anyone with her rings.[84]

Back to her revelations: What promises had St. Catherine and St. Margaret made her? She protested that this had "nothing at all to do with your trial," but said that among other things they had told her that the king would be restored to his kingdom whether his enemies wished it or not. And they promised to take Joan to paradise, as she had asked them to do. Had they promised her anything else? They had made other promises, but she would not tell them—they had nothing to do with the trial. But within three months she would reveal another promise. Had the saints told her that within three months she would be freed from prison? (Perhaps Joan had confided her hopes of release to Loiseleur or to John Gray.) She replied, "That has nothing to do with your trial; I do not know when I will be freed." She added that those who wanted to remove her from this world might well themselves go first. When Cauchon persisted, she said, "One day I will be freed"; she could not tell when until she had permission.[85]

Did her voices forbid her to tell the truth? "Do you want me to tell you that which concerns the king of France? There are many matters that have nothing to do with the trial." She was sure, however, that the king would regain his kingdom. And if it were not for the daily comfort of her revelation, she would die.[86]

In hope of catching Joan off guard, Cauchon took a sudden turn: What had she done with her mandrake? The mandrake was a medicinal plant used in both black (maleficent) and white (beneficent) magic. Joan replied that she had never had one; she had heard that there was one near her village, but she had never seen it. She had heard that it was a dangerous and evil thing to keep, but she did not know what it was used for; she had heard that it attracted money, but she did not believe it. Her voices had never told her anything about it.

Back to St. Michael: In what form did he appear? Joan answered that she did not see his crown, and knew nothing about his clothing. Was he naked? Another riposte: "Do you think God cannot afford to clothe him?"

Did St. Michael have hair? "Why should they have cut it?"

She added that she had not seen St. Michael since she had left the castle of Crotoy, nor had she seen him very often; she did not know whether he had hair. Did he have his scales? (St. Michael was often pictured at the Last Judgment weighing the souls of the dead.) "I don't know." She felt great joy when she saw him, and felt that she was not in mortal sin. She had confessed to both St. Catherine and St. Margaret. When she confessed, did she ever believe she was in mortal sin? She did not know, but "Please God that I never was, and that I never will act so that my soul will be thus burdened."[87]

The matter of the king's sign was introduced once more, and once more Joan refused to discuss it, saying that it had nothing to do with the trial. Was anyone with the king when she had shown him the sign? She thought not, but there were many people fairly near. Had she seen a crown on the king's head when she showed him the sign? "I cannot tell you without going against my oath."[88]

Sixth Session, Saturday, March 3

Beaupère opened the interrogation by asking Joan about the appearance of her saints. Did St. Michael have wings? What about the bodies and limbs of the other saints? "I have told you everything I know; and I would rather you cut my throat than tell you more." Did Michael and Gabriel have natural heads? "I saw them with my own eyes, and I believe it was they, as firmly as I believe that God exists."* Did she believe that God made them in the shape and form in which she saw them? Yes. Did He create them that way from the beginning? "You will have nothing

*During the previous session, Joan had said that she "did not remember" whether Gabriel had appeared to her; at this point she seems to have accepted the fact that he had, and hereafter Gabriel was added to her roster of saints; later she said that he comforted her early in May and her voices identified him.

else from me for the present, because I have already answered."[89]
She was asked about the revelation that she would escape. "That does
not touch on your trial. Do you want me to speak against myself?"
Pressed further about what her voices had promised, she said, "They told
me that I would be freed, but I do not know the day nor the hour; and
they told me to put a cheerful face on it."[90]
Again the male dress: Had the commission at Poitiers asked whether
she had assumed it at the instruction of her voices? "I do not remember."
They had, however, asked her where she had first worn it, and she had
told them that it was at Vaucouleurs. Had the king or queen or others
of her party asked her to change to woman's dress? "That is not in your
trial." Was she not asked to do so at Beaurevoir? "Yes, indeed. And I
answered that I would not change it without God's permission."[91]
Beaupère asked whether her men-at-arms had had standards made
like hers. She answered that some of her companions-in-arms did, but
only to identify themselves as of her party. Beaupère tried to exact from
her an admission that she had claimed her standards were lucky. Had
she sprinkled holy water on them or caused them to be so sprinkled? "I
know nothing of it; if it was done, it was not done by my order." Had
she seen it done? "That is not in your trial. And if I saw it done, I am
not now advised to answer."[92]
She was questioned about Brother Richard and their meeting at
Troyes, and then about the cult that had formed around her. Did she
know that the people of her party had had a mass and prayers said for
her? She answered that she did not know, but if they did, it was not at
her command; and if they had prayed for her, she was sure that they had
done nothing wrong. Did the people of her party believe firmly that she
was sent by God? "I don't know what they believe, and I refer to their
opinion; but even if they do not believe it, I am sent by God." What were
people thinking when they kissed her feet and hands and clothing? She
answered that when people came to see her, she prevented their kissing
her hands as far as she could, but poor people came to her because she
welcomed them and helped them.[93]
A number of questions followed that were designed to show that she
had performed sorcery: Had women touched her ring with their own
rings? Many women had touched her hands and rings, but she did not
know their intentions. Had her people caught butterflies (used in magic)
in her standard near Château-Thierry? It was a story made up by her

enemies.* Had she found gloves for one of the knights at Reims who had lost them? No, one knight had lost his gloves, but she did not say she would find them.[94]

Had she received the sacraments in men's clothing? Yes, but she did not remember that she had received them in armor.

An absurdly trivial incident was introduced: Why had Joan taken the bishop of Senlis's horse? When Joan had arrived at Senlis, the bishop, a Burgundian partisan, had fled to Paris, and his carriage horse had been seized for Joan's use. Joan discovered, however, that the horse was not strong enough to bear the weight of armor, and it was given to La Tremoille to return to the bishop. Joan explained to the court that she had bought the horse for 200 gold saluts, but she did not know whether the bishop had ever received the money. She had written him that he could have the horse back if he preferred.[95]

She was asked about the infant at Lagny who had revived after her prayers and those of the girls of the town. Did not the townspeople say that her prayers had brought the baby back to life? "I never inquired."[96]

The subject of Catherine of La Rochelle was raised, and Joan told about Catherine's pretensions and how she had tested them.[97]

A theme was now introduced to which the court was to return again and again, the role of her voices in her failures and defeats. Why did she not succeed in capturing La Charité, since she had God's command? Joan replied defensively, "Who told you that I was commanded to enter?" Did her voice not counsel her to go there? Joan answered that she had wanted to go "into France," but the men-at-arms told her that it was better first to attack La Charité.[98]

She was asked about her leap from the tower at Beaurevoir. The preliminary inquiry had apparently turned up a report that Joan had been angry and had used profanity when the Burgundian guards found her. Joan denied it. There was another report that she had blasphemed when she learned that Guiscard Bournel had sold the town of Soissons to the Burgundians; she denied this too, and said that those who had reported it were mistaken.[99]

At this point, Cauchon adjourned the court. He had predicted a "beautiful trial," and had invited a number of prominent people to watch

---

*The *Chronique de la Pucelle* (p. 318) says that at Troyes "some simple folk said that they saw the Maid's standard surrounded by an infinity of white butterflies."

him prosecute what he believed would be a clear case against an illiterate nineteen-year-old peasant girl who was either a fraud or possessed by evil spirits, or both. But at the end of the sixth session, it was clear that his strategy had failed. He now called a series of conferences in his house to go over the minutes of the trial and determine how to proceed further. The conferences, held every day for a week, produced two conclusions: that Joan should be questioned henceforth privately in her cell, and that the number of assessors in attendance should be limited to a selected few. The explanation given publicly for limiting the attendance was that the "various occupations" of the assessors made it difficult for them to be present. The real reason was evidently that Cauchon wished to eliminate assessors sympathetic to Joan and at the same time to make the trial less public.[100]

It seems to have been at this point that a distinguished Norman cleric, Jean Lohier, arrived in Rouen. Consulted by Cauchon, Lohier told the bishop what he did not want to hear. After reading the record of the proceedings, he pronounced the trial invalid for several reasons: its form was questionable; it was held not in the ecclesiastical court but in the castle behind closed doors, and in a place where the participants were not free to speak; the honor of the king of France, whose cause Joan upheld, was at issue, but neither he nor anyone supporting him had been summoned; the prisoner had not been informed of the evidence against her; and although she was "a simple girl," she had no counsel to help her answer "so many masters and doctors in profound matters, especially having to do with her revelations."

Cauchon was furious; he ordered Lohier to remain for the trial, but the Norman announced that he was leaving. Notary Guillaume Manchon reported that Cauchon then went to some of the University masters who were assessors and vented his frustration on them. "Here's Lohier, who wants to ruin our trial by giving his interlocutory judgments! He condemns the whole thing and says it is worth nothing. If you are to believe him, we ought to start all over again, and everything that we have done is worthless. It's easy to see which side he's on. By St. John, we'll do nothing of the sort; we'll go on with our trial as we have begun."

According to Manchon's testimony at the Rehabilitation, Lohier spoke to him the following morning in the cathedral: "You can see how they'll proceed. They will catch her if they can by her own words—that is, when she says, 'I know for certain,' touching her apparitions [it is one thing], but if she says, 'It seems to me,' instead of 'I know for certain,' I do not believe that any man can condemn her. I think they are proceeding more from hate than anything else, and therefore I will not stay here any longer, for I want to have no more to do with it." Shortly afterward, Lohier repaired to Rome, where he served on the Rota, the papal appeals court, and was its dean at the time of his death.[101]

Cauchon's new tactic was a success. The second phase of the trial marked a change in Joan's demeanor, whether it was the prison setting in which the court was held and the limitation of the participants to a small number, most of them implacably opposed to her, or whether fetters and captivity and the pressure of the trial had worn her down. In the earlier phase, Joan had been determined, resistant to suggestion and leading questions, and matter-of-fact; in the second she showed flashes of spirit, but where she had once replied, *"Passez outre,"* or denied the questioners the answers they tried to extract, she now began to furnish them with what they wanted. Her answers became vague and sometimes extravagant. Nevertheless, and despite everything, she stood her ground on the essential questions.

Seventh Session, Saturday, March 10

Only half a dozen assessors were present when the court assembled in Joan's cell and Jean La Fontaine began the interrogation with questions about her capture at Compiègne. Like the queries about La Charité, this line of questioning was meant to discredit her voices. Had they told her to make the sally in which she was captured? Joan said that they had not. She did not know that she would be captured that day, although she had always been told she would eventually be taken prisoner.[102]

La Fontaine questioned her about her coat of arms, her horses, and her "treasure," with the intention of showing that her lifestyle had become lavish and pretentious.[103] Then he returned once more to the king's sign. Up to this point Joan had refused to divulge anything about it, or even that there had been such a phenomenon. She had only made "revelations" to the king.

Evidently either the preliminary inquiries or Loiseleur's spying had led her inquisitors to believe that Joan had shown the king some concrete object, something magical, perhaps a crown, that caused him to place his confidence in her. Now Joan suddenly gave them the answer they sought:

her sign was "fine and honorable, and very believable, and good, and the richest thing in the world." Why was she unwilling to disclose it, when she herself had required a sign from Catherine of La Rochelle? Joan replied that if Catherine had shown her sign as Joan had, to "notable churchmen, bishops and archbishops, the archbishop of Reims and others whose names she did not know, and Charles of Bourbon, La Tremoille, and several other knights, who saw and heard it as clearly as she saw those to whom she was talking at that moment," Joan would not have asked Catherine for a sign. But in any case, she knew from St. Catherine and St. Margaret that as for the matter of Catherine of La Rochelle there was absolutely nothing in it.

Did the sign still exist? "*Il est bon à savoir,* and it will last a thousand years. It is in the king's treasury." Was it gold, silver, or precious stone, or crown? "I will tell you no more; and no man could devise anything as rich as the sign. In any case, the sign you need is for God to deliver me from your hands, and that is the one He will most surely send you."

When the sign came to the king, how did Joan respond? She thanked the Lord for delivering her from the questions of the churchmen at Poitiers "who were arguing against her" and knelt. In previous sessions, the court had asked several times whether an angel had been present when Joan showed the king the sign, and Joan had either refused to answer or denied it; now she said that an angel had indeed brought the sign to the king. "The churchmen stopped arguing when they witnessed the sign." When the king and his retinue had seen the sign and the angel that brought it, she asked the king if he was satisfied, and he said yes. And then she went into a little chapel nearby, and she heard that after she left more than 300 people saw the sign. And God was willing to let them see the sign for love of her, so that they might stop questioning her.[104]

Eighth Session, Monday, March 12, Morning

Once more only a handful of assessors were present, with La Fontaine doing the questioning, again about the sign and the angel. Had the angel who brought the sign said anything? Yes, he told the king that he should put Joan to work, and the country would soon be relieved. Was this angel the same one that first appeared to her? It was always the same one, and he never failed her. Did not the angel fail her when she was captured?

It was God's will. Had not the angel failed her with respect to her spiritual well-being? "How could that be, when he comforts me every day?" She believed that the comfort came from St. Catherine and St. Margaret. Did she call them, or did they come without being called? They often came without being called, and if she needed them, she asked the Lord to send them. Did she ever call them when they did not come? She had never had need of them but they had responded.[105]

Had St. Denis ever appeared to her? Not that she knew. Had she spoken to God when she promised to keep her virginity? "It ought to be enough to promise it to those whom He sent, that is, to St. Catherine and St. Margaret."[106]

The subject of Joan's vow of virginity led to a new line of questioning: Why had Joan cited "a certain man of Toul" for breach of promise? "I did not cite him, he cited me, and I swore to tell the truth before the judge." She had made the man no promise. The first time she heard her voice, she swore to remain a virgin as long as it should please God, and she was then about thirteen.[107]

Had she talked about her voices to her parish priest or any other churchman? No, only to Robert de Baudricourt and the king. The voices had not compelled her to keep them secret, but she was afraid the Burgundians might prevent her from making her journey, and she was especially afraid that her father would stop her. Had she done well to leave without saying goodbye to her parents? One must honor one's mother and father. She answered that she had obeyed them in everything else but this, but that she had written them a letter and they had forgiven her. Had she not sinned when she left her father and mother? Since God had commanded it, she had to obey, and if she had had a hundred fathers and a hundred mothers, if she were a king's daughter, she would still have gone. Had she asked her voices whether she should tell her father and mother that she was leaving? The voices had been willing for her to tell them, except for the trouble that they would have made; as for herself, she would not have told them for anything. Her voices left it up to her whether to tell her father or mother or to be silent.[108]

She was now asked a curious question: Had she ever received letters from St. Michael or her voices? Possibly a trap had been laid with letters sent her in prison purporting to be from her voices. Her answer is as puzzling as the question: "I have not had leave to tell you this, but within a week I will gladly tell you what I know."[109]

Had her voices ever called her "daughter of God, daughter of the Church, great-hearted Maid"? They had often called her "Joan the Maid, daughter of God." Why should she be unwilling to say the Pater Noster (Our Father) if she called herself daughter of God? She would willingly say it, and she had refused previously with the intention that my lord of Beauvais would hear her confession.[110]

Ninth Session, Monday, March 12, Afternoon

When the interrogation resumed that afternoon, Cauchon was absent (perhaps consulting with Sub-Inquisitor Le Maitre, who had returned to Rouen). Again Jean La Fontaine conducted the questioning. The inquiry in Domremy had unearthed the fact that her father had had premonitory dreams about Joan's going off with soldiers, and Joan was now asked about them. She said that her father and mother had nearly lost their minds when she went away to Vaucouleurs. Had these thoughts or dreams come to her father when she had her visions? Yes, more than two years after she heard the first voices.[111]

Again she was asked whether Robert de Baudricourt had suggested that she wear man's dress; she answered that she had done so at her own will and not at the request of any man in the world. Had her voices commanded her to do so? "Everything I have done that is good, I have done by command of the voices." Did she not believe that she had done wrong in wearing man's dress? No, and even at that moment if she were with her own people in the same male dress, she believed that it would be for the great good of France to do as she had done before her capture.[112]

How would she have liberated the duke of Orleans? She would have taken enough English prisoners to exchange for him, and if not, she would have crossed the sea to rescue him. Had St. Margaret and St. Catherine told her that she would do so within three years? (Here again Loiseleur's prison spying was in evidence.) Yes, and she had told the king to let her take prisoners. If she had lasted three years without hindrance, she would have liberated him—even a shorter term than three years, but longer than one year, she did not know exactly.[113]

Tenth Session, Tuesday, March 13

Le Maitre, the Rouen Sub-Inquisitor who had resisted participation, joined Cauchon as judge at this session, having been pressured to do so by an appeal from Cauchon to the Inquisitor General in Paris.[114] Once more Joan was asked what the sign was that she had given the king. She replied, "Do you want me to break my vow?" Le Maitre asked her whether she had sworn to St. Catherine not to reveal the sign. "I have sworn not to reveal the sign of my own accord, because I have been pressed to tell about it too much."

Here the trial record added that Joan said to herself, "I promise that I will say no more about it to anyone." But she immediately volunteered the information that the sign consisted in the angel's assuring the king, "by bringing him the crown," that he would have "the whole kingdom of France through God's help and her labor, and that he should put her to work, that is, give her soldiers, or else he would not so soon be crowned and anointed."

This was Joan's first mention of a crown, the theme La Fontaine had introduced the day before, and it was immediately seized upon. How did the angel bring the crown, and did he put it on the king's head? It was given to an archbishop, the archbishop of Reims, it seemed to her, and he received it and gave it to the king, and she herself was there, and it was put in the king's treasury. Where did this take place? In the king's chamber in the castle of Chinon. On what day and at what hour? "I do not know the day, but as for the hour, it was late." The month was March or April, she thought, almost two years before, and it was after Easter.

The first time that she saw the sign, did the king see it? Yes, and he received it himself.

What was the crown made of? "Be assured that it is of fine gold, and is so rich that I do not know how to describe its richness," and the crown meant that the king would hold the kingdom of France. Did it have precious stones? "I've told you what I know about it." Did she handle it or kiss it? No.

Joan now told the story in some detail: she had prayed for God to send the king a sign; the angel had come to her lodging and they had gone together to the king; they had gone up the stairs together to the king's room, Joan had said, "Sire, here is your sign"; the angel had bowed to the king and spoken to him as she had already described and also praised the king's "fine patience . . . in the great tribulations he had suffered." It was "about a lance's length from the door to the king," and the angel had walked across the floor to him; "afterward [the angel] went out by the way he came in." A number of people saw the crown, and some saw the angel. The angels that had accompanied them appeared in various forms, some with wings, some with crowns; St. Catherine and St. Margaret had been among them, and had gone into the king's room with the angel. When they had left the king, the angel took his leave from her "in a little chapel," and she had wanted to go with him, and had wept. The interrogator asked sarcastically whether God had sent the angel on account of Joan's merits. Joan replied that he had been sent for a great purpose, in hope that the king would believe the sign, and so that they would stop arguing with her, and to help the good people of Orleans, and because of the merits of the king and the good duke of Orleans.

Why had Joan been chosen, rather than another? She answered that it pleased God to use a simple maid to drive out the king's enemies.

Did the crown glitter, and did it have a pleasant odor? She did not remember, but she would think about it. A moment later she said that it did and always would, but it must be guarded well.

Had the angel written her letters? This time she answered no.

Why had the king and his retinue believed it was an angel? Because the churchmen had said so, and because of the crown. How did the churchmen know it was an angel? "Because of their learning, and because they were clerics."[115]

She was asked whether her voices had told her to make the assault on Paris. No, she had gone "at the request of some gentlemen who wanted to make a skirmish or an assault-at-arms," and she had fully intended to go further and cross the moats. Had she done well to assault Paris on the day of the Nativity of the Blessed Mary? Joan answered merely that it was good to keep the festivals of our Lady. Had she not commanded the Parisians to surrender in Jesus's name? No, she had said, "Surrender to the king of France."[116]

Eleventh Session, Wednesday, March 14, Morning

Jean La Fontaine questioned Joan at length about her jump from the tower at Beaurevoir. Why had she jumped? She answered that one reason was that she had heard it said that all the people of Compiègne, from the age of seven, would be put to fire and sword, and that she would rather die than survive after such a destruction of good people. The other was that she knew she would be sold to the English, and she would rather die than be in their hands. Had her voices consented to the leap? St. Catherine had told her almost every day that she must not jump, and that God would help her and the people of Compiègne, but Joan had retorted that if God was going to help them, she wanted to be there. St. Catherine had then said, "You must take this in good part; you will not be freed until you have seen the king of the English." Joan had answered, "Truly, I do not want to see him. I would rather die than fall into the hands of the English." After her leap, there had been two or three days when she did not want to eat or drink. St. Catherine had comforted her and had told her to confess and ask God's forgiveness for jumping (implying that her motive had been suicide), and that undoubtedly the people of Compiègne would be sent help before St. Martin's Day in the winter. Then she began to recover and began to eat once more and was soon cured.

La Fontaine then asked directly if she had meant to kill herself. No, but in jumping she commended herself to God and hoped to escape and avoid being delivered to the English. Once more she was asked whether she had blasphemed against God and her saints when she was recaptured after the leap "as is found in the evidence [of the preliminary inquiry]"; once again she denied it, but said she could not remember what she had said or done. Did she want to refer to the court's information? "I refer to God and none other, and to good confession."[117]

Did the voices ask for a delay before they answered? Sometimes St. Catherine answered at once, but sometimes Joan had to listen carefully because of the noise made by other people, and by her guards. When she asked St. Catherine something, St. Catherine and St. Margaret at once asked our Lord and then answered Joan at His instruction. Did a light accompany them? There was never a day when they did not come to the castle, and it was always with a light. She had asked three things of her voices: that they should deliver her, that God should help the French and guard the towns in their possession, and for the salvation of her own soul.[118]

Of the court she had one request: that if she were taken to Paris, she might have a copy of her questions and answers so that she could give them to the people of Paris and say to them, "Here is how I was questioned at Rouen, and my answers," and would not be troubled with so many questions.

Why had she told Cauchon that he was putting himself in danger by trying her? What she had said to my lord of Beauvais was "You say that you are my judge; I do not know whether you are or not, but I advise you not to judge badly, which would put you in great danger, and I warn you so that if our Lord punishes you I will have done my duty by warning you." What was this danger? St. Catherine had said that she would have help, and she did not know whether it would deliver her from prison, or if while she was being tried there would be some disturbance by which she would be delivered, but she thought it would be one or the other. And her voices had told her that she would be delivered by a great victory, and later her voices said to her, "Take everything in good spirit, do not despair in your martyrdom; you will finally come to the kingdom of paradise." And her voices told her this simply and absolutely, without faltering; and she believed that her martyrdom was the pain and adversity that she was suffering in prison, and did not know if she would suffer more, but put her faith in God.

Since her voices had told her she would go to the kingdom of paradise, was she sure of salvation, and that she would not be damned in hell? She firmly believed it when her voices told her that she would be saved, as firmly as if she were already there.

After this revelation, did she believe that she could not commit a mortal sin? "I know nothing, but rely entirely on God." The court remarked that this was a "weighty answer," to which Joan replied that she held it as "a great treasure."[119]

Twelfth Session, Wednesday, March 14, Afternoon

When the questioning resumed where it had left off, Joan added a qualification to the statement she had made about her salvation—she would be saved provided she kept her oath to "keep well her virginity of body and soul."

She was now asked a key question: If her voices had assured her of salvation, did she need to make confession? Joan answered that if she were in mortal sin she believed that St. Catherine and St. Margaret would immediately abandon her. But as for her confession, "one cannot cleanse one's conscience too much."[120]

Had she ever denied or cursed God in prison? No, never. Sometimes she had said "God (or St. John, or our Lady) willing," and those who reported it had misunderstood.[121]

The court introduced the subject of Franquet d'Arras: Was not taking a man prisoner for ransom and then having him killed a mortal sin? Joan protested that she had done no such thing. Had she paid the man who had taken Franquet prisoner? Joan replied that she was not a master of the mint or treasurer of France to give people money.[122]

At this point the interrogator read to her a list of charges. She had made an assault on Paris on a feast day, had taken the bishop of Senlis's horse, had jumped from the tower at Beaurevoir, wore male dress, and had consented to the death of Franquet d'Arras. Did she not believe that she was in mortal sin? First, as for the assault on Paris, "I do not believe I am in mortal sin, and if I am, it is for God to know it, and for the priest who hears my confession." Second, as for the bishop's horse, it was not she who had taken it, she had tried to pay for it, and she had tried to return it. Third, she had jumped at Beaurevoir not out of despair but to save her life and escape so that she could help others. Afterward she had confessed, and St. Catherine had revealed to her that she was forgiven. Had the voices given her a heavy penance for disobeying them? The hurt she had received in falling had been a large part of the penance. As for whether she had committed a mortal sin in jumping, "I do not know, but I refer myself to our Lord." Fourth, as for wearing male dress, "Since I do it by God's command and in his service, I do not believe I do wrong; and when it pleases God so to command, I will immediately put it aside." Joan did not reply to the fifth charge, that of consenting to Franquet's death.[123]

Thirteenth Session, Thursday, March 15, Morning

At this session the crucial question was introduced: If she had done anything contrary to the faith, would she submit to "the judgment of the Church"? Along with the matter of male dress, which became a symbol of her refusal to submit to the Church, this theme dominated the rest of the interrogations. It was not simply a matter of Joan's saying, "I submit," but of her accepting the Church's, by which Cauchon meant the court's, pronouncements and admitting that her revelations had been lies, her saints and angels evil spirits, that everything she had done was not good but evil, and that she was in mortal sin.

Joan's reply was that her testimony should be examined by clerics, and if they said there was anything in it contrary to the Christian faith, she would consult her voices. But if there was anything wrong in it and against the Christian faith ordained by God, she would not wish to uphold it, but would be very anxious to change to the contrary opinion.

This rather confused response—the ecclesiastics should judge, but their judgment must be submitted to Joan's voices, while on the other hand she had no wish to adhere to unorthodox belief—led the court to explain to her a favorite concept of the medieval Church, the distinction between the "Church Militant" and the "Church Triumphant." The Church Militant was the Church on earth, the pope, the cardinals, the prelates, the clergy, and all good Christians engaged in the struggle against the enemies of Christ; the Church Triumphant was the Church victorious in heaven, God, the saints, and the souls that had been saved. Joan must submit what she had said and done to the judgment of the Church Militant, the Church's earthly representatives—in other words, to Cauchon, Le Maitre, and the assessors. Joan listened to the explanation and replied, "I will not give you any other answer for the present."[124]

The questioning turned to Joan's attempted escape from the castle of Beaulieu. Had God or her voices given her permission to escape from prison whenever she pleased? "I have asked for it many times, but so far I have not had it." Would she escape if the chance presented itself? She replied that if the door was open, she would go, for that would be God's permission. Without such permission, she would not go, although she might make an attempt to escape, to test out God's permission and see if He sent her help. "Help yourself, and God will help you."[125]

The court reminded her that she had asked to hear mass. Would it not be more appropriate to hear it in woman's dress? "Promise me that I may hear mass if I wear a woman's dress, and I will answer you." "I promise you that you may hear mass, but you must be in a woman's dress." "And what do you say if I swore and promised our king not to change these clothes? All the same, I say, make me a dress, long down to the ground, without a train, and let me go to mass; and when I return I will put back on the clothes I now am wearing." The interrogator told her sternly that she must adopt woman's dress "simply and absolutely." "Then give me a dress like that of a burgher's daughter, that is, with a long skirt, and I will wear it, and also a woman's hood, to go to mass." But a moment later she begged them to let her hear mass in the clothes she was wearing.[126]

Was she willing to submit everything she had said and done to the determination of the Church? "All my deeds are in the hands of God, and I commend myself to Him, and assure you that I do not wish to do or say anything counter to the Christian faith."[127]

The questioning returned to the things that she said she had done without the permission of her voices—the assault on Paris, the siege of La Charité, the leap from the tower at Beaurevoir. How did she know her voices were good spirits? "St. Michael assured me of it before the voices came to me." How did she know it was St. Michael? "By the speech and language of angels." How did she know it was the language of angels? She replied that she believed it immediately, "and wanted to believe it." If the Enemy appeared in the form of an angel, how would she know the difference? She answered that she could easily tell if it were St. Michael or a counterfeit. What doctrine had St. Michael taught her? First to be a good child, and that God would help her, and among other matters that she would go to the help of the king of France, and of the misery in the kingdom of France.[128]

Fourteenth Session, Saturday, March 17, Morning

The final day of the preparatory interrogation opened with questions about St. Michael and the angels that appeared with him. "He was in the form of a very true and upright man [*très vrai prud'homme*]," Joan said. As for the angels, she saw them with her own eyes, and she believed as firmly in the deeds and words of St. Michael as she believed that our Lord Jesus Christ suffered and died for us. And what made her believe in him was that he had given her good counsel, comfort, and sound doctrine.[129]

Again she was asked if she was willing to submit all her words and deeds, good or evil, to the judgment of our Holy Mother Church. She answered that she loved the Church and would support it with all her power, and she should not be prevented from going to church or hearing mass. As for the good works she had done, she commended herself to the King of Heaven who had sent her to Charles. "And you will see that the French will soon win a great action that God will send to them, which will shake the whole kingdom of France." When this came to pass, they must remember that she had said it.

Would she submit to the decision of the Church? "I refer to our Lord, who sent me, to our Lady, and all the blessed saints of paradise." She believed that God and the Church were one and the same, and there was no need to make difficulties about it.

Once more the difference between the Church Militant and the Church Triumphant was explained to her; she must submit to the Church on earth, represented by the court. Joan answered that it was by the commands of the Church Triumphant—God, the Virgin Mary, and the saints—that she had been sent to the king of France, and to it she submitted all her good deeds and everything she had done or would do.[130]

When it was evident that she would not change her answer, the questioning returned to the subject of her clothing. She explained that she would not take a woman's dress unless she was found guilty. Then she would beg them to grant her a dress and a hood. Why, if she wore man's dress by God's command, did she ask for a woman's dress at her death? Joan answered only, "It is enough for me if [the dress] be long."

Was it pleasing to God for her to say that she would take a woman's dress if they let her go? Joan answered that if they let her go in a woman's dress, she would at once put on a man's dress and do what our Lord commanded her, and not for anything would she take an oath that she would not arm herself and wear male dress to do our Lord's will.[131]

Did St. Catherine and St. Margaret hate the English? "They love what our Lord loves, and hate what He hates."

Did God hate the English? As for the love or hate that God had for the English, or what He would do for their souls, she knew nothing; but she knew that they would be driven out of France, except for those who would die there.

Had God been for the English when they were successful in France? She did not know whether God had ever hated the French, but believed that He would punish them for their sins, if they were in sin.[132]

The session closed with a succession of short questions: Had she put her armor on the altar at St. Denis so that it would be worshiped? No. Why did the sword from St.-Catherine-de-Fierbois have five crosses on

the handle (possibly sorcery)? She did not know. Who had suggested the
design of her standard—the angels with "arms, feet, legs, and wearing
clothing"? She had already answered that question. Were they painted
the way the angels appeared to her? She had had them painted as they
were painted in churches. Had she seen them as they were painted? "I
will tell you nothing more." Why had she not had the light painted that
came to her with the angel or the voices? It had not been commanded
her.[133]

Fifteenth Session, Saturday, March 17, Afternoon

The final session, that afternoon, continued the questioning about the
standard. Joan explained that her saints had told her how it should be
painted. Had they told her that with it she would win all her battles?
They told her to carry the standard boldly, and God would help her. Did
she help the standard the most, or did it help her? She answered that
whether the victory was her standard's or hers, it was all for our Lord,
and the hope of victory was based on our Lord and no one else. If
someone else had carried it, would he have had as good fortune as she
did when she carried it? "I do not know, and I refer to our Lord." If she
had carried someone else's standard, would she have had as much faith
in it as in the one given her by God, or even that of her king? "I always
more willingly carried the one given me by our Lord."[134]

Why had she put JESUS MARIA on her letters? The clerks who wrote
the letters put it there, and they said it was appropriate.[135]

Had she been told that if she lost her virginity she would lose her good
fortune, and that her voices would come no more to her? "That has not
been revealed to me." If she were married, would her voices no longer
come to her? "I do not know, and I refer to our Lord."[136]

Did her king do right in killing or causing to be killed my lord of
Burgundy? Joan answered that it was a great tragedy for France, and
that whatever was between them, God had sent her to help the king of
France.[137]

The court pointed out that although she had told Cauchon that she
would answer him and his commissioners as she would the pope himself,
there were a number of questions which she refused to answer. Was she
not bound to tell the truth to the pope, vicar of God, about everything
she was asked touching the faith and her conscience? She answered that

she asked to be taken to him, and she would answer everything that she ought to answer.[138]

She was asked once more about the ring that bore the words JESUS MARIA. Why did she gaze at it when she went into battle? It was in honor of her father and mother, and because she had touched St. Catherine with her ring when she appeared. The interrogator now asked her about embracing the saints, and where she had touched them. Did they smell good? *"Il est bon à savoir,* they did." In embracing them, did she feel warmth or anything else? She could not embrace them without feeling and touching them. Had she given them garlands? She had often given garlands to their pictures and statues in churches, but not to the actual apparitions, as far as she could remember.[139]

Was her standard flown at the king's side? Not that she knew. Why was it brought into the church of Reims, at the coronation, rather than those of the other captains? Another answer that became famous: "It had the trouble, it was only right that it should have the honor."[140]

The preparatory interrogation was concluded, and the court adjourned to prepare their indictment.

12. The Trial: Charges and Judgment

ON MARCH 18 AND 22, Cauchon convoked a group of the assessors at his house to discuss future procedure. It was decided that the charges against Joan should be drawn up by the promoter, Jean d'Estivet.[1]

In the following days, Cauchon and some of the assessors visited Joan in her cell (March 24 and 25). To her request that she be allowed to hear mass on Palm Sunday, she was again told to change to woman's dress, and on her refusal the request was denied. She declared that she would not change even to hear mass on Easter. Her manner of dress did not burden her soul, she said, and to wear it was not contrary to the Church.[2]

The day after Palm Sunday, some of the assessors met again at Cauchon's house to consider the articles of accusation which Estivet had now prepared. There were seventy, set down in random order, the grave with the petty, some repetitive. These were to be read to Joan, who would then be given an opportunity to reply to them.[3]

The following day the court assembled in the room next to the great hall of the castle where the first part of the trial had taken place. Some forty assessors were present. Most had attended only the first six (public) sessions, so that much of Joan's testimony was available to them only in the foreshortened and prejudiced form of the seventy articles.

The prisoner was brought in, and promoter Estivet swore to proceed against her without fear or favor, but only by zeal for the faith. For the first time Joan was offered counsel, with the explanation that since she was not learned in letters and theology, she might choose one of those present to advise her how to answer. Joan was evidently suspicious of their advice; she thanked Estivet, but refused: "I have no intention of separating myself from the counsel of God."[4]

Nevertheless she obtained help. A Dominican friar of Rouen, Isambart de la Pierre, Sub-Inquisitor Le Maitre's assistant, had been present at the sessions in Joan's cell. Evidently troubled by the course of the inquiry, he felt compelled to help Joan in spite of her refusal of counsel. Brother Isambart had arrived at the session late, with another friar from his monastery, Guillaume Duval; and since there was no room left among the other assessors, they had found places close to Joan, who was seated at a table. As she was questioned, Isambart indicated to her what he thought she should say, now nudging her with his elbow, now making a sign with a hand. What attention she gave the Dominican's signals is conjectural. Her testimony remained consistent with what she had said before, and always in character.[5]

The reading of the articles took two days; each article began with an accusation, supported by evidence from the trial, with the date of the testimony. Most of Joan's responses were either denials or referrals to her previous testimony, but occasionally she gave a fuller answer.

The accusations summed up the testimony of the trial, covering the same ground and sometimes repeating the same words, but now unmasking the purpose behind the questions. Those about Joan's baptism and religious education were transformed into a charge that Joan had not been taught the Christian faith in her childhood, but "sorcery, divination, and other superstitious practices or magic arts," that the people of Domremy had long been known for such practices, and that Joan's own godmother, the mayor's wife, had consorted with fairies. Joan replied that she knew nothing about fairies, that she had been "as well taught as a good child ought to be," and as for her godmother, she referred to her previous statement (that her godmother had merely said she had seen them). She was accused of "dancing and chanting spells, and of hanging garlands" on the Ladies' Tree, and of "keeping a mandrake in her bosom, hoping by it to have prosperity in wealth and temporal things." She firmly denied both charges.[6]

She was accused of going to Neufchâteau without her parents' permission and of leading an immoral life in La Rousse's house, to which the failure of her alleged marriage plans was ascribed. Joan denied the tale.[7] Next came the dangerous charge about her mode of dress. She had "given up and rejected female dress, had her hair cut round" like a soldier, wore "a shirt, breeches, a doublet with hose attached by twenty laces, leggings laced on the outside, a short robe, to the knees, a cap, tight boots, long spurs, a sword, a dagger, a coat of mail, a lance, and other arms . . . and with these, she had gone into battle, claiming that she was sent by God through revelations made to her, and that she did this on behalf of God." This was "in violation of canon law, abominable to God and men, and prohibited by the sanctions of the Church under penalty of anathema." She had worn "sumptuous and ostentatious clothes, of expensive material and cloth of gold and fur, and not only short tunics, but tabards [long loose coats worn over armor] and robes slashed up the side; and it was well known that when she was captured she was wearing a cloth-of-gold *hucque,* open on both sides." To attribute the wearing of such clothes to the command of God, the angels, or the Virgin was blasphemy. Joan replied, "I have blasphemed neither God nor His saints."[8]

She was reminded that she had repeatedly refused to wear a woman's dress at Beaurevoir and at Arras, and that she continued to refuse clothing "suitable to her sex . . . and to womanly duties." Joan admitted that she had been admonished and had refused; as for womanly duties, she said, "there were enough other women to do them."

She was accused of having made promises to the king and of having used divination and occult means to fulfill them. Joan brushed aside this charge; she had told the king that she was God's messenger and that if he would put her to work, she would raise the siege of Orleans and God would restore his kingdom, have him crowned at Reims, and drive out his enemies—"*all* the kingdom, and if my lord of Burgundy and the other subjects of his kingdom did not return to obedience, the king would make them do so by force."[9]

She was charged with dissuading the king from negotiations and inciting her party to murder and the effusion of human blood, and saying that peace could only be obtained by the lance and sword. She replied by citing the letters and ambassadors she had sent to the duke of Burgundy.[10]

A number of lesser charges followed: she had found the sword at St.-Catherine-de-Fierbois by divination—or she had hidden it there herself for the priests to find; she had put spells on her ring and her standard; she had blasphemously put the names of Christ and our Lady on "presumptuous and bold" letters to Bedford and Henry VI; her letters to the English had been written under the counsel of evil spirits; she had blasphemously used the sign of the cross on her letters. Joan denied all the charges, and referred to her previous answers.[11]

Her reply to the count of Armagnac's letter about the three popes was introduced, and she referred the court to her previous testimony.[12]

The court adjourned for the day. Isambart de la Pierre, Guillaume Duval, and Jean La Fontaine had been detailed to visit and admonish Joan in her cell during the afternoon. The friar found himself confronted there by a furious Warwick, who demanded, "Why did you help that wicked woman this morning, making all those signs to her? *Par la morbleu,* if I see you trying to help her again and warn her, to her profit, I will have you thrown in the Seine!" Duval, testifying at the Rehabilitation, reported that Isambart's "two companions [himself and La Fontaine] fled in terror." The incident was one of several reported by Rehabilitation witnesses in which assessors were threatened or intimidated by Cauchon or by Warwick and his aide Stafford for trying to help Joan or for merely expressing opinions mildly favorable to her.[13]

On Wednesday the court reconvened. At the outset of the second day's hearing, Joan interjected a fresh statement about her controversial clothing. She would not change it without God's leave, even if they cut off her head.[14]

The charges resumed. She had refused sufficiently to explain her visions or the sign she had given the king; therefore the court was forced to conclude that her revelations came from evil spirits. Joan replied that her revelations had come from St. Catherine and St. Margaret, and she would maintain this until death.[15]

She was accused of rashly and presumptuously insisting that she could recognize archangels, angels, and saints, and could distinguish their voices from human voices; she replied that she held to what she had already said, and as for her rashness and presumption, she referred to our Lord, her judge.[16]

It was charged that when she had acted contrary to the command of the voices, as when she jumped from the tower at Beaurevoir, she had exhibited a kind of fatalism, a lack of recognition of human free will and of the possibility of falling into sin. Did she not believe that in acting contrary to the command of her voices she was committing mortal sin? "I have already answered that, and I refer to that answer." As for the question about free will, she referred to our Lord.[17]

A number of other charges followed. She had, since her youth, said, done, and perpetrated many crimes and sins, but she insisted that she had acted at God's command and in His behalf, through revelations of the angels and St. Catherine and St. Margaret. She had said that she hated Burgundians, and that her voices were in favor of the king of France, and that they did not love the Burgundians. She had "performed all acts customary to men of war, and more." She had turned Franquet d'Arras over to civil justice to be executed. She wore men's clothing even while receiving the sacraments. She had attacked Paris on a feast day. She had seized the bishop of Senlis's horse. She had claimed that the saints, angels, and archangels were not in favor of the English but the French, thus claiming that the saints in glory hated a Catholic kingdom and people. She boasted that St. Catherine and St. Margaret had promised to take her to paradise if she kept her virginity. She swore and blasphemed when she leaped from the tower at Beaurevoir and in prison at Rouen. And yet she claimed that she had never committed mortal sin. Concerning all these accusations, Joan referred to her previous testimony.[18]

Next came the most significant charges. She claimed that the spirits that appeared to her were sent by God, although she gave no signs to prove it, and sought no spiritual advice on the matter, but had wanted to hide her revelations from the clergy while showing them to lay people. Joan replied that as for signs, if those that demanded them were not worthy, it was not her fault; she had often prayed that it would please God to reveal them to people of her party; but she asked the advice of no bishop, curate, or anyone else as to belief in her revelations. She believed as firmly as she believed that our Lord Jesus Christ had suffered and died to save us from the pains of hell, that it was Saints Michael, Gabriel, Catherine, and Margaret whom our Lord had sent to comfort and counsel her.[19]

A related charge: she was accused of worshiping evil spirits, kissing the ground where they walked, kneeling to them, embracing and kissing them, thanking them with clasped hands, invoking them daily. Again she referred to her previous testimony, and added that she would call her voices to her aid as long as she lived. How did she summon them? She prayed: "Most sweet God, in honor of Your holy passion, I beg You if You love me, to reveal to me how I should answer these churchmen. I well know, as to my dress, the command by which I took it, but I do not know how I should leave it off. Therefore, may it please You to inform me." She added that she "had often had news from her voices about my lord of Beauvais." What did they say about him? "I will tell you privately." Her voices had come three times that day. Were they in her room? "I have told you so; I heard them well." They had told her how she should answer about her clothing.[20]

The accusations continued: her "presumptuous, rash, and lying" story about the angel at Chinon; her "seduction" of Catholic people, who worshiped her and had masses said for her; her "presumptuous and proud" assumption of leadership of the army. She was charged with rejecting the company and service of women and wishing "to be served by men in the private offices of her room and her secret matters— something unheard of to a modest and devout woman." She replied that her household was governed through men, but when she was in lodgings she usually had a woman with her. And in war, when there was no woman to be found, she lay fully dressed and armed.[21]

She was accused of using her revelations and prophecies, which she claimed came from God, for her own temporal gain—riches, office, horses, ornaments—which had extended even to her family. She referred to her previous answer.[22]

As part of the preliminary inquiry, the ecclesiastical court of Paris had questioned Catherine of La Rochelle, who had furnished information with which Joan was now confronted. Joan had "two counsellors whom she called the counsellors of the spring" (a reference to the springs in the Bois Chenu) who visited her in prison; they would help Joan escape from prison "with the aid of the devil, unless they watched her well." Joan said that she did not know what Catherine meant by her "counsellors of the spring." Perhaps she had once heard St. Catherine and St. Margaret at the spring in the Bois Chenu. But she would not want the devil to rescue her from prison.[23]

What about her military failures at Paris, La Charité, Pont l'Evêque, and Compiègne, when her voices had promised her success? Had she not said then that Jesus had broken His promise to her? She referred to her previous answers and denied that she had ever said that God had failed her.[24]

She was accused of placing her armor on the altar at St. Denis to be worshiped as a relic, and of pouring melted candle wax on children's heads to tell the future, and of making many divinations. She denied it.[25]

Her refusal to take the oath was brought up against her, along with her requests for delays and other misconduct during the trial. She had threatened the judge, she had repeatedly refused to answer, saying, *"Passez outre,"* or "I won't tell you everything," or "I will say no more," or "That has nothing to do with your trial." Joan replied that she had asked for delays only so that she might answer questions more surely, and so that she might know whether she ought to answer what they asked.[26]

This relatively minor charge was immediately followed by one that was deadly serious. Warned that she must submit to the Church Militant, and informed of the distinction between the Church Militant and the Church Triumphant, she had said that she would submit only to the Church Triumphant, referring her deeds to God and the saints, and not to the judgment of the Church on earth. Joan replied that she wished all the honor and reverence in her power to the Church Militant, but as for submitting her deeds to it, "I must ask God, who caused me to perform them." The question was repeated and she said, "Send me the clerk next Saturday, and I will answer you."[27]

She was accused of assuming for herself the authority of God and the angels and elevating herself above the power of the Church; she had lied during the trial, violating her oath; she had been governed by evil spirits and not by the counsel of God and the angels as she claimed; she had frequently said that she would ask God for revelations, for example, as to whether she should tell the truth about something, which was to test God and require from Him what no one should ask. Joan denied the allegations and said that she had not called on God except when necessary.[28]

She was accused of sorcery, divination, superstitious practices, heretical belief, sedition, disturbing and impeding the peace, inciting to the shedding of human blood, and blasphemy. She replied that she was a good Christian, and as for all the charges, she referred to the Lord.[29]

Finally, she was charged with making no attempt to amend her ways, although she had been warned of her errors. She replied that she had not

committed the crimes with which the promoter charged her, but hoped
that she had done nothing against the Christian faith. If she had done
anything against the faith, would she submit to the Church and to those
appointed to correct her? She replied that on Saturday, after dinner, she
would answer.[30]

On Saturday, March 31, Joan was interrogated in her cell about the
matters on which she had requested a delay.

Was she willing to submit to the judgment of the Church on earth
everything she had done and said, whether good or evil, especially the
crimes and wrongdoing with which she was charged? Joan answered that
in everything they asked she would submit to the Church Militant, as
long as it did not ask her to do the impossible—that is, to revoke the
things she had said and done by God's command, and her visions and
revelations; she would not revoke them for any man alive. Would she
submit to the Church Militant if it told her that her revelations were
illusions or diabolical superstitions, or evil? She answered that she would
refer to our Lord, whose commands she always obeyed.

Did she not believe that she was subject to the Church of God on earth,
that is, to our holy lord pope, the cardinals, the archbishops, bishops, and
other prelates of the Church? Yes, God first being served.

Had her voices commanded her not to submit to the Church Militant
on earth, or to its judgment? She replied that she did not say whatever
came into her head, but spoke at the command of her voices, and they
did not command her not to obey the Church, God first being served.[31]

On the following Monday, it was decided to reduce Estivet's seventy
articles to twelve, summarizing the principal points of the testimony.
Who was entrusted with the task we do not know. At the Rehabilitation,
the assessors who were still living were intent on disassociating themselves from it. Thomas de Courcelles, who later translated the trial
record into Latin, credited the summation to University of Paris master
Nicolas Midi. These twelve articles, encapsulating all the testimony
given in the trial, were the basis of the deliberations that followed.[32]

Joan's answers were briefly summarized on twelve subjects:

Her revelations and apparitions, and her assertion that they came from
God;

The sign she had showed the king, and the contradictory things she
had said about it;

Her statement that she had recognized the saints and angels by their good advice and the comfort they had brought her;

The foreknowledge of events and recognition of people (such as the king and Robert de Baudricourt) which she attributed to the aid of her voices;

Her insistence on male dress;

Her use of the sign of the cross and the words JESUS MARIA on her letters;

Her disobedience to her parents and the anxiety she had caused them;

Her leap from the tower of Beaurevoir, here termed suicidal;

Her assertion that St. Catherine and St. Margaret had promised to take her to paradise if she kept her virginity, as she had vowed;

Her statement that the saints were on the side of the French, and that since she had learned this, she had not loved the Burgundians;

The reverence she had shown "those whom she called St. Michael, St. Catherine, and St. Margaret," believing they came from God, without asking advice from any churchman;

And finally, her statement that she was unwilling to refer the matters contained in her trial to the judgment of the Church on earth, nor of any man alive, but to God alone, although it had several times been explained to her that everyone must believe in the Catholic Church, and that every good Catholic Christian must submit all his deeds to the Church, especially concerning revelations.[33]

Much of this summary accurately reviewed Joan's testimony, but there were discrepancies, as notary Guillaume Manchon pointed out at the Rehabilitation. Joan had denied that her leap at Beaurevoir was suicidal; and her refusal to submit her deeds and words to the judgment of the Church was always qualified—she had said she would submit as long as her submission was not contrary to God's command. Joan was never given an opportunity to reply to the summary.

On April 5, the articles were presented to a group of assessors, mostly University of Paris masters, who were asked to state their opinions in writing.[34] Some of them expressed reservations about Joan's guilt. Three of the assessors, Pierre Minier, Jean Pigache, and Richard Grouchet, wrote that if the revelations came from an evil spirit or demon, it seemed to them that many of Joan's statements were "suspect, injurious, and against good practices," but "if these revelations come from God or from a good spirit, which however is not certain to us, we should not interpret

them as evil."[35] This very qualified statement infuriated Cauchon. Grouchet testified at the Rehabilitation that the bishop demanded of the three
assessors, "Is *this* what you've been doing?";[36] while Nicolas de Houppeville reported that Cauchon told Minier that he should not confuse law
with theology, and should leave law to the jurists.[37] The abbots of Jumièges and Cormeilles requested that the record of the trial be submitted
to "our mother, the University of Paris," or to a general council, but
above all, that Joan be admonished charitably and informed of the
dangers that threatened her. "Whether she is in mortal sin, God only
knows, who sees into the hearts of men; and since there are facts unknown to us which we are not prepared to judge, especially since we were
not present at the examination of the said woman, we refer to the
theologians for further judgment."[38] Still another University of Paris
theologian, Raoul Sauvage, gave a long unfavorable opinion, but concluded that the case should be taken to Rome.[39] A statement which did
not appear in the court record was that of the bishop of Avranches, "a
very ancient and good cleric," reported Brother Isambart de la Pierre,
Jean Le Maitre's assistant. Asked his opinion, the bishop in turn asked
Isambart what Thomas Aquinas would have said "about the submission
one must make to the Church." Isambart supplied him with St.
Thomas's opinion: "In doubtful matters touching the faith, one must
always have recourse to the pope or to the general council." The bishop's
pronouncement never entered the proceedings. "It was left out by mal-
ice," Isambart said.[40]

During this period of deliberation, Joan fell ill. Physicians were at
hand, including some serving as assessors, the medical profession being
commonly practiced by churchmen. One of these, Guillaume de Chambre, testified at the Rehabilitation that Warwick explained to him and
to the duchess of Bedford's physician, Jean Tiphaine, that they were to
take care of Joan, "for the king did not want her to die a natural death;
he held her dear, for he had paid dearly for her, and he wanted her to
die only at the hands of justice, and that she should be burned." Tiphaine
took her pulse and asked her what was the matter and where it hurt;
Chambre palpated her abdomen. She was feverish, and a guard reported
that she had vomited.

They decided to bleed her. Warwick warned, "Watch out when you
bleed her, for she is cunning and might kill herself." The bleeding was

carried out, and Joan began to recover. During her convalescence, promoter Estivet came to see her, and in his hearing Joan said that it was
a carp that Cauchon had sent her that had caused her illness. Estivet
declared angrily that she was lying: "You, wanton, have eaten shad and
other things that have made you sick." Joan denied it, and she and
Estivet exchanged "many harsh words." Chambre said that Joan was so
upset that she became feverish again. Warwick, following every detail,
bade Estivet not to insult Joan further (lest she escape the executioner).[41]

On April 18, Cauchon, Sub-Inquisitor Le Maitre, and six assessors
visited Joan, still recuperating in her cell, to make the "charitable admonition." They found her weak and occupied with thoughts of death, but
by no means subdued. Once more she was advised, since she was an
"illiterate woman ignorant of the Scriptures," to choose a counsel from
among the theologians and jurists present; if she did not accept counsel
and follow the Church's advice, she was in the greatest danger.

Joan's response was, "It seems to me, considering the illness I am
suffering, that I am in great danger of death. And if God thus wishes to
do His pleasure with me, I beg you to hear my confession, and [give me]
my Saviour too [in communion] and [let me be buried] in consecrated
ground."

Cauchon replied, "If you wish to have the rights and sacraments of
the Church, you must behave like a good Catholic and submit to the holy
Church," to which Joan answered, "I have nothing more to say to you
now."

She was told that the more she feared death from her illness the more
she must amend her life, and that she would not have the privileges of
the Church unless she submitted to the Church.

"If my body dies in prison, I trust that you will bury it in consecrated
ground; if you do not, I put my trust in our Lord."

She was reminded that during the trial she had said that if she had
done anything against the Christian faith, ordained by our Lord, she
would not uphold it. "I refer to the answer I have given, and to our
Lord."

Cauchon recalled that she had said she had had many revelations from
God, from St. Michael, and Saints Catherine and Margaret. Could "any
good creature" come to her saying that he had revelations from God
concerning her, and she would believe him? Joan answered that no
Christian in the world could come to her claiming that he had revelations

without her knowing whether it was true or not, and she would know it from St. Catherine and St. Margaret.

Could she not envisage that God could reveal something to a good creature unknown to her? She answered, *"Il est bon à savoir,* yes. But I would not believe man or woman unless I had a sign."

She was asked if she believed that the Holy Scriptures were revealed by God. "You know it well, and *il est bon à savoir,* yes."

Finally she was asked whether she submitted to the Holy Mother Church. "Whatever happens to me, I can do or say no other than I have already said in the trial."

The assessors present then told her that it was her duty to submit, citing authorities and scriptural examples to prove their point. University of Paris master Nicolas Midi quoted Matthew 18 : 15–17: "Moreover if thy brother shall trespass against thee, go and tell him his fault between thee and him alone; if he shall hear thee, thou hast gained thy brother. But if he will not hear thee, then take with thee one or two more, that in the mouth of two or three witnesses every word may be established. And if he shall neglect to hear them, tell it unto the Church; but if he neglect to hear the Church, let him be unto thee as an heathen man and a publican." Unless Joan obeyed the Church, Midi warned, she would be abandoned as a heathen. Joan replied that she was a good Christian and had been baptized, and she would die a good Christian.

Since she wanted the Church to administer communion to her, would she submit to the Church? Joan replied that as to her submission, she could answer no other way than as she had done. She loved God, served him, and was a good Christian, and would aid and sustain the Holy Church with all her power.

Cauchon asked her if she would like "a fine and notable procession to restore her to a good estate, if she were not already there." Joan replied that she wished very much that the Church and the Catholics would pray for her.[42]

A number of the assessors seem to have felt a growing concern about Joan's continued refusal to submit to the Church. They believed that she did not understand the implication of her stand, the fact that she was threatened with death. Friar Isambart de la Pierre believed that Joan understood the Church Militant to mean the present court—the judges and assessors, her mortal enemies—and that if it were made clear to her that it included the pope and the general council, then assembled at

Basel, she would submit as she had been advised. At some point after the first admonition,* probably around the first of May, Cauchon's deputy, Jean La Fontaine, Isambart de la Pierre, and Friar Martin Ladvenu visited Joan and urged her to submit to the pope and the general council, "at which there were many prelates and doctors of the king's party." Joan cried, "Oh, if there are clerics from our side there, I would like to submit to the Council of Basel." According to notary Manchon, Joan seized on the advice and the next day announced that she would readily submit to the pope and the council. Cauchon demanded to know who had spoken with her the day before, and he sent for Joan's guards to find out. The guards named La Fontaine and the two monks. Cauchon vented his fury on Sub-Inquisitor Le Maitre, promising that he would do them harm. When La Fontaine heard of the incident, he quitted Rouen at once, and his name no longer appears in the trial records. The two monks, on the other hand, begged Le Maitre to intercede for them, and he did so with vigor, threatening to absent himself from the remainder of the trial, thus removing the prestige of the Inquisition's authority. Otherwise, Manchon said, "they would have been in mortal danger." Thenceforward no one was allowed to visit Joan except Cauchon or someone approved by him; Cauchon visited her at will, but even the Sub-Inquisitor could not do so without him.⁴³

On May 2, when Joan was brought before the court in the room adjoining the great hall to hear the public admonition, she had completely recovered from her illness and was once more ready for battle. Jean de Chatillon, archdeacon of Évreux, was delegated to address her, beginning with a general admonition that explained the articles of the faith and asked whether she was willing to "amend her faults in accordance with the deliberations of the venerable doctors and magistrates." Joan replied simply, "Read your book [the document containing the admonition which the archdeacon was holding] and then I will answer you. I trust in God, my Creator, in everything; I love Him with all my heart."

Chatillon asked her if she had any answer to the general admonition. "I trust in my judge, the King of Heaven and earth."

Chatillon then reiterated all the familiar admonitions against Joan's

*The story is told several times both by Isambart and Guillaume Manchon, with variations and inconsistencies that make it difficult to pinpoint the time, or determine whether there was a single incident or two.

pride and arrogance: her belief "that she understands more about matters of faith than learned and lettered men"; her refusal to submit her deeds and words to the Church Militant; her stubbornness in wearing a man's clothing; the "lies and vanities" of her belief in her apparitions; her insistence that she had not sinned.

Once more the Church Militant was explained to her. Joan's response was, "I believe in the Church on earth; but for my deeds and words, as I have said before, I refer to God. I believe that the Church Militant cannot err or falter; but as for my words and deeds, I refer them all to God, who made me do everything I have done."

Did she have no judge on earth, and was not our lord pope her judge? "I will say nothing more about this. I have a good master, that is, God, whom I trust in everything, and not anyone else."

If she did not believe in the Church, she would be a heretic and would be punished by being sentenced by other (secular) judges to be burned. "I will say no more; and if I saw the fire, I would say what I have said, and nothing else."

If the general council, the pope, the cardinals, and the rest were there, would she submit? "You will drag nothing more from me."

Would she submit to our holy father, the pope? "Take me there and I will answer him." "And she would answer no further," the record said.[44] Isambart de la Pierre testified at the Rehabilitation that Joan said that she submitted to the general council, at his persuasion, but Cauchon shouted at him, "Be silent, in the name of the devil!" When notary Manchon asked whether he should write down Joan's submission, Cauchon declared that it was not necessary. Then Joan said, "Ah, you are careful to write down what is against me, but you will not write down what is for me." Her words were not recorded, "and there was a great murmur among those assembled," Isambart reported.[45]

It is important to note that there was more than one point of view about Joan's submission. The English wanted her convicted and executed as an unrepentant heretic, and therefore did not want her to submit. Cauchon would doubtless have preferred her dead, since failure to execute her would have embarrassed him with the English. Yet his exertions, quite as much as those of a number of the assessors, make it evident that he sincerely sought her submission, which would have made her execution impossible and substituted a heavy penance, probably life imprisonment. Clearly, both as churchmen and as a matter of conscience, Cauchon and his colleagues felt obligated to save her soul.

Another, smaller group of assessors went further, believing that Joan should be given the chance of an appeal to the pope or the general council. This group believed that the paramount question—Were her voices from God and was her mission holy, or were they otherwise?—should be left to the highest authority. Since Joan's endorsement by the commission at Poitiers had been mainly negative—she seemed virtuous, things were desperate, and the king might as well give her a trial—there was logic in the idea of an examination by high and impartial Church authority.

Joan herself did not really wish to be judged by anyone. She was convinced of her mission, of the identity of her saints and angels, and that she had committed no mortal sin. For her to accept the judgment of the present court was impossible, a negation of everything she had lived for during the past two years. The judgment of pope and council was a straw she grasped in desperation. Perhaps she even saw in it an opportunity to escape, since she quickly turned down the suggestion that the trial record be submitted to the pope.

The questioning continued. She was asked again to change from male clothing, and again she answered that she was very willing to put on a long dress and a woman's hood to go to church and take communion, provided that when she returned she could take it off and resume what she was wearing. It was explained to her that she no longer needed to wear a man's clothing, especially since she was in prison. "When I have done what I was sent by God to do, I will put on a woman's clothing."

She was reminded that, as had already been explained, it was blasphemy to say that God and the saints made her wear a man's clothing, and that in doing so she erred and did evil; she replied that she blasphemed neither God nor the saints.

Admonished again about her revelations, she answered that she referred to her judge, that is, God, and her revelations came from God without any intermediary.

Concerning the sign she had given the king, would she be willing to refer to the archbishop of Reims, the knights who were present, and others of the party? Joan replied that the court should bring them there and she would answer; otherwise she would not refer or submit to them about the trial.

Would she refer or submit to the Church of Poitiers, where she was

examined? "Do you think you can catch me this way and draw me to
you?"

Finally she was admonished once more to submit under pain of being
abandoned by the Church; and if the Church abandoned her, she would
be in great danger, her soul of incurring the danger of eternal fire, her
body of temporal fire. Joan replied, "You will not act as you say against
me without your suffering evil in body and soul."

Asked to give one reason why she would not submit to the Church,
she declined to answer.

She was admonished and exhorted again, by "several doctors and
experts of various sciences and faculties," to submit to the Universal
Church Militant, to our lord pope, and to the holy general council.
Cauchon then warned her to give serious thought to the admonitions.
"How long do I have to think?" She must consider then and there, and
respond. When Joan did not answer, the meeting dispersed and she was
taken back to her cell.[46]

A week later, on Wednesday, May 9, Joan was brought to the keep
or donjon of the castle, its central stronghold, and shown the instruments
of torture, in the presence of Cauchon and Le Maitre, nine of the assessors,
and the executioner of Rouen, Maugier Le Parmentier, and his
assistant.

Torture was used by the Inquisition primarily to extort confession. In
Joan's case, she had provided so much information about her thoughts
and beliefs that torture could hardly add to it, or improve the court's
case. Nevertheless, Cauchon decided to confront her with the threat.

Some of the critical points of the testimony were read to her, and she
was admonished and exhorted to tell the truth about them. Joan replied,
"Truly, if you were to tear me limb from limb and drive my soul from
my body, I could tell you nothing different; and if I said anything
different, afterward I would say that you made me say it by force."

Joan added that on Holy Cross Day (May 3, the day after the public
admonition), St. Gabriel had comforted her, and her voices had told her
that it was he. She had asked them whether she should submit to the
Church, since the churchmen were strongly advising her to do so, and
the voices told her that if she wanted God to help her, she must trust
Him for all her deeds. She well knew that He had always been master
of all her deeds, and that the Enemy had never had any power over them.
She had asked her voices if she would be burned, and they had answered

that she must trust our Lord, and He would help her.

She was questioned once more about the "sign of the crown" which she said she had given the archbishop of Reims and asked whether she would be willing for him to be consulted about it. "Have him come here, and then I will answer you; but he would not dare say the contrary of what I have told you."[47]

The executioner reported that "everyone present marveled" at the prudence of her responses, and he and his assistant left "without doing anything."[48]

The judges, however, remarked not on her prudence but "the obduracy of her spirit and the mode of her answers," and decided to delay while they discussed whether to apply the torture or not; Joan was returned to her cell.[49] Three days later the judges and thirteen assessors met at Cauchon's house to deliberate. Their conceptions of the purpose of torture were divergent. Some of them envisioned torturing her into submitting to the Church, others to extract the truth or a confession. Only two voted unconditionally for torture—University of Paris master Thomas de Courcelles and Aubert Morel, a doctor of canon law. Courcelles said that she should be tortured and "questioned as to whether she would submit to the judgment of the Church"—in other words, tortured into submission. (Courcelles suppressed this statement when he translated the text of the trial into Latin, and it is to be found only in Guillaume Manchon's original French minutes; at the Rehabilitation Courcelles testified that he had "never given an opinion as to her being tortured."[50]) Morel said that she should be tortured in order "to learn the truth about her lies." Nicolas Loiseleur, who had spied on Joan in prison, thought that "for her soul's health" she should be tortured, but indicated that he would go along with the majority. Sub-Inquisitor Le Maitre said that she should be "questioned repeatedly as to whether she would submit to the Church Militant," but did not mention torture. The others unanimously voted against it, most of them because it was "not expedient at the moment," and one assessor, Raoul Roussel, treasurer of Rouen cathedral, said that to torture Joan would "calumniate" the trial.[51]

On Sunday, May 13, Warwick entertained guests in his residence at the castle, including Cauchon; Jean de Mailly, bishop of Noyon and counsellor to the English king; Warwick's daughter, whose husband

Talbot was still prisoner; Joan's captor, John of Luxembourg; his brother, chancellor Louis of Luxembourg; "two Burgundian knights" (one of whom may have been Haimond de Macy, the knight who annoyed Joan at Beaurevoir); and "other various squires and pages, 110 persons in all."[52] It was probably on this day, either before or after the meal, that John of Luxembourg paid a visit to Joan, accompanied by his brother and Warwick, Stafford, and Haimond de Macy. Joan's former custodian addressed her with sadistic jocularity: "Joan, I've come to ransom you, on condition that you promise never to bear arms against us." Joan replied, "In God's name, you are making fun of me, for I know well that you have neither the wish nor the power." John repeated his joking offer several times, and Joan made the same reply, adding, "I know well that these English will kill me, believing that after my death they will win the kingdom of France; but even if there were a hundred thousand *godons* more than are here at present, they will not gain the kingdom." Haimond de Macy reported that Stafford was indignant, and half drew his dagger as if he were going to strike Joan, but Warwick held him back.[53]

The judges now consulted the University of Paris for its opinion on the case, but only in a very limited sense. The twelve articles of indictment were sent to Paris, unaccompanied by any other material of the trial, and on May 14 the University masters met to deliberate on them.

On Saturday, May 19, Cauchon assembled the assessors in the archbishop's chapel to hear the reading of the University's conclusions. They were uncompromising:

That Joan's statements about her visions were pernicious lies, and her apparitions and revelations were from evil and diabolical spirits, Belial, Satan, and Behemoth;

That her testimony about the king's sign was a presumptuous lie, derogatory to the dignity of angels;

That the reasons Joan gave for recognizing her angels and saints were insufficient, and that she believed too easily and boldly, and inasmuch as she said she believed in her apparitions as firmly as in the faith of Jesus Christ, she erred in the faith;

That her foreknowledge and precognition were superstition and divination, presumptuous assertion, and vain boasting;

That she blasphemed God and held His sacraments in contempt when

she said that she wore male clothing by His order and took communion
thus dressed, and condemned herself by imitating the customs of the
heathen in her clothing;

That her letters, in which she had used JESUS MARIA and the sign of
the cross to indicate that instructions contained therein should not be
followed, and in which she had boasted that God would give her victory,
proved that she was a cruel and cunning murderess thirsty for human
blood, seditious, inciting to tyranny, blaspheming God;

That by leaving her parents without their permission, thereby causing
them great anxiety, and going to Robert de Baudricourt, who gave her
a man's garments and a sword and men to take her to the king, to whom
she had promised victory and said that God had sent her to install him
in his kingdom, she had transgressed the commandment to honor thy
father and mother, had behaved scandalously, blaspheming God and
erring in the faith, and had given a rash and presumptuous promise;

That her leap from the tower of Beaurevoir was suicidal and her
conclusion that God had forgiven the sin was presumptuous and showed
that she failed to understand the doctrine of free human will;

That her belief that she had not committed mortal sin and that her
saints would bring her to paradise was presumptuous and rash and a
pernicious lie;

That her assertion that her saints were for the French and not the
English, and that since she had learned the voices were on her king's side
she had not loved the Burgundians, was blasphemy against the saints and
transgression of the commandment to love one's neighbor;

That the reverence she had made to her saints, and her belief that they
came from God, without asking the advice of any churchman, and her
vow of virginity to them, showed her as an idolator, an invoker of
demons, who erred in the faith, who made bold assertions, and took an
unlawful oath;

That her refusal to refer her words and deeds to the judgment of the
Church on earth or to "any man alive," saying that she would be judged
by God alone and that her answers at the trial were given not by her own
intelligence but by God's command, showed her as schismatic, with no
understanding of the unity and authority of the apostolic Church, and
up to this time perniciously erring in faith.

The University concluded that Joan was schismatic, erring in faith,
apostate, a liar and a divinator, and suspect of heresy; she must be

"charitably exhorted" and abjure, or be turned over to secular justice.[54]

After the University's conclusions had been read, the assessors were called upon to give their reactions. One after the other they concurred. Only Isambart de la Pierre expressed a mild reservation, by referring to a previous opinion (which however does not appear in the records).[55]

On Wednesday, May 23, Joan was once more admonished, this time in a room near her cell, by Pierre Maurice, a canon of Rouen cathedral, in the presence of a half dozen assessors. "Joan, dearest friend," the admonition began, "it is now time, near the end of your trial, to think carefully of what you have said." She was informed of the University's opinion, and warned "not to choose the way of eternal damnation with the enemies of God, who are always endeavoring to disturb men, transforming themselves into the likeness of Christ, the angels, and the saints, saying and asserting that they are such. . . . Therefore, if such things appear to you, do not believe in them, but reject and repel the belief or imagination of such things and follow the opinion of the University of Paris and other learned men who know the law of God and the sacred Scriptures." Such apparitions were not to be accepted unless they were justified in Holy Scripture or by a miraculous sign. "You have believed too lightly, not praying to God for certainty or having recourse to a prelate or other learned ecclesiastic to inform you of the truth, which you should have done, considering your condition and the simplicity of your knowledge."

Couching his message in a metaphor that Joan would understand, he asked her to suppose that her king had put her in command of a fortress, forbidding her to allow anyone to enter. Someone came saying that he was sent by the king's authority, but she would not believe him or allow him to enter unless he had letters or some other sign. Thus our Lord Jesus Christ, when He ascended into Heaven, entrusted the government of His Church to Blessed Peter the Apostle and his successors, forbidding them to receive any men who came in His name unless sufficiently assured other than by their own words. Similarly, if in her king's dominion a knight born under his rule rebelled and said, "I will not obey the king or submit to any of his officials," would she not condemn him? Then what of Joan, born in Christ's faith, baptized, daughter of the Church and bride of Christ, if she refused to obey the officers of Christ, the prelates of the Church? If she persevered in her error, her soul was damned to perpetual punishment, and her body to perdition. She must not be constrained by shame or the fear of losing the "great honors" she had formerly held, but must put God's honor and the salvation of her soul first. If she obeyed and submitted to the Church, she would save her soul and deliver, he hoped, her body from death; but if she persevered, her soul would be damned, "and I fear also the destruction of your body. From which, may Jesus Christ preserve you."[56]

When the admonition was concluded, Joan replied, "As far as my words and deeds, to which I testified in the trial, are concerned, I refer to it and maintain them."[57]

Pierre Maurice then asked her if she believed that she was not compelled to submit her words and deeds to the Church Militant or other than to God. "I will maintain what I have always said and held in the trial." She added that if she were in judgment, and saw the fire lighted, and the flames mounting, and the executioner ready to cast her in the fire, and even if she were in the midst of the fire, she could say nothing other, and she would maintain what she had said in the trial until death.

The judges then declared the trial ended and announced that on the following day they would give their verdict, "and proceed further according to law and reason."[58]

13. Abjuration, Relapse, Death

IN THE CEMETERY OF THE ABBEY OF ST. OUEN, not far from the cathedral, two scaffolds had been erected, one as a tribune for the judges, notaries, prelates, and other officials, the other for Joan. Three documents had been prepared: an abjuration, ready to be signed; and alternate sentences, one if she abjured, the other if she failed to do so. The outcome in this latter event was signified by the presence of the executioner and his cart. At the Old Market, the stake was already prepared.

Early on the morning of Thursday, May 24, Jean Beaupère, canon of Rouen cathedral, obtained special permission to visit Joan, to warn her of what was about to happen: she would now be taken to the scaffold, where a sermon would be preached to her. He advised her that if she was a good Christian she would then agree to place all her deeds and words under the judgment of the Church, "and especially the ecclesiastical judges." According to his testimony at the Rehabilitation, Joan said that she would do as he instructed.[1]

Later, as she was being taken to St. Ouen, perhaps in the abbey itself, Nicolas Loiseleur drew her aside "in a certain small doorway" and gave her similar advice: "Joan, trust me and you will be saved. Accept your [woman's] dress, and do everything they tell you, or you are in danger

211

of death. And if you do as I say, you will be saved, and will have great
benefit, and no harm, but will be turned over to the Church."[2]

Joan was led to the platform, which she shared with the usher Massieu
and Guillaume Erard, the University of Paris master who was to preach
the sermon. Among the notables on the other platform were Cardinal
Beaufort; chancellor Louis of Luxembourg; William of Alnwick, bishop
of Norwich, a member of the English king's great council; three abbots,
and the principal assessors.[3]

A large crowd had gathered, including a number of English soldiers.
What the feelings of those present were we can only speculate. Master
Erard, a friend of Cauchon's, and like him politically connected with the
English, told his servant, who testified at the Rehabilitation, that he
wished he were far away in Flanders.[4] He chose as his text John 15 : 4:
"As the branch cannot bear fruit of itself, except it abide in the vine; no
more can ye, except ye abide in me." In the trial record the sermon was
summed up in a sentence: "[Erard] said solemnly that all Catholics ought
to remain in the true vine of the Holy Mother Church, planted by the
right hand of Christ; he showed Joan that she was separated from the
unity of the Holy Mother Church by her many errors and grave crimes,
and had scandalized Christian people in many ways, and he admonished
and exhorted her and the people to salutary doctrines."[5] The record
omitted part of the sermon described by several of the Rehabilitation
witnesses; Erard rhetorically addressed King Charles: "Ah, noble house
of France, always the protectress of the Faith, and you, Charles, who call
yourself king and governor, have you been thus deluded, to attach yourself to a heretic and schismatic, to the words and deeds of a wicked
woman, ill-famed and dishonored? And not only you, but the entire
clergy and nobility of your party, by whom she was examined and
approved, as she has said?" Then he turned to Joan, raised an admoni-
tory finger, and said, "I am speaking to you, Joan, and I tell you that
your king is heretic and schismatic." Joan replied, "By my faith, sir, with
all respect, I say and swear to you, on pain of my life, that he is the most
noble Christian of all, and no one loved the faith and the Church better
than he, and he is not at all what you say." The preacher turned to Jean
Massieu and said, "Make her be quiet."[6]

Erard then addressed Joan again: "Here are the lord judges, who have
many times summoned and required you to submit all your words and
deeds to the Holy Mother Church, warning you that in those words and

deeds were many things which, it seems to the clerics, are not good to say or maintain."

Joan replied, "I will answer you. On submission to the Church . . . I have said that all the works which I have said and done should be submitted to Rome to our lord the supreme pontiff, to whom, after God, I refer myself. And as for my words and deeds, I did them on behalf of God." She added that they were hers alone, not any other person's, neither the king's nor any other's, and if there were any fault in them, it was hers and no one else's.

Was she willing to revoke her deeds and words which had been reproved? "I refer myself to God and our holy father the pope."

It was explained to her that this was not enough, and that she could not be taken to the lord pope, because he was too far away, and that the bishops were judges, each in his own diocese; therefore she must yield to the Holy Mother Church, and accede to what the clerics and learned men had said and determined.

This exhortation was repeated to Joan three times. Then Cauchon began to read the sentence.[7]

As he read, Massieu and Nicolas Loiseleur urged Joan to submit and save her life, and Erard addressed her: "Joan, do as you are advised. Do you want to die?"[8] Cauchon paused, and Cardinal Beaufort's secretary told him to hurry up, saying, "You're too favorable to her";[9] according to notary Manchon, the Englishman called Cauchon a traitor. Cauchon was heard to say, "You shall pay for that!" and to demand an apology for the insult.[10]

One witness said that Joan agreed to submit if the clerics advised her to;[11] another that she said, "You have gone to great pains to lead me astray," and that "to avoid the danger" she would agree to do whatever they wanted.[12] Erard replied, "Do so now, or you will end your life by fire today," and Joan agreed that she would rather submit than burn.[13] Another witness said that she clasped her hands and prayed aloud to St. Michael, asking him to counsel and direct her.[14]

Cauchon turned to Cardinal Beaufort and asked him what he should do. The cardinal replied that Joan should be accepted as a penitent.[15]

The abjuration was then produced. Haimond de Macy, the Burgundian knight, says rather surprisingly that one of the English king's secretaries, a man named Lawrence Calot, took it out of his sleeve and handed it to Joan to sign. Joan at first said that she did not understand what it meant to abjure, and asked for advice; Massieu explained it to her. She then protested, somewhat disingenuously, that she could not read or write.[16]

Jean Massieu read the document. It was very short—"six or seven lines," on a piece of folded paper.[17] Massieu said that it promised that she would not bear arms or wear male clothing, "and many other things he could not remember," but that it was not the abjuration inserted in the court record.[18] The Orleans manuscript of the trial record, which is believed to be a version of Guillaume Manchon's French minutes, gives a brief abjuration which may be the document Joan signed; it confesses that she is "a miserable sinner," who recognizes the "snare of error" in which she has fallen, confesses that she "falsely pretended" that she had revelations from God, angels, and saints, "revokes all her words and deeds contrary to the Church, and asks to live in unity with it."[19] The abjuration which appeared in the Latin version of the court record was much more detailed, specifying the charges of "superstitious divinations," male dress, presumption, sedition, idolatry, and the rest, and renouncing it all, submitting to "the correction . . . of our Holy Mother Church and God's good justice."[20]

Joan's attitude as she signed the abjuration aroused comment. According to Jean de Mailly, bishop of Noyon, a number of those present remarked that she seemed to pay little attention to what she was doing.[21] Several assessors believed that she did not understand what she was signing.[22] Haimond de Macy testified that when Lawrence Calot handed her the document to sign, and a pen, she "mockingly drew a kind of circle" on the paper.[23] One witness said that she smiled, another that she laughed as she repeated some of the words of the abjuration.[24] Then Calot took her hand and forced her to "make some sign"—one witness thought it was a cross, which might explain Joan's smile, since she had testified that on her letters a cross signified that the contents were false.[25]

Because of her apparent contempt for the abjuration, Beaufort's secretary protested that Cauchon was wrong to accept it—it was a mockery. Cauchon replied, "You are lying. My profession compels me to seek the health of Joan's soul and body." Beaufort ordered the secretary to be silent.[26]

The crowd had grown increasingly restless, and there was "a great tumult," Jean Massieu said, as Joan signed. Stones were thrown, "but by whom he did not know."[27]

Cauchon then read the sentence: perpetual imprisonment, "on the bread of sorrow and the water of affliction, so that she could weep for her sins and nevermore commit them."[28]

One witness testified that after the sentence Loiseleur said, "Joan, you have done well this day, if God pleases, and have saved your soul." "Come, now, you churchmen," Joan replied, "take me to your prisons, and I'll no longer be in the hands of the English."[29] Jean Massieu said that she made the same request to promoter Estivet; he echoed her appeal, and it was passed on to Cauchon. The bishop said only, "Take her back where she came from."[30]

As Joan was led back to her cell in the castle, the English soldiers shouted insults at her. The English leaders and common soldiers alike were furious both at Cauchon and at the assessors. One witness said that as the assessors returned from the castle, some of the English threatened them with their swords, declaring that the king had wasted his money on them; Warwick complained to Cauchon and some of the assessors that the English king was in a bad situation, and Joan was escaping him, to which one of the assessors answered, "My lord, don't worry—we'll soon catch her again."[31]

In her cell, Joan was given a woman's clothing, which she put on. To mark her as a penitent, her hair, still in the round haircut she had worn since Vaucouleurs, was shaved off.[32]

What happened in Joan's prison cell during the three days that followed remains a mystery, not from lack of evidence, but from bewildering and contradictory overabundance.

On Friday or Saturday, Cauchon, hearing a rumor that she was about to resume male dress, sent two of the assessors, University masters Jean Beaupère and Nicolas Midi, to visit her, intending to urge her to "persevere and continue in the good resolution which she had made on the scaffold, and to take care that she did not relapse," but they could not find anyone with a key to admit them to the prison. While they were waiting in the castle courtyard for the guard, some English soldiers spoke menacingly to them, threatening to throw them in the river. The two assessors retreated to the castle drawbridge, where they were threatened by another group of soldiers, and finally fled without talking to Joan.[33] No other attempt seems to have been made at this point.

On Monday, May 28, it was revealed that Joan had resumed male clothing, the symbol of her refusal to submit to the court and, in the court's eyes, to the Church.

Witnesses at the Rehabilitation gave several different explanations. The most elaborate story was that of usher Jean Massieu; he said that Joan had told it to him on the following Tuesday. According to him, Joan's guards had put her male clothing into a bag and kept it in the cell. On Sunday, when Joan prepared to rise, she asked the guards to free her from her chains. Instead, one of them forcibly removed her woman's clothing, emptied the sack, and flung the male clothing at her, ordering her to get up; the woman's clothing was stuffed into the sack. Joan covered herself with the clothing they had given her, protesting, "Sirs, you know it's forbidden—I can't wear it." But they would give her nothing else to wear. She remained thus until noon, when finally she was forced "by bodily necessity" to put on the male clothes; when she returned, they would give her no other, no matter how much she begged.[34]

Friar Martin Ladvenu, one of the assessors, on the other hand, said that he had heard from Joan herself that "a great English lord" had entered her cell and tried to rape her; that was why she had put on male clothing.[35]

Jean de Mailly, bishop of Noyon, said that he had heard, he could not remember from whom, that male clothing was slipped into her cell by the window.[36]

Guillaume Manchon said that Joan had explained that if she had been sent to ecclesiastical prison, she would not have resumed male dress, but that she did not dare remain in the custody of the English in a woman's clothing.[37] His statement was echoed by Isambart de la Pierre, who reported that on Monday Joan, "disfigured and outraged," her face wet with tears, had said that the English had done her much wrong and violence in prison when she was dressed as a woman.[38]

Rumor had already begun to circulate on Sunday that what Beaupère and Midi had feared had taken place. Several of the assessors hurried to the castle to find out if it was true, but were met in the courtyard by eighty or more English soldiers, Friar Martin Ladvenu said, who shouted at them that they were false, traitorous Armagnacs and false counsellors and drove them away.[39] Later that same day André Marguerie, a canon of Rouen cathedral who had English connections and was by no means sympathetic to Joan, went to find out how and why Joan had resumed male dress. It was not enough to see her thus dressed, he said. An Englishman barred his way, called him an "Armagnac traitor," and threatened him with a spear. The canon left hurriedly.[40]

Joan was given the opportunity of explaining herself on Monday when Cauchon, Le Maitre, and eight of the assessors presented themselves at the prison. They found her dressed in "a tunic, a hood, a robe, and other male garments." Asked to explain, she declared that she had done so of her own free will, without constraint, and that she preferred man's dress to woman's. She had never intended to take an oath to abandon it. It was more suitable and convenient to wear man's clothing, being with men, than to wear a woman's dress. Furthermore, she had resumed it because the judges had not kept their promise to allow her to hear mass and take communion, and to remove her fetters. She would rather die than be kept in irons. But if they would promise that she could go to mass and have her fetters removed, and be placed in a pleasant (*gracieuse*—gracious) prison (the French minutes of Guillaume Manchon added, "and have a woman [with her]"), she would do everything the Church ordered.[41]

Here was evidently the crux. What Joan expected when she signed the abjuration we have no way of knowing—perhaps that she would be given a penance and released; certainly that since she had been sentenced by the Church she would be kept in a Church prison. She had evidently believed that she would be freed from the fetters she had worn during her imprisonment at Rouen, and that she would no longer be treated as if she were excommunicated. The English guards, frustrated that their victim had escaped death, had probably treated her roughly, as Manchon and Brother Isambart had said. Taken together, the prospect of continuing in this condition seemed worse than death.

One thing was clear, and decisive. Her voices had again spoken. She once more insisted on what the court record called the "illusions of her pretended revelations." The judges asked her if she had heard the voices of St. Catherine and St. Margaret, and Joan replied, "Yes." God had sent the two saints to her to tell her that she had done a great wrong and had consented to treason by her abjuration and revocation, in order to save her life, and that she had damned herself to save her life.

In the margin of the court record, the notary wrote the words *"Responsio mortifera"*—fatal answer.

Joan went on: Her voices had told her on the scaffold to answer the preacher boldly; he was a false preacher, and he had said that she had

done many things which she had not done. In saying that God had not
sent her, she had damned herself; it was true that God had sent her. Her
voices had told her since that she had done great harm by confessing that
what she had done was not well done. Everything she had said and
recanted that Thursday she had done only out of fear of the fire.

Did she believe that her voices were St. Margaret and St. Catherine?
She answered, "Yes, and from God." The judges asked her about the
crown. "I told you the truth about everything in the trial, as best I
could."

The judges reminded her that in front of the judges and officials and
the crowd, when she abjured, she had admitted that she had lyingly
boasted that her voices were Saints Catherine and Margaret. Joan replied
that she did not mean to say so. She did not understand that she was
denying her apparitions. Everything she had said was because of fear of
the fire, and any revocation she had made was false.

She said that she would rather do her penance all at once—that is, to
die—rather than endure any longer the agony of imprisonment. She had
never done anything contrary to God and the faith, no matter what she
had been made to say, and as for what was in the abjuration, she did not
understand it. She had not meant to recant anything, unless it was
pleasing to God. Finally she said that if the judges wanted her to, she
would put on woman's clothing again; but for the rest, she would do
nothing.

The court record concluded: "Having heard this, we left her, to proceed further according to law and reason."[42]

A crowd of English notables and soldiers were waiting in the castle
courtyard, among them the earl of Warwick. Two witnesses reported
that Cauchon greeted him, laughing, with the words, "Farewell, be of
good cheer, it is done," another that he said, "We've got her! [*Capta est!*]"[43]

Some of the assessors shared Cauchon's pleasure; but many were
troubled.[44]

On the following day, May 29, the judges and principal assessors met
in the archbishop's chapel to deliberate on Joan's relapse. Cauchon
opened the meeting by asserting that Joan had been admonished again
and again to "return into the way of truth," and had signed an abjuration
with her own hand, but "being persuaded by the devil," she had declared
that her voices had come again, and she had taken off her woman's dress
and resumed man's clothing.

The assessors were called on one after the other to give their opinions. Three of them pronounced for handing Joan over immediately to secular justice. The rest recommended that she should be given one more chance, another sermon should be preached to her, the abjuration should be once more read and explained to her—and if then she was still obdurate, the judges would have no recourse but to declare her a heretic and turn her over to secular justice to be burned. Isambart de la Pierre added that it should be made clear to Joan that it was a matter of life or death. Their opinions were merely advisory, and Cauchon and Le Maitre were not compelled to accept them.

Cauchon thanked the assessors and announced that Joan would be proceeded against "as a relapsed heretic according to law and reason."[45]

That afternoon all the assessors were notified by letter that Joan would be taken next day to the Old Market at eight o'clock in the morning to be declared "relapsed, heretic, and excommunicate."

On the morning of Wednesday, May 30, two of the assessors, Dominican friars Martin Ladvenu and Jean Toutmouillé, were sent by Cauchon to Joan's cell to tell her of her approaching death, to urge her to "true contrition and penitence," and to hear her last confession. They found that all the stoicism of Joan's interview with the judges on Monday was gone, as well as the mocking mood of the day when she had signed the abjuration.

As Toutmouillé described the scene at the Rehabilitation, "the poor woman" wept and tore her hair, lamenting, "Alas! they treat me thus horribly and cruelly, that my body, whole and entire, which has never been corrupted, will today be consumed and turned to ashes! Ah, I would rather be beheaded seven times than burned! Alas! if I had been in the Church prison to which I submitted myself, and guarded by the people of the Church, not by my enemies and adversaries, things would not have come to this miserable pass. Oh, I appeal to God, the great judge, the wrongs and grievances that have been done me." And she continued to complain of "the oppressions and violences" that had been done her in prison by her jailers and others.[46]

After her confession, she asked Ladvenu to administer communion. He sent a messenger to ask Cauchon's permission, and Cauchon granted it.[47] The sentence of excommunication had not yet been pronounced, although Joan had been treated during the trial as if it had. The notary

Manchon was asked at the Rehabilitation why Cauchon had acceded to this last request. He replied that the judges and assessors deliberated about it and decided to "absolve her at the tribunal of penitence."[48]

Ladvenu was annoyed when the communion bread was brought unceremoniously—"very irreverently," Jean Massieu said—"on the plate which bore the chalice, covered with the same cloth as the chalice, without a light, and without a procession, or surplice or stole [for the priest]." Ladvenu sent back for torches and a stole, and administered the sacrament.[49]

When the two monks had finished, Cauchon arrived on the scene. Joan addressed him: "Bishop, I die through you." He began to remonstrate with her, saying, "Ah, Joan, be patient. You die because you did not keep your promise but returned to your former evil-doing." Joan replied, "Alas! if you had put me in Church prisons and in the hands of competent and suitable Church guards, this would not have happened; that is why I appeal to God about you."[50]

Included at the end of the trial record is a document entitled "Posthumous Information," purporting to describe a scene that occurred either before or after Joan's confession and communion. The circumstances are puzzling. Throughout the trial, every meeting of the assessors, every interrogation, every visit to Joan's cell of a group, was carefully recorded by the notaries and authenticated by their signatures. No notary, however, was present at the interview recorded in the "Posthumous Information," and when Cauchon asked the notaries to sign the document, they refused. The document consists of a series of statements purportedly made a week after Joan's death by seven of the assessors, including Martin Ladvenu and Jean Toutmouillé, the two friars who heard Joan's confession, Thomas de Courcelles, Pierre Maurice, and Nicolas Loiseleur. Rehabilitation testimony makes no mention of the interview or of the admissions Joan is supposed to have made, although most of the assessors involved were Rehabilitation witnesses.

The burden of the assessors' statements, each of which contained the words "and it seemed to him that Joan was at that time of sound mind," was that while Joan insisted that she had really heard her voices and seen her visions—"Good or bad, they appeared to me"—she now admitted that her voices had deceived her; they had told her that they would free her from prison, but they had not done so. She further confessed that the story about the angel who had brought the crown was nothing more than a figure of speech. She herself was the angel, who promised to have the king crowned at Reims. Whether her spirits were good or evil she left to the clerics. Her voices most often came to her with the sound of the bells at compline or matins. As for the "multitude of angels" she said had accompanied the angel with the crown, what she actually saw on that occasion was "some kind of little things." She believed in God alone, and would put no more faith in her voices "which have deceived me." "Exhibiting great signs of contrition and penitence for the crimes which she had perpetrated," the document concluded, Joan "begged indulgence of the English and Burgundians for having them killed, put to flight, and often damned."[51]

Ladvenu and Toutmouillé were certainly present in Joan's cell that morning, and a Rehabilitation witness said that Pierre Maurice, one of the seven assessors, visited Joan at that time. According to this witness, she asked him, "Master Pierre, where will I be tonight?" and he replied, "Do you not have a good hope in God?"[52] Some of the admissions have a certain verisimilitude. The document, in fact, reads like the solution to a detective story (though a disappointing one). It has been grasped at by many writers to explain Joan's visions in terms of natural phenomena: the metaphorical crown, the voices heard in the sound of the bells (auditory hallucination), the "little things" that she interpreted as a multitude of angels (migraine). On the other hand, the admissions sound like plausible explanations of Joan's visions which might have occurred to the skeptical judges.

As for Joan's disillusion with her voices, she had testified at the trial that she hoped to be rescued, but also that her voices had told her not to despair in her martyrdom, that she would come to the "kingdom of paradise." Joan hoped the martyrdom of which they spoke was nothing more than "the pain and adversity she was suffering in prison," but she put her faith in God. Did that faith temporarily fail her, so that like Christ on the cross she cried, "God, why hast Thou forsaken me?" Or was the whole story the invention of the judges, to discredit her? Martin Ladvenu, whose deposition in the "Posthumous Information" echoed his colleagues, testified at the Rehabilitation that Joan had believed to the end that her voices came from God and that they had not deceived her.[53]

When the others had left, Joan was led weeping from the castle by Jean Massieu and Martin Ladvenu, who were unable to restrain their own tears, and placed in the executioner's cart.[54] A Rehabilitation witness said that Nicolas Loiseleur, seeing Joan in this extremity, felt a sudden compunction and, weeping, tried to climb into the cart to ask her pardon, but the English shoved him away and might have killed him but for the intervention of the earl of Warwick, who warned him to leave Rouen at once.[55]

Eighty to a hundred armed English soldiers accompanied the cart through the streets to guard against any threat of rescue. In the large open space of the Old Market, four platforms had been set up, one for the judges and notables, one for Joan and Nicolas Midi, who was to preach the sermon, one for the bailiff of Rouen and secular judges, and, high above the crowd so that everyone could see, the scaffold with the stake and the wood ready for burning.[56] The records of the Paris Parlement tell us that a pointed hat, like a bishop's miter, was placed on Joan's head, bearing the words "Heretic, relapsed, apostate, idolator," and a sign was fixed to the platform where she stood to hear the sermon and sentence: "Jehanne, called the Pucelle, liar, pernicious, seducer of the people, diviner, superstitious, blasphemer of God, presumptuous, misbelieving the faith of Jesus Christ, braggart, idolator, cruel, dissolute, invoker of devils, apostate, schismatic, and heretic."[57]

Nicolas Midi used as his text I Corinthians 12 : 26, in which the unity of the members of the body is compared to that of the Church: "And whether one member suffer, all the members suffer with it." The sermon was not preserved in the court records; we know only that it was long.[58]

By the time Nicolas Midi concluded, it was about nine in the morning. Cauchon once more admonished Joan to "repent her evil deeds and show true contrition," directing Martin Ladvenu and Isambart de la Pierre to counsel her.

He then pronounced the sentence: "We, Pierre, by divine pity, humble bishop of Beauvais, and we, Jean Le Maitre, deputy of the Inquisitor of the Faith, judges competent in this matter, declare that you, Joan, called the Pucelle, have been found by us relapsed into diverse errors and crimes of schism, idolatry, invocation of devils, and various others. . . . Since the Church never closes her arms to those who would return to her, we did believe that, with full understanding and unfeigned faith, you had abandoned all the errors which you had renounced, vowing, swearing, and publicly promising that never again would you fall into such errors. . . . Nonetheless, time and time again you have relapsed, like a dog that returns to its vomit, as we state with great sorrow.

"Wherefore we declare that you have again incurred the sentence of excommunication and are again fallen into your previous errors, wherefore we now declare you to be a heretic. And by this sentence . . . we cast you forth and reject you from the communion of the Church as an infected limb, and hand you over to secular justice, praying the same to treat you with kindness and humanity in respect of your life and limbs."[59] The last qualification was an insincere formality always added to the sentences of the Inquisition.

Nicolas Midi then turned to Joan and said, "Go in peace, the Church can no longer defend you, and delivers you up to secular justice."[60]

Joan fell on her knees and began to pray. She commended her soul to God, the Virgin Mary, and the saints; she asked forgiveness of the judges, the English, the king of France, and "all the princes of the kingdom," and once more declared that she alone and not the king was responsible for everything she had done, good or bad.[61]

Her lamentations and prayers lasted perhaps half an hour; a witness tells us that they were so moving that Cauchon, Louis of Luxembourg, and Cardinal Beaufort wept and many other Englishmen were moved to tears, though some of them laughed.[62]

By Inquisition procedure, Joan should have been turned over at this point to the sheriff and his assistant, on the platform with the bailiff, for the sentence of execution. Several Rehabilitation witnesses pointed out that a heretic condemned in Rouen a short time later was treated according to this formality (what secular justice did with him, we are not told); in fact the bailiff was warned by Louis of Luxembourg that he must not proceed in the second case as he had done with Joan.[63] Instead, Joan was seized by two sergeants and hustled from the platform to the bailiff, who made a gesture with his hand: "Take her away." She was handed over to the executioner: "Do your office."[64]

Joan begged Jean Massieu for a cross. An English soldier won anonymous immortality by fashioning a little wooden one for her. Joan kissed it and placed it in her bosom.[65] She also asked Massieu to bring the ceremonial cross from the nearby church of St. Sauveur, so that she could look at it until she died. Massieu sent the parish clerk for it, and Joan embraced it closely, clinging to it until she was bound to the stake.[66]

Some of the soldiers grew impatient. One asked Massieu derisively, "Well, priest, will you make us dine here?"[67] At last Joan was led to the

Execution

scaffold. At this point many of the assessors left. Their duty was completed, but many admitted that they could not bear to watch.

Joan was bound to the stake and the fire kindled. Brother Isambart
held the cross high so that she could see it.[68] In the midst of the flames,
she cried, "Rouen, Rouen, am I to die here?" and then, "Ah, Rouen, I
fear you will suffer for my death!"[69] She was heard to ask for a missal,
and for holy water. Then she invoked her saints, and several times called
out, "Jesus!" Martin Ladvenu said that the executioner usually dispatched his victims so that they did not suffer too long, but the English
had built the scaffold so high that he could not reach her.[70] At last Joan
gave a great cry of "Jesus!" and died.[71]

When he was assured of her death, the executioner swept aside the
smoldering wood so that all could see that she had not escaped.[72]

By the order of Cardinal Beaufort, her ashes were carefully collected
and thrown into the Seine.[73]

14. Afterward

OF THE EFFECT OF JOAN'S DEATH, we have only distant echoes registered in the Rehabilitation record. Some of the stories reflect an already emerging belief that she was a saint. Brother Isambart de la Pierre stated that Joan's heart and entrails would not burn, no matter how much oil, sulfur, and charcoal the executioner applied, "at which he was astonished as at an evident miracle." The tale was reminiscent of many accounts of the martyrdom of saints, but the executioner, who also testified, did not mention the miracle.[1]

Brother Isambart also told the story of an English soldier who had hated Joan and had sworn that he would with his own hand add wood to the fire, but who as he did so heard Joan call the name of Jesus and was thunderstruck to see, as her spirit left her body, a white dove fly "in the direction of France." The Englishman was led off "almost in ecstasy" to an inn near the Old Market. When a drink had restored his strength, he sought out a priest to confess.[2]

Pierre Cusquel, the mason of Rouen who had visited Joan in her cell, was the source of a story involving another Englishman. John Tressart, one of Henry VI's secretaries, left the scene of the execution weeping and groaning, "We are all lost, for we have burned a saint."[3] The story

supplied Shaw with the basis for his character Chaplain John de Sto-
gumber. Jean Riquier, at the time of Joan's execution a fifteen-year-old
member of the cathedral choir, testified in similar vein that he heard Jean
Alepée, a cathedral canon who had been strongly antipathetic to Joan,
say, "Would that my soul were where I believe that woman's is!"[4]

The notary Manchon reported his own remorse. He "had never wept
so much about anything that happened to him, and for a month afterward he did not recover." With part of the money earned by his participation in the trial he bought "a little missal," which he still had at the
time of the Rehabilitation, and with which he prayed for Joan.[5]

While some of the lesser participants in the trial felt remorse, the
principals experienced uncomfortable premonitions. On June 12 Cauchon and the leading assessors obtained "letters of warranty" from
Henry VI promising that if any of them were sued for what had happened, the English king would defend them.[6]

Henry wrote to the duke of Burgundy announcing that Joan had been
burned "for the benefit of the faith and the extirpation of pestilent error,"
an accurate summary of the court's finding.[7] But just as on the French
side the idea that Joan was a saint began to take hold, on the English
the idea that she was a witch flourished. When the duke of Bedford
attributed English defeats to Joan's "false enchantments and sorcery" he
was voicing an accusation that the judges had dropped. In their judgment, she had been a dupe of the devil, not his partner. The idea that
Joan was a witch persisted only in England. The Burgundian writers in
the generation after her death merely treated her mission with skepticism.

On the political-military plane, Bedford sought to follow up Joan's
execution by a maneuver that would counter the effect of the coronation
of Charles at Reims. Reims unfortunately remained in French hands, so
to anoint young Henry VI Bedford was forced to make do with Paris.
Even this project presented a military obstacle, Louviers, a small town
on the Rouen–Paris road that La Hire had taken by surprise attack two
years earlier. Several Rehabilitation witnesses said that the English
feared to move on Louviers while Joan lived. A siege operation was now
pressed, and in October the town fell.

At last, early in December, nine-year-old Henry VI was able to ride
into Paris, where he was given a ceremonious welcome, the guilds and

the aldermen taking turns in holding a blue canopy starred with golden fleurs-de-lis over his head. One of the features of the procession was poor Guillaume the shepherd, Regnault of Chartres's protege, who had fallen into English hands and, as the Bourgeois of Paris noted with satisfaction, was "safely tied up with strong rope, like a thief." According to rumor, Guillaume was drowned in the Seine shortly after, without benefit of publicity or ritual.[8]

On Sunday, December 16, Henry was crowned at Notre-Dame, and a banquet was held at the palace on the Île de la Cité. Despite a large turnout—the notables were jostled by "cobblers, mustard sellers, packers, winestall keepers, stonemasons' lads"—the Bourgeois gave a sour report: the food, cooked the previous Thursday (an English custom, he thought), was unspeakable. "Many a time the marriages of children of Paris citizens have done more for the guilds, goldsmiths, goldbeaters, all the luxury trades, than the king's consecration did." The boy king was whisked out of Paris the day after Christmas, without having granted any of the traditional pardons and releases from taxation.

As public relations, Bedford's coronation ceremony was a fiasco. "No one in secret or in public was heard to praise [the king]."[9] Hardly was it over when the English cause suffered a stunning setback. The use of Paris for the coronation had been possible only through the passive cooperation of the duke of Burgundy. But Philip had no more assisted in Henry's consecration than he had in that of Charles. Now he coolly gave his allies notice of a preliminary agreement he had made with Charles. "The war for the pursuance of which you have not aided or supported me as you should" had become too expensive to continue, he wrote Bedford. Henry VI's great-uncle, Cardinal Henry Beaufort, made a last-minute attempt to reconcile the two dukes. When it failed, he proposed that England join in the Burgundian truce with the French, but Henry VI's chancellor, Louis of Luxembourg, vetoed the idea.[10]

That spring (1432) the English suffered fresh setbacks around Paris. Chartres was taken by ruse, and an English force trying to recover Lagny was driven off by Dunois.

Rouen itself was momentarily seized by a boldly raiding Armagnac band, but was quickly retaken when reinforcements for the attackers failed to arrive and the citizens rallied to the English. The leaders of the raid were ransomed, but 114 common soldiers were beheaded in the Old Market where Joan had died ten months before.[11]

In November 1432 Anne of Burgundy, who had for years kept peace between her husband Bedford and her brother Philip, died, severing a dynastic link that had fortified and formalized the Anglo-Burgundian alliance. Shortly after, Philip reopened full negotiations with Charles at Arras. Unable to prevent the talks, the English were now forced to join them, but could accomplish nothing except to delay the inevitable. Charles offered to allow Henry VI to retain Normandy and Aquitaine as fiefs of the French crown, a come-down Henry and his councillors were not ready to accept. In fact, so far was Bedford, mortally ill in his palace in Rouen, from appreciating the ebb of English power that his counter offer was a mirror image of Charles's: Charles could keep the provinces he held by paying homage to Henry VI as king of France.[12]

The negotiations dragged on interminably until on September 9, 1435, the English delegation left Arras, and on September 29 the French and Burgundians concluded a treaty. By its terms, Philip recognized Charles as king of France. In return, Philip was allowed to keep all the territorial concessions the English had made to him, except for Champagne and Brie. The fortified "towns of the Somme," to the north, guarding Philip's Flemish territories and threatening Paris, remained in his hands but could be redeemed by the king for 400,000 crowns. During Charles's lifetime, Philip was exempted from paying homage for his French fiefs. Finally, Charles solemnly denied complicity in the murder of Philip's father at Montereau and promised to punish the guilty parties, have masses said for the soul of the victim, and erect a monument to him.[13]

Charles has been criticized by modern historians as yielding too much to Burgundian demands in the treaty of Arras, but the great purpose of all his diplomacy toward the duke of Burgundy was finally accomplished, and the English were permanently deprived of the ally on whom their French enterprise depended.

News of the treaty was greeted in London with appropriate fury. Merchants from Bruges (in Philip's Flanders) were seized and their goods confiscated. Philip's ambassadors were arrested and narrowly escaped death, and in October Parliament was instructed to provide money for an army to punish Burgundian treachery. The gesture was futile.[14]

During the following winter, the English were driven out of their remaining footholds of the Île de France, and in February Richemont blockaded Paris, whose sentiments were changing in tune with those of its Burgundian protector. The English garrison, deprived of Burgundian aid and isolated in the now hostile city, took refuge in the Bastille. In April a nearly bloodless insurrection permitted French troops led by Dunois and Richemont to effect an entry into the city. The English garrison was allowed to withdraw on payment of "a large sum" for safe conduct, and to the accompaniment of the jeers of the Parisians. According to the Bourgeois, Richemont issued a proclamation thanking the citizens "for having so peaceably returned the chief city of his realm" to the king, and saying that if any man had wronged Charles, he was forgiven; he also forbade his men, on penalty of hanging, to quarter themselves in any Parisian's house without his consent, or "to insult or in any way annoy or rob anyone" except Englishmen. "The Parisians loved them so for this that before the day was over, not a man in Paris but would have risked his body and goods to destroy the English," said the Bourgeois. ". . . Whatever evil he had done against the king, nobody was killed for it."[15]

Not long after the recovery of Paris by Charles, a bizarre incident revealed that Joan was far from forgotten. A woman appeared in Metz claiming to be Joan and evidently resembling her. She won recognition by Joan's brothers (apparently willing dupes) and enjoyed a brief career speaking in parables as she traveled around accepting plaudits and presents. In 1439 she visited Orleans, and was wined and dined and given a gift of money "for the good she did the town during the siege." The charade ended when she was invited to a dinner to meet the king and failed to appear. Shortly after, she was seized in Paris by the University and Parlement and unmasked as a certain Claude des Armoises, with a colorful career behind her (if her new story was true) as a soldier in the pope's army. The Bourgeois reported that she joined the Paris garrison for a short time and then vanished.[16]

A second impostor appeared in 1452 in Champagne dressed in boy's clothing and won acceptance or toleration until she reached Saumur, where she was imprisoned for three months and then banished by René of Anjou. She later married and was allowed to return to Saumur but had to promise to abandon male dress.[17]

Whatever popular credulity was willing to attribute to Joan, the significance of her intervention on the political and military scene grew increasingly clear. With Paris in his hands and Burgundy neutralized,

Charles unmistakably had the upper hand in his kingdom. The English, confined to their twenty-year-old possession of Normandy and their three-hundred-year-old province of Aquitaine, no longer posed a threat to his lands or crown; and in fact, on the contrary, his own power threatened even these last English enclaves. The very delay that intervened pointed up the historic change that had now taken place in the government of France as it had earlier in that of England. Charles concentrated on improving his administration, refilling his treasury (with the aid of the moneyman of Bourges, Jacques Coeur), and rebuilding his now thoroughly professional and national army.[18] Whether by divine purpose or not, Joan had been guided by a sure instinct in focusing her enterprise on the person of the king. Monarchy was the path of the future for centuries to come.

The transition from feudal to monarchic power was evident most significantly in the military field. Joan's epic is filled with evidence of the rise of the new money-based royal military power amid the disappearance of the old anarchic feudal fighting class. As the army became professionalized, knights disappeared not so much out of it as into it, blending with plebeian "men-at-arms" who wore the same armor, rode the same horses, and received (by 1440) the same pay. Great nobles—dukes, counts, earls—continued to maintain their own military forces, but though they could hire captains, archers, and men-at-arms, the new artillery arm was beyond any but a king's means.

Thus the artillery, whose military value Joan had appreciated, became, because of its cost, an element of significance in the social-political evolution. The pioneering artillery force of Charles VII was strengthened and improved under the direction of the Bureau brothers (like Joan non-noble in origin), until it became an effective arm in the field as well as in siege operations. When the Hundred Years War entered its final phase in 1449, it took on for the first time the character of a French invasion of English territory. The walled towns and castles of Normandy fell with astonishing rapidity to the Bureau brothers' bombardments, and the English field army was destroyed at the battle of Formigny (April 15, 1450).

Charles at once turned his attention to Aquitaine (Gascony-Guienne) in southwest France, English since Henry of Anjou married Eleanor of Aquitaine and became king of England in 1154. Where the Normans had welcomed the French as liberators, the Gascons resisted them as conquerors, but the result was the same, climaxed by the last battle of the war, at Castillon (July 17, 1453), where Joan's old antagonist Talbot was found among the piles of English dead.[19]

In accordance with Joan's prediction, the English had been "driven out of France." For another hundred years they retained Calais, which Charles refrained from attacking out of consideration for the duke of Burgundy, whose Flemish wool-producing towns wanted it left in English hands.

Meantime, the Rehabilitation proceedings had been set in motion.[20]

When Rouen opened its gates to Charles and Dunois in 1449, the record of Joan's trial fell into the king's hands. What his feelings had been in the years since her death is a subject for conjecture, but documents of varying reliability report that the event had shocked him. A letter from an Italian merchant in Bruges written immediately afterward (June 1431) asserts that the news afflicted the king with "very bitter sorrow," and that he "threatened to wreak a terrible vengeance on the English and the women of England."[21] Pius II, writing in 1461, says that Charles grieved bitterly,[22] and chronicler Pierre Sala, writing in 1516, but recalling the conversations of a king's chamberlain he had known as a boy, says the king felt sad but helpless.[23]

Whether out of his own curiosity and concern or in response to public opinion or both, Charles appointed one of his councillors, Guillaume Bouillé, dean of Noyon cathedral, to study the trial record. Bouillé himself brought an active interest in Joan's fate that evidently contributed to enlarging the scope of his mission, originally limited simply to ascertaining the facts about the trial. That a vindication of Joan would benefit Charles by removing the stigma of heresy and witchcraft from the instrument by which he had gained his crown was also evident.* Yet this factor was not mentioned until some months later when Bouillé submitted his initial report. If self-interest argued for Charles's opening Joan's trial to public scrutiny, self-interest also argued against it. He had gained Paris by promising amnesty, a promise he had scrupulously kept, and he had promoted the spirit of national reconciliation to the extent of forbidding the use of the old epithets "Armagnac" and "Burgundian." A

*In their introduction to the first volume of the Rehabilitation record, Paul Doncoeur and Yvonne Lanhers even suggest that Charles's mistress Agnes Sorel might have played a role in initiating the inquiry: "Is it more than coincidence that the date (February 15) of the order to Bouillé is that of the arrival of Agnes Sorel at Jumièges?"[24]

reopening of Joan's case threatened to revive all the old bitterness.

Officially, the inquiry was initiated by a letter from Charles to Bouillé on February 15, 1450, instructing him to inquire into the trial by which his enemies, because of "the great hate they had for [Joan], had wickedly and unjustly had her killed, with great cruelty."[25]

Bouillé summoned seven participants in the trial to make depositions about its fairness and propriety: the notary Guillaume Manchon, the usher Jean Massieu, University master Jean Beaupère, and four Dominican friars of Rouen who had been assessors: Martin Ladvenu, Isambart de la Pierre, Guillaume Duval, and Jean Toutmouillé. Six gave closely similar testimony: that Joan had been persecuted and mistreated by the English, who hated and feared her, that Cauchon had been their particular instrument, that Joan had appealed to the pope and the general council but her appeal had been ignored, that those who had tried to help her or who had disagreed with Cauchon had been persecuted in their turn, that she had been executed without a proper sentence by lay justice, that she had not understood the questions she was asked, that she had been held illegally in a military prison, and that Erard in his sermon at St. Ouen had attacked the king and Joan had defended him.[26] The only dissenter was the University's Jean Beaupère, who did not directly contradict the others, but expressed skepticism about Joan's visions (he believed that they were "more from natural cause and human intention than supernatural") and said that, "as for her innocence, she was very subtle, with a woman's subtlety."[27] Councillor Bouillé drew up a summary of the testimony discounting Beaupère's evidence and, to encourage the king's continued participation, declared that it was in Charles's interest to look further into "the iniquitous, scandalous sentence which threatens his crown," with the implication that the sentence should be annulled.[28]

Charles was willing, but there was a problem. The sentence had been pronounced by the Church, and only the Church could nullify it. To the papacy such an inquiry and possible overturn of Church justice could not be very welcome. The trial had been conducted in conformity with Church law by a properly constituted court. In the calculations of the present pope, Nicholas V, two extraneous considerations were also present. In 1438 Charles had proclaimed a degree of independence for the French church in the "Pragmatic Sanction of Bourges," whose validity the pope naturally contested. At the same time the Turks were threatening Constantinople, and Nicholas hoped to enlist Charles's aid in a crusade. Apart from these specifics, Charles's position of power in the Europe of 1451 was such that no pope could afford to treat him lightly.

Seeking a compromise to the thorny problem, Nicholas appointed as his legate to France Cardinal Guillaume d'Estouteville, a Norman with a strong record of Armagnac loyalty, and entrusted him with the double mission of convoking an assembly to annul the Pragmatic Sanction and dealing with the trial of Joan of Arc.

In February 1452 Estouteville visited the king at Tours and two months later went to Rouen, both to summon the conference on the Pragmatic Sanction and to take up the case of Joan of Arc. He at once contacted the Inquisitor General of France, Jean Bréhal. Bréhal assembled the two-year-old depositions from Guillaume Bouillé's inquiry and the twenty-year-old trial documents and handed the whole mass of data over to two canon lawyers whom Estouteville had brought from Rome.

Early in May 1452 Estouteville and his lawyers produced a critique of the 1431 trial consisting of twelve articles designed to form a basis for further inquiry. The propositions were:

That Cauchon had hated Joan because she fought against the English, and had sought her death by every possible means;

That he had demanded her delivery primarily to the king of England and only secondarily to the Church, and had been willing to pay any price for her;

That the English feared Joan and wanted her dead;

That Cauchon had kept her in a secular prison and in the hands of her enemies;

That he was not legally competent to try her;

That she was a simple, honest girl and a good Christian;

That she had several times during the trial said that she would submit to the judgment of the Church and the pope, and that her testimony seemed to proceed from a good rather than an evil spirit;

That she did not understand the questions about the Church Militant;

That she was condemned as relapsed though she was willing to submit;

That she had been compelled to resume male clothing;

That though her submission to the Church was clear to the judges, they had given in to English pressure and condemned her as a heretic;

That all these facts were matters of common note in Rouen and in the kingdom of France.[29]

Five witnesses were examined with reference to these twelve articles. Three had already testified in the king's inquiry: notary Guillaume Manchon and friars Martin Ladvenu and Isambart de la Pierre. To them were added Pierre Miget, another assessor, and Pierre Cusquel, the mason. With the aid of their testimony, the twelve articles were expanded to twenty-seven, and the following week seventeen more witnesses were summoned to testify.

The new list, which formed the basis of all the inquiries that followed, elaborated on some of the earlier charges and added new ones:

That pressure had been exerted on the notaries to falsify the record and to omit Joan's testimony favorable to her;

That the English had used agents provocateurs to stimulate Joan's resistance to submission;

That the questioning had been "difficult and insidious" and Joan did not understand it;

That it exhausted her so that she made slips of the tongue which were then seized upon;

That the translation of the court record into Latin was inaccurate and suppressed things that might have been favorable to Joan;

That Joan was given no facilities for defending herself;

That without a proper sentence from a secular judge Joan was turned over to the English who "inspired by rage against her" immediately led her to the stake;

That she had died commending her soul to God and invoking Jesus in a manner that evoked tears from everyone present;

That the English had thus acted against Joan in order to discredit "the most Christian king."[30]

Some of these charges were never substantiated, even by the testimony of the witnesses most sympathetic to Joan. The notaries were proud of the accuracy of their record, and other witnesses backed them up. The only points on which the record was actually challenged were its suppression of Joan's statement that she would submit to the judgment of the pope and the general council (a statement, however, that if omitted at one point was entered in the record at least twice elsewhere), the form of the abjuration she signed, and the "Posthumous Information," which the notaries had refused to authenticate.

Thus the trial record was very largely vindicated. The Latin translation seems to have been faithful (except for Courcelles's suppression of his own vote in favor of torture) and some minor divergences from the Orleans manuscript—if it is indeed a copy of the French minutes. Further, Loiseleur's activities seem to have been directed toward information and confession rather than provoking Joan's resistance, and while the questioning was indeed exhausting and difficult, the record showed that Joan fended very well for herself.

The inquiry concluded, Inquisitor Bréhal drew up a digest of the case and submitted it to a series of theologians and lawyers to study and give their opinion; they pronounced in Joan's favor.

Two years passed without any further action.

A new phase of the inquiry was initiated by Joan's own family, evidently at the suggestion of one of the theologians who had been consulted about the case. Joan's mother and brothers petitioned the new pope, Calixtus III, to institute a Rehabilitation process, to restore Joan's honor and redress the injustice, and to cite her judges or their heirs and successors. In June 1455 the d'Arc family's petition was granted, and three commissioners were appointed to produce the verdict.

On November 7, 1455, the inquiry opened in the cathedral of Notre-Dame in Paris, crowded with spectators. The petition of Joan's mother, Isabelle Romée, was read:

"[The plaintiff] had a daughter born in lawful marriage, to whom the sacraments of baptism and confirmation were given, and who was raised in the fear of God and respect for the tradition of the Church. . . . Nevertheless, although [Joan] never thought, conceived, or did anything contrary to the faith . . . certain enemies . . . had her arraigned in Church court . . . and despite her disavowals and appeals . . . they condemned her in a damnable and wicked trial, and put her to death most cruelly by fire. . . ."[31]

Three delegates were appointed by the pope to carry out the new investigation. The most important was the archbishop of Reims, Jean Jouvenel des Ursins, a longtime supporter of Charles VII, and convinced of Joan's innocence. But the situation was delicate. Fortunately for the inquiry, Pierre Cauchon and Jean d'Estivet, the judge and the promoter, were dead, as were Nicolas Loiseleur, the prison spy, Nicolas Midi, who had preached the last sermon in the Old Market, and many others. Sub-Inquisitor Jean Le Maitre, whom Cauchon had dragooned against his will into taking part in the trial, had disappeared. But the assessors who were still alive occupied important Church positions, and some were in the king's service. Jean de Mailly, bishop of Noyon, was councillor Guillaume Bouillé's own superior; several canons of Rouen cathedral who had acted as assessors were still alive, as were several of the University masters. Thomas de Courcelles, who had voted in favor of torturing Joan, had been Charles's representative at the Council of Basel (defending the Pragmatic Sanction).

Hearings were recommenced, some covering the same ground as the first inquiry, but this time extending to Domremy, Vaucouleurs, Toul, Orleans, and Paris.

For the interrogations in Domremy, Vaucouleurs, and Toul, a special list of questions was developed with several specific purposes: identifying Joan, in the absence of parish records, by giving her place of origin and parish and the names of her parents and godparents; providing information about her piety and virtue; examining the activities of Joan and her friends at the Ladies' Tree; establishing the fact that an inquiry had been made in her place of origin before the trial; and investigating the rumors about Joan's sojourn with La Rousse in Neufchâteau in 1428.[32]

At Beauvais, the new bishop, promoter, and Sub-Inquisitor were summoned to appear in behalf of their 1431 predecessors. They protested that they could not be held answerable, but eventually the new promoter appeared to declare that he would not contest the inquiry or attempt to defend Cauchon's trial.

Some of the Rouen witnesses were reluctant and gave unresponsive answers—"I know nothing," "I do not remember"— or denied that they had taken much part in the trial. But for the most part they gave the investigators what they wanted, in their replies often repeating the words of the articles.

The depositions were concluded at Rouen on May 14, 1456. In June, Inquisitor Bréhal studied the documents and produced a review of the case.

Finally on July 7, in Rouen cathedral, Jean Jouvenel des Ursins pronounced his official verdict: "We say, pronounce, decree, and declare the said trial and sentence to be contaminated with fraud, calumny, wickedness, contradictions, and manifest errors of fact and law, and together with the abjuration, the execution, and all their consequences, to have been and to be null, without value or effect, and to be quashed. . . . We proclaim that Joan . . . did not contract any taint of infamy and that she shall be and is washed clean of such. . . ."

One of the copies of the original articles of accusation was then torn up. The court moved to the cemetery of St. Ouen and there the verdict was solemnly repeated. The next day it was pronounced for the third time in the Old Market, and there, on the site of the scaffold, a cross was erected in Joan's memory.[33]

No individual was condemned in the verdict except by implication. The result was an intelligent compromise; Joan was absolved, and at the same time the possibilities of renewed civil conflict were minimized. Joan's exhaustively formal trial had required four months. The trial was condemned in an even longer process, seven years from the first inquiry to the final judgment, two years for the official investigation. The testimony of over a hundred witnesses was heard and recorded, some testifying several times, and an enormous array of opinion from jurists and theologians was compiled.

The unfairness of Joan's trial, the bias of the judges, the pressures of the English, the techniques of the Inquisition, have received much criticism. In spite of the impressive physical weight of testimony, the Rehabilitation is scarcely more defensible in terms of objectivity. The articles on the basis of which witnesses were questioned in effect told them what they were to answer, and understandably enough, for the most part they obliged. The key question remained: Joan's willingness to submit to the judgment of the Church. Her deeds, both large and small, were of infinitely less significance to Joan, the court, and the Church than were her visions and her mission.

On this subject the archbishop avoided judgment. One reason for his silence might have been concern about offending the assessors who had taken part in the trial. But beyond that must have been an uneasy feeling of ambiguity about Joan's voices, which he shared with other churchmen, Armagnac or not, and doubtless with laymen such as Charles. Where her voices came from they did not know. Perhaps not from heaven, certainly not from hell. The question ultimately was in God's hands.

The Church recognized that direct communication with God could take place, but reserved to itself the right to examine mystics and give or withhold approval. Joan was reluctant in the extreme to have her visions examined, even by the clergy at Poitiers, even by her parish priest. Her belief in them was so strong that it is difficult to conceive that she would have accepted anyone's judgment that they were illusions or lies

—pope, council, or anyone else. Her visions were her reason for being, the meaning of her life.

Certainly Joan was no heretic in the sense of the contemporary English Lollards, followers of John Wycliffe, or of the Bohemian Hussites. She was no reformer, either social or ecclesiastical, no pre-Protestant, no social revolutionary. She accepted the social system, she zealously observed the rites and sacraments of the Church. She surely belonged to no dissident group.

Yet Joan was not an ordinary Catholic Christian, or an ordinary anything. She was something else—intensely individualistic, inner-directed, believing so strongly in her own revelations that after a year of imprisonment and months of questioning and pressure, and in the shadow of the scaffold, she maintained unflinchingly that her voices were those of St. Catherine and St. Margaret and that they had been sent to her by God. Joan's clash was not only with Church authority, but with the authoritarian character of the Church, the fact that it reserved for itself the power of deciding what was the truth.

Thus the Church-conducted Rehabilitation found the Church-conducted trial unjust and fraudulent. The popular view, however, blamed not the Church but the English, the French obverse of the English conviction that Joan was a witch. François Villon, at almost this moment, was writing in *Ballade des Dames du Temps Jadis* (Ballad of the Ladies of Yesteryear):

> *Et Jehanne, la bonne Lorraine,*
> *Qu'Englois brulerent à Rouan . . .*[34]
> *(And Joan, the good Lorrainer,*
> *Whom the English burned at Rouen. . . .)*

By archbishop Jean Jouvenel's pronouncement, the sentence against Joan had been revoked. It was less than her family had sought, but it was enough, and Joan's name had been cleared. For the Church, a more positive expression of change in attitude took more than four centuries, during which Joan was by no means forgotten, and during which she became almost more a literary than a historical figure.

The rising European nationalism of the century following the French Revolution revived interest in Joan as a patriotic figure, and simultaneously as a Catholic heroine. In 1869 an illustrious bishop of Orleans,

Felix Dupanloup, launched an initiative toward Joan's canonization. In the 1890s a great liberal pope, Leo XIII, opened the investigation that led in 1909 to her beatification. Canonization followed in 1920. The Church raised Joan to sainthood strictly for her virtues. No mention was made of her military accomplishments, her martyrdom, her voices, or her visions.[35]

By a reverberating irony, while Joan is now a saint, both Catherine and Margaret have been stricken from the Church calendar because of doubts that they ever really existed.

15. Five and a Half Centuries of Joan of Arc

OPINION ABOUT JOAN has a history of its own, spanning the centuries between her death and the present day, from the contemporary chronicles, French and Burgundian, through the nationalistic English histories that culminated in Shakespeare's *Henry VI, Part 1,* the Voltairean skepticism of the Renaissance and Enlightenment, the new patriotic ideology of the French Revolution, to the concepts and fashions of the present day, including the anthropological, the Freudian, the mystical, and the faddish and freakish.

The French chronicles written shortly after Joan's death—the *Chronique de la Pucelle,* the *Journal du Siège d'Orléans,* and the chronicles of Perceval de Cagny, Guillaume Gruel, Jean Chartier, and others—represent what might be called the providential viewpoint. That is, they assume or imply that Joan was sent by God to save Charles VII and France. This conviction was shared by the famous feminist poet Christine de Pisan, who in her last poem, written in July 1429, hailed the victory at Orleans:

> *Esther, Judith, and Deborah*
> *Were ladies of great worth*

240

By whom God restored
His people when they were hard-pressed,
And others I have heard of
Who were valiant, none more so,
But many more miracles
Were done by the Pucelle.
Ah, what honor to the feminine sex!
Which God so loved that he showed
A way to this great people
By which the kingdom, once lost,
Was recovered by a woman,
A thing that men could not do. [1]

The Burgundian chroniclers took a more skeptical view. The most important of them because of his influence on later writers, particularly English, was Enguerrand de Monstrelet. Picturing Joan as a former servant at an inn* who rode horseback and otherwise comported herself in a fashion unseemly for young girls, Monstrelet recorded that she was "said to be inspired by divine grace," but quoted with approval the letter from Henry VI to the duke of Burgundy describing Joan's condemnation as "a fortification of our faith and extirpation of pestilent errors."[2] Another Burgundian, Le Fèvre de St.-Rémi, described Joan as a shepherdess who said she had revelations of the Virgin Mary, accompanied by angels and saints and "the prophet David," and asserted that word of Joan's revelations had reached "a certain gentleman" (Robert de Baudricourt) who had armed her and given her a horse and taken her to the siege of Orleans, where she had performed apparent miracles and frightened the English.[3]

The fact that the Burgundian chronicles were all written after the treaty of Arras of 1435 had reconciled the two French factions and ended the Burgundian alliance with England probably accounts for their relatively mild tone. A better illustration of contemporary Anglo-Burgundian sentiment is afforded by the *Journal d'un Bourgeois de Paris,* which summarized Joan's story immediately after her execution in distinctly hostile terms. Freely garbling the testimony at the trial, the Bourgeois wrote that Joan went about with soldiers every day, "no woman with her," dressed like a man, and carrying a great stick, with which she struck any of her men who did anything wrong, "like a very cruel

*An idea derived from Joan's stay at La Rousse's establishment in Neufchâteau.

woman." She took communion dressed in men's clothes, which she refused to stop wearing, boasted that she could produce "thunder and other marvels if she wished," once jumped from the top of a high tower without hurting herself at all, and had people, both men and women, killed if they did not obey her instantly. She scandalously claimed that God spoke to her personally through St. Michael, St. Catherine, and St. Margaret, and predicted secret things to her.

The Bourgeois also reported the substance of a sermon preached by a Dominican in Paris shortly after Joan's execution. The Dominican said that Joan had worn male clothing "since she was about fourteen years old," that her father and mother had been so angry with her that they "would like to have killed her if they could have done so without qualm of conscience," and therefore she had left them, "in the devil's company, and had ever since been a murderer of Christian people, full of fire and blood, till at last she was burned." In prison, the preacher continued, "the devil appeared to her as three people, that is, St. Michael, St. Margaret, and St. Catherine, as she called them." These devils in the shape of saints urged her not to change her male dress: "Don't be afraid, we will take good care of you." Joan immediately put on her old clothes "that she used to wear on horseback, which she had hidden in the straw of her bed." She was sentenced to die for her obstinacy, but when she called on the devils, "not one of them appeared again after her sentence, invoke them though she might. Then she changed her mind, but it was too late."[4]

Historians have searched hard to find scanty contemporary English references to Joan. Two edicts, of August 1429 and May 1430, against mutinying English soldiers were published by seventeenth-century historiographer Thomas Rymer in his collection of documents, the *Foedera,* under the title "Proclamations against captains and soldiers who have abandoned their post terrified by the incantations of a Pucelle"; however, the title is Rymer's and nothing in the documents themselves connects them with Joan.[5] The only documentary reference to Joan in English archives is in the letter written in 1433 by the duke of Bedford to the English council defending himself against charges of negligence for the English defeats, in which he refers to Joan as a "disciple and limb of the Fiend" who used enchantments and sorcery to win battles.[6]

Contemporary English chronicles are almost as silent about Joan as first-century Latin historians are about Jesus. Only a 1430 version of the municipal history known as the *Great Chronicle of London* refers to "a woman . . . called the Pucelle de Dieu, the false witch through whose power the dauphin and all our adversaries trusted to have conquered all France, and never to have had the worst of it in a place she was in, for they held her amongst them for a prophetess and a worthy goddess."[7] (One rendering of this chronicle juxtaposed the news of Joan's capture with a local item: "Also this same year, about Candlemas, Richard Hunden, a wool packer, was damned as a false heretic and Lollard, and burned at the Tower Hill, who was of so large [free] conscience that he would eat flesh on Fridays.")

Joan received more space in an English chronicle dating from a generation later, the *Brut,* purporting to record the annals of Britain from its mythical founding by Brutus. Printed by William Caxton in 1480 as *Chronicles of England,* England's first published history, it narrated a version of Joan's story based on hostile Burgundian sources.

This year [1430] on St. George's day, King Henry [VI] passed over the sea to Calais toward France. About this time and before, the realm [France] being in great misery and tribulation, the Dauphin with his party began to make war, and gained certain places, and made distresses upon Englishmen, by means of his captains, that is to say, La Hire and Poton de Xaintrailles, and in especial a maid which they named *la Pucelle de Dieu.*

This maid rode like a man and was a valiant captain among them, and took upon her many great enterprises, in so much that they had a means to have recovered all their losses by her. Notwithstanding, at the last, after many great feats, by the help and prowess of Sir John Luxembourg, which was a noble captain of the Duke of Burgundy, and many Englishmen, Picards, and Burgundians, which were of our party, before the town of Compiègne, the 22nd day of May [actually the 23rd], the foresaid Pucelle was taken in the field, armed like a man, and many other captains with her. And were all brought to Rouen, and there she was put in prison, and there she was judged by the law to be burnt. [Here the chronicler added a lurid detail found neither in Burgundian sources nor in the legal record.] And then she said that she was with child, but in conclusion, it was found that she was not with child, and then she was burnt in Rouen. And the other captains were put to ransom and treated as men of war are accustomed.[8]

English historians of the sixteenth century—Robert Fabyan, John Stowe, Richard Grafton, Edward Hall—followed the *Brut* and the Burgundian tradition. Hall's chronicle (1548) sounded a new note of patri-

Charles VII had undertaken to regain his kingdom, Hall
⸱ his spies informed him that "many and divers cities and
Ϝrance, abhorring the English liberty, and aspiring to the
ʋondage and native servitude (according to the nature of asses,
the more they be charged with, the more they desire) would (when
ι ⁄ saw their time) not only rebel and return to his faction and part,
but also were ready to aid and assist him in recovery of his desired realm
and ancient dominion, in expelling also the English nation out of the
territories of France."

Like Monstrelet, Hall described Joan as "a chambermaid in a common
hostelry . . . a ramp [tomboy] of such boldness that she would course
horses and ride them to water and do things that other young maidens
both abhorred and were ashamed to do." She preserved her virginity,
however, either "because of her foul face, that no man would desire it," +
or because she had vowed to live chaste. Hall repeated a story told by
Jean Chartier in his chronicle about a courtier's posing as the king at
Chinon and Joan's penetration of the deception, although she had never
seen the king before. When he came to Joan's capture and trial, Hall
omitted the *Brut*'s story of the pretended pregnancy, but concluded that
Joan had offended by lack of modesty and of the pity that should be in
a woman's heart. "Where was her womanly behaviour, when she clad
herself in a man's clothing, and was conversant with every common
soldier, giving occasion to all men to judge and speak evil of her and her
doings?" Her story was a "blot to the French nation"—that "all the
notable victories, and honorable conquests . . . were gotten and achieved
by a shepherd's daughter, a chambermaid in a hostelry, and a beggar's
brat. . . . For surely, if credit may be given to the acts of the clergy
. . . this woman was not inspired with the Holy Ghost, nor sent from God
(as the Frenchmen believe) but an enchantress, an organ of the devil, sent
by Satan. . . ."[9]

The *Brut*-derived chronicles culminated in a work which had the
distinction of becoming one of the main sources of Shakespeare's history
plays: the *Chronicles* of Raphael Holinshed, published in 1587. Holinshed described Joan as "a young wench of eighteen years," whose
father was "a sorry shepherd," and whose parents "brought [her] up
poorly in their trade of keeping cattle." In appearance she was "counted
likesome, of person strongly made and manly, of courage great, hardy
and stout withal; an understander of councils though she were not at

them; great semblance of chastity both of body and behaviour; the name of Jesus in her mouth about all her businesses; humble, obedient, and fasting divers days in the week. A person (as their [the French] books make her) raised up by power divine, only for succor to the French estate then deeply in distress. . . . In warfare she rode in armor cap-a-pie and mustered as a man, before her an ensign all white wherein was Jesus Christ painted with a flower-de-luce in his hand."

Holinshed repeated, with fewer details, Hall's account—Joan's miraculous identification of the king at Chinon, the "bold enterprises which to our great displeasure" she pursued for two years, and finally her capture at Compiègne, where she was "sold into the English hands," and Bedford's inquiry, through the agency of Pierre Cauchon, into her life and belief. He revived the *Brut*'s story of the false pregnancy, and echoed Hall's opinion that through Joan the dauphin's "dignity abroad was foully spotted" by profaning his estate with "devilish practices with misbelievers and witches."[10]

Shakespeare's chronicle play *Henry VI, Part 1,* first performed in 1592, is believed by some scholars to be the work of a combination of playwrights, by others to be entirely Shakespeare's.[11] It owed much of its information about Joan to Hall and Holinshed, but added touches of its own, both for dramatic effect and to enhance the role of the play's hero, the English captain John Talbot. Whether because of shared authorship or contradictory purposes, the Joan of *Henry VI, Part 1* emerges as an even more schizophrenic personality than in Holinshed: in the early scenes a brave and dignified woman, in Act V a virago who invokes demons and denies her father, insisting that she is "descended of a gentler blood and issued from the progeny of kings," a notion that found an echo in twentieth-century writings about Joan. The play goes beyond its sources to blacken her character, and freely rearranges history to do so. Shakespeare's Joan captures Rouen by ruse (as it was in fact captured a year after her death), puts it to the torch, and taunts the dying regent Bedford (who actually died four years after Joan). Talbot answers her:

> Foul fiend of France, and hag of all despite,
> Encompass'd with thy lustful paramours!
> Becomes it thee to taunt his valiant age
> And twit with cowardice a man half dead?

Yet in the following scene an eloquent Joan parleys with the duke of
Burgundy and persuades him to abandon his English alliance and join
the dauphin's forces (an improvement on history which was adopted by
several of Shakespeare's literary heirs):

> *Brave Burgundy, undoubted hope of France!*
> *Stay, let thy humble handmaid speak to thee. . . .*
> *Look on thy country, look on fertile France,*
> *And see the cities and the towns defac'd. . . .*
> *Behold the wounds, the most unnatural wounds,*
> *Which thou thyself hast given her woeful breast.*
> *O, turn thy edged sword another way.*

In the play, Talbot and his son are killed in Joan's lifetime, rather than
twenty-two years after her execution, and Joan flings gratuitous insults
at their bodies. Summoning her "fiends" in Act V, she promises to "lop
a member off and give it to you . . . so you do condescend to help me
now," and when her "ancient incantations are too weak,/and hell too
strong for me to buckle with," she offers them "my body, soul, and all,"
declaring when they refuse her, "Now, France, thy glory droopeth to the
dust." Sentenced to burn, she announces, as in the *Brut* and Holinshed,
that she is with child, whereupon York and Warwick debate the child's
paternity: "She and the Dauphin have been juggling." Realizing that
they will not scruple to kill "a bastard of Charles's", she offers them first
Alençon, then René of Anjou as the father. York replies:

> *Why, here's a girl! I think she knows not well,*
> *There were so many, whom she may accuse.*

Warwick: 'Tis sign she hath been liberal and free. *York:* Strumpet, thy
words condemn thy brat and thee.

Joan replies with a curse:

> *May never glorious sun reflex his beams*
> *Upon the country where you make abode,*
> *But darkness and the gloomy shade of death*
> *Environ you, till mischief and despair*
> *Drive you to break your necks or hang yourselves!*

To which York returns a curse of his own:

> *Break thou in pieces and consume to ashes,*
> *Thou foul accursed minister of hell!*

Charles VII thereupon agrees to a truce with the English, ending the play.

Thus, while French chroniclers had concluded that Joan's role was providential, a hostile line of historians that led from contemporary Burgundians to later English chroniclers and finally to the nationalistic *Henry VI, Part 1* credited her with an opposite, diabolical inspiration.

A new note was sounded by a neutral commentator: Pius II (Aeneas Silvius Piccolomini). This great humanist pope, who reigned from 1458 to 1464 and played an influential role in European politics, left memoirs which included a summary of the history of the fifteenth century. His account of Joan's story was generally sympathetic, though it included some misinformation. He made her a swineherd, named her place of origin as neighboring Toul rather than Domremy, had her meet the dauphin at Bourges rather than Chinon, and simplified and foreshortened her career. He asserted that the court at Rouen "could find nothing to correct except the man's dress she wore," and therefore put her back in prison where her guards tempted her with "now a military cloak, now a cuirass, now a breastplate or other armor" until she succumbed to temptation and put them on, "not knowing that she was putting on death." He concluded: "Thus died Joan, that astonishing and marvelous maid who restored the kingdom of France when it was fallen and almost torn asunder; who inflicted so many heavy defeats on the English; who being made general over men kept her purity unstained among companies of soldiers; of whom no breath of scandal was ever heard. . . . Whether her career was a miracle of heaven or a device of men I should find hard to say."

Here Pius II introduced a theme which the Burgundian chronicler Le Fèvre de St.-Rémi had hinted at, a political conspiracy using Joan as a tool.

Some think that when the English cause was prospering and the French nobles at variance among themselves thought no one fit to be commander, one shrewder than the rest evolved the cunning scheme of declaring that the Maid had been sent by heaven and of giving her the command she asked for, since there was no man alive who would refuse to have God for his leader. Thus it came about that the conduct of the war and the high command were entrusted to a girl. . . .

This at any rate is beyond question: that it was the Maid under whose command the siege of Orleans was raised, by whose arms all the country between Bourges and Paris was subdued, by whose advice Reims was recovered and the coronation celebrated there, by whose charge Talbot was routed and his army cut to pieces. . . . It is a phenomenon that deserves to be recorded, although after-ages are likely to regard it with more wonder than credulity.[12]

It has often been asserted that in France in the sixteenth and seventeenth centuries Joan's reputation underwent first a decline and then an eclipse. The idea derives largely from the historical work of a French contemporary of Shakespeare, Bertrand de Girard, Seigneur du Haillan, one of a school of humanists who treated history as a literary exercise, inventing characters and mixing fabricated speeches, letters, and conversations with documented facts. Du Haillan's *De l'Estat et succez des affaires de France,* first published in 1580, expressed humanist doubt about the authenticity of Joan's visions, repeated Pope Pius II's suggestion that she had been introduced by French captains to aid morale, and prefigured *Henry VI, Part 1* on the subject of her morals (though Shakespeare evidently arrived at the same conclusion independently of du Haillan). "Some say Joan was the whore of Jean, the Bastard of Orleans, others of the Sire de Baudricourt, and others of Poton [de Xaintrailles]."[13]

Du Haillan, however, had little impact on French opinion. In 1639 the first serious scholarly treatment of Joan's life, *L'Histoire de la Pucelle d'Orléans,* was written by University of Paris doctor Edmond Richer. In a manuscript that remained unpublished until 1912, Richer used the trial and Rehabilitation records to vindicate Joan, endorse her visions, refute the charges against her, and condemn the court that found her guilty. Several published seventeenth-century accounts—monographs by local historians of Orleans, Rouen, Reims, essays of antiquarians, poetical works—also extolled her. Charles du Lys and Jean Hordal, descendants of two of Joan's brothers, published books about her. Several plays in French and Latin cast Joan as heroine, freely romanticizing her story.[14]

In 1646 a reference in a volume of published letters to du Haillan's slur on Joan's morals provoked the famous novelist and *précieuse* (woman intellectual) Madeleine de Scudéry, to write an energetic refutation stating that Joan's purity was not to be questioned and that the "chaste warrior" was sent by God to save her country; her sentence in Rouen was "the most unjust ever pronounced." Not all women could become warriors, said Mlle. de Scudéry, but sometimes it was God's decision that women should bear arms.[15]

The best-known seventeenth-century work about Joan was Jean Chapelain's long poem *La Pucelle,* which, pedestrian itself, inspired Voltaire in the following century to compose a work which enjoyed a tremendous *succès de scandale,* appearing on the Church Index from the date it was published, and outraging generations of the devout.

Chapelain, one of the intellectuals who helped found the Académie Française, conceived his work as a poem in twenty-four cantos, combining allegory, romance, and epic. Its real hero was Joan's comrade-in-arms Dunois (whose descendant was Chapelain's patron). Charles VII's mistress Agnes Sorel (actually not a contemporary of Joan) and the English regent Bedford were the villains, with poisoned apples, duels, doubles, and other non-historical details abounding. The first volume of Chapelain's poem, published in 1656, was a popular success, but received so severe a review from the arbiter of criticism Boileau, that the remaining cantos remained unpublished until 1882.[16]

Although local historians, antiquarians, and Church scholars of the eighteenth century continued to admire Joan, a skeptical attitude was adopted by Voltaire and his fellow *philosophes,* who viewed history as a weapon in their war against Church, monarchy, and nobility.[17] Joan belonged to the Middle Ages, in their eyes a period of darkness when "barbarism, superstition, and ignorance covered the face of the world," to be studied only to avoid its recurrence.[18] Montesquieu voiced the Enlightenment's rejection of the "providentialist" view of Joan's story, the idea that Joan was guided and helped by Divine Providence rather than by natural forces. "The English took her for a sorceress; the French for prophetess and envoy of God. She was neither. . . . If the story of the Maid is a fable, what can one say of all those miracles that all the monarchies claim, as if God governed a kingdom with a special providence from that with which he governed its neighbors!"[19]

In his *Essai sur les moeurs* (1756) Voltaire praised Joan's courage and resolution, but attributed her appearance on the stage of history to political conspiracy, a notion he apparently derived from Le Fèvre de St.-Rémi: Charles VII had been reduced in 1429 to such a deplorable state that he had not only devalued the currency, but had been forced to "have recourse to a stranger expedient, a miracle. A gentleman of the frontiers of Lorraine, named Baudricourt, believed that he had found in a young servant of a cabaret of Vaucouleurs a person fit to play this role of warrior and mystic." Charles's councillors and the clerics of Poitiers who examined Joan found her inspired, "whether they were mistaken, or whether they themselves were clever enough to enter into this pretence: the masses believed it, and that was enough." She inspired the soldiers at Orleans "with the courage and enthusiasm of men who believe they see the Divinity fighting for them." After her capture, Bedford decided to punish her; "she had feigned a miracle, Bedford feigned to believe her a sorceress." The University of Paris in charging her with heresy and magic "committed a detestable act of cowardice." Thus was condemned to die by fire "the woman who, having saved her king, would have had altars erected to her in ancient times when men elevated them to their liberators. Charles VII cleared her reputation afterward, sufficiently honored by her punishment itself. . . . Cruelty is not enough to drive men to such executions, what is also needed is this fanaticism composed of superstition and ignorance which has been the malady of almost every age." In a later work, Voltaire lamented the fact that there had not been a philosopher on the faculty of theology of the University of Paris at the time of Joan's trial; no philosopher would have allowed this girl, who should instead have been honored, to be burned alive.[20]

Such were Voltaire's serious thoughts on the subject of Joan. They were soon obscured by the publicity and scandalized comment that surrounded his mock-heroic poem, La Pucelle (1755).

According to a contemporary, Voltaire was impelled to write La Pucelle by a challenge at a dinner party during which Jean Chapelain's work had been the subject of critical merriment; Voltaire suggested that the theme might better be handled as a farce, and set to work to compose it for the sole amusement of his circle of intimates.

The poem was designed as a burlesque at the expense of Voltaire's enemies-to-the-death, superstition and bigotry. Rhymed in a lively iambic pentameter, La Pucelle has as its main theme the mystical importance allegedly attached to Joan's virginity. The daughter of a chambermaid by a priest, Voltaire's Joan is a strong, vigorous, active girl who fetches and carries, waits on table, and distributes slaps to "the indiscreet hand that touches her thigh or bare throat"; she "works and laughs from night to morning, leads horses, tends them, curries them, waters them, and pressing them with her gentle thigh mounts them bareback like a Roman soldier."

France's patron, St. Denis, introduces Joan's virginity as a mystical weapon against the English. This "rare jewel" is challenged on all sides, threatening the success of the French cause, and nearly falls to a series of demons, sorcerers, and assorted males, including even the winged donkey which St. Denis gives her as a steed. Finally Dunois himself courts her, but St. Denis intervenes in the nick of time. The war between the French and English is finally settled by an epic combat, first physical, then verbal, between St. Denis and St. George in heaven. St. Denis wins, and the saints decree that the English shall be conquered by the French. Mounting her long-eared Pegasus, Joan rides off to defeat the English at Orleans, while St. George gnashes his teeth and St. Denis applauds. Joan's story occupies less than half the poem; the rest is concerned with the adventures of Charles VII, Agnes Sorel, Dunois, Tremoille, and a number of fictional characters, as well as with lengthy satirical digressions.[21]

The leaders of the French Revolution shared Voltaire's views on politics and religion, but not his antipathy to nationalism. As patriots, they saluted Joan as a national heroine, a role confirmed by the nationalist spirit of nineteenth-century Europe. Voltaire's death date (May 30) by chance coinciding with Joan's, on Voltaire's centennial in 1878 a French republican newspaper published on its front page large portraits of Joan and Voltaire side by side, entitled, "Patriotism" and "Tolerance." The caption ascribed Joan's death not to the English but to the "Catholic clergy who burned her alive at Rouen, May 30, 1431."[22]

The French Revolution's view was echoed abroad, first of all in 1793 in a long, florid poem by the nineteen-year-old Oxford undergraduate Robert Southey. Forty years later, as a middle-aged poet laureate, Southey was embarrassed at having written "in a republican spirit," as a youth "ignorant enough of history and of human nature to believe that a happier order of things had commenced with the independence of the United States, and would be accelerated by the French Revolution." Young Southey may have been present at the very moment of a turnaround in English public opinion about Joan. He had seen a pantomime in Covent Garden Theater in which Joan "was carried off by devils, and precipitated alive into hell. . . . The feelings of the audience revolted at such a catastrophe; and after a few nights, an angel was introduced to rescue her." He had also "had the patience to pursue" Chapelain's poem, but, he boasted, "had never been guilty of looking into Voltaire's." But though he cited many sources—Monstrelet, Hall, Holinshed, the *Journal d'un Bourgeois de Paris,* Stowe—his poem had no more historical merit than Chapelain's or Voltaire's. Like them he introduced Agnes Sorel as a principal character and, adding a touch of his own, gave Joan a shepherd sweetheart who was killed in battle. The poem ended with Joan's crowning the king at Reims with her own hands, to the odd accompaniment of a republican speech adjuring him not to oppress his people.[23]

German poet Friedrich Schiller likewise portrayed Joan as a heroine of national liberation. His verse drama *Die Jungfrau von Orleans* (1801) turns Joan into a sort of Valkyrie, a "lion-hearted maid" who as a shepherdess fought a wolf with her bare hands to rescue a lamb. Borrowing liberally from Chapelain and Shakespeare, Schiller provided enough plot complications for several plays. Charles VII's mother, Isabelle, is the villain, Agnes Sorel is Joan's friend and supporter, Dunois is in love with Joan, Joan is in love with Lionel, duke of Clarence. After the coronation at Reims Joan's father declares that she is the instrument of the devil and curses her; she takes refuge with her childhood sweetheart in a charcoal burner's hut in the forest of Ardennes, where the wicked Queen Isabelle captures her. Bound in triple chains, Joan listens while a soldier in a watch tower reports that the French are fleeing, Dunois is wounded, English troops surround the king. She begs God to "change these fetters into spiders' webs," bursts them asunder, rallies the troops, drives out the English, and rescues the king. Mortally wounded, she seizes her banner as heaven's portals open before her. "Brief is the sorrow, endless the joy," she cries, and falls dead.[24]

Schiller's romantic farrago (which Tchaikovsky turned into an opera in 1881) marked the climax of Joan as legend. Up to this moment the only truly historical treatment was Edmond Richer's work of 1621, unpublished but known to scholars, and forming the basis of a brief biographical sketch (1753) by Abbé Nicolas Lenglet-Dufresnoy. Another serious scholar, Clement l'Averdy, published in 1790 *Extraits des manuscrits des procès* (Extracts from the Manuscripts of the Trials), supplementing the work of Edmond Richer.

In 1841 the historical Joan suddenly emerged in a popular form when Jules Michelet, head of the historical section of the French National Archives, published his monumental *History of France.* The three chapters covering Joan's story stirred such widespread interest that they were reprinted as a separate volume. Based on the documents, Michelet's work was a true historical treatment, though its tone reflected the patriotic legend.[25]

The growth of interest in Joan as a historical figure, part of the nineteenth-century flowering of historical scholarship, was climaxed by a decisive event. Jules Quicherat, a professor (later director) at the École des Chartes in Paris, published his *Procès de condamnation et de réhabilitation de Jeanne d'Arc, dite la Pucelle* (1841–1849), in five volumes, containing not only the complete texts of the trial and the Rehabilitation, but virtually every document of interest pertaining to Joan—excerpts from chronicles, literary works, letters, public documents, extracts from accounts—one of the great early efforts to assemble historical resource material on a single subject.

Quicherat's work created both a scholarly and a popular revolution in respect to the historical Joan of Arc: the realization that the half-legendary heroine of a distant past existed as a genuine historic figure, about whom much real information was available, and one whose life and personality were far more mysterious and challenging than the caricatures of Shakespeare, Voltaire, and Schiller.

In one way, the moment of Joan's emergence was awkward. French and European politics were polarized between liberal republican nationalism and conservative Catholic monarchism. Both parties could lay claim to Joan, and did. Michelet, republican and anticlerical, wrote his volume about Joan as a hymn to patriotism at the moment of an Anglo-French diplomatic crisis in the Mideast. Alexandre Dumas père added a fictionalized biography, *Jehanne la Pucelle* (1842), the next year.[26] The 1860s saw several biographies by French historians, notably those of Henri-Alexandre Wallon[27] and Marius Sepet,[28] and chapters about Joan in a biography of Charles VII by A. Vallet de Viriville,[29] all in the same vein as Michelet. The Franco-Prussian war inspired a new spate of books about Joan, a native of the "marches" (frontiers) of Lorraine (though Joan's part of the province remained inside France).

A century after Southey, another student poet, Charles Péguy, of the École Normale in Paris, read Quicherat and composed a verse play. A native of Orleans, Péguy was acquainted with the annual local celebration of the relief of Orleans. By the time he fell leading his platoon in the battle of the Marne in 1914, Péguy had won fame as an avant-garde poet and Catholic socialist; but as a poor student in 1897 he had to get his *Jeanne d'Arc* printed at his own expense. Péguy's Joan reflects its author's meditative, deeply religious concern with human suffering, hungry children, and other victims of war. She states her purpose: "to kill war."

As a mature poet Péguy returned several times to Joan of Arc. A second play, *Le Mystère de la charité de Jeanne d'Arc* (1909) (Mystery Play of the Charity of Joan of Arc), was an expanded version of the Domremy part of the earlier play. In *Tapisseries de Sainte Geneviève et de Jeanne d'Arc* (1913) (Tapestries of St. Geneviève and Joan of Arc) Péguy drew a parallel between the two shepherdesses, Geneviève from Nanterre and Joan from Domremy. Joan reappeared with St. Geneviève in the concluding verses of his long religious poem *Ève* (1913):

> *And one died thus in a solemn death*
> *In her ninetieth or ninety-second year*
> *And the hard villagers and the hard peasants*
> *Watching her grow old believed her eternal.*
>
> *And the other died thus in a solemn death.*
> *She had not outlived her humble nineteen years*
> *By more than four or five months, and her carnal ashes*
> *Were dispersed in the winds.*[30]

Quicherat's influence also reached America.

Fifteen-year-old Mark Twain was serving his apprenticeship as a printer when one day a page from a book about Joan of Arc—whose it was, he did not say—blew across his homeward path. He read about Joan's persecution in prison by her English captors and was enthralled. Querying his mother, he was surprised to discover that Joan was a real person. Subsequently he read everything he could find about her and about medieval history, and even taught himself a little Latin and French. He later claimed that the stray leaf from the book had opened the world of literature to him.[31]

Twain did not actually embark on the writing of his fictional biography, *Personal Recollections of Joan of Arc,* using translations of Quicherat, until almost forty years later (the book was published in 1896).

When he did, it was as an escape from potboilers. The book was "private and not for print, it's written for love and not for lucre." He was afraid to append his name to it for fear people would think it was meant to be funny. His Joan was a liberator, but much more important, a symbol of virginity and purity, modeled after his own daughter Susy (who died tragically the year the book was published). He read the manuscript aloud every night to the family. "Many of Joan's words and sayings are historically correct," Susy wrote a friend, "and Papa cries when he reads them." As he read the closing chapters to the family, they were all in tears.[32] Bernard Shaw described Mark Twain's heroine as "an unimpeachable American school teacher in armour," who, however, "being the work of a man of genius, remains a credible human goodygoody in spite of her creator's infatuation."[33]

The same year (1896), another American, Francis Cabot Lowell, great-grandson of the Boston merchant of the same name who revolutionized textile manufacture in the United States, published a different kind of biography of Joan. Lowell was a judge of the U.S. district court for Massachusetts whose legal training gave his work an academic value that Mark Twain's lacked, while robbing it of emotional appeal.[34]

Another writer of world stature to explore Quicherat was Anatole France, who in 1908 published a full-scale formal biography. The ironic pen of the author of *The Revolt of the Angels* found congenial targets in medieval mysticism and the Church, especially in digressions about its saints, all of whom emerge sounding like St. Maël of *Penguin Island.* But the main thrust of his *Vie de Jeanne d'Arc* is its reduction of Joan's importance by depicting her, à la Voltaire, as an innocent tool in the hands of conspirators. This time the conspirators are not the French captains or the political powers, but the Church. On the military plane, Anatole France credits the victories to Dunois and relegates Joan to the role of good luck charm. The idea of offering herself as a military leader was put into her head by priests who heard of her "hallucinations" and decided to make use of them. Her words to the king at Chinon were not her own (she was too simple) but those of the priests. These anonymous priests also rewrote a prophecy attributed to Merlin to make it apply to Joan, and circulated books containing the forgery in the years before Joan's appearance at Vaucouleurs and Chinon. Joan's generalship was limited to driving prostitutes out of camp, curbing the soldiers' blasphemy, seeing that they went to confession, and issuing vain ultimatums to the English.[35]

The following year the Scottish scholar-poet Andrew Lang published a reply to Anatole France. Lang's *Maid of France,* equally grounded in Quicherat's documentation, effectively refuted the Church conspiracy thesis and, though sentimentalized and marred by an outrage at Charles VII, Cauchon, and the University of Paris so excessive that it rendered his final chapters almost incoherent, added a work of stature to the literature.[36]

The year Lang's book was published (1909) witnessed Joan's beatification. Her canonization in 1920 was fittingly celebrated by Shaw's great *Saint Joan,* whose impressive and touching picture of a frank, strong, brave, common-sensical woman has been realized by a number of gifted actresses. The persuasive character of Shaw's portrait makes Joan's death perhaps even more moving than does Péguy's poetry.

If Shaw's interpretation remains one of the best, one of the oddest appeared the following year, 1921, also in England. Anthropologist Margaret Murray, writing amid the new scholarly interest in folklore and myth that bred *The Golden Bough* and *From Ritual to Romance,* declared in her *Witch Cult in Western Europe* that Joan really was a witch, a priestess in an old "Dianic" religion that had survived underground after the triumph of Christianity. Dr. Murray believed that the severity of Joan's punishment was the result of the near success of the Peasant Revolt of 1381 in England, which she believed had been staged by the same cult. Half a century later, when Joan united France against the English, the rulers of Church and State determined that the cult must be stamped out. Joan's "saints" and "angels" were real human beings, who hid in the cell next door when she was in prison and talked to her through a hole in the wall. The wearing of male clothing was a sign of membership in the witch cult, as was the refusal to take an oath or to give direct answers. Joan's death by burning and the throwing of her ashes into running water were rites of the same religion, "after the sacrifice of the Incarnate God," whom Joan represented.[37]

A bizarre version of the political conspiracy theory of Pius II, Voltaire, and Anatole France emerged in France in the 1950s, 1960s, and 1970s, with nearly a dozen books advancing essentially the same "bastardy theory."[38] The idea, expressed in embryonic form in 1810 by a writer named Pierre Caze, flowered fully in Maurice David-Darnac's *Histoire véridique et merveilleuse de la Pucelle d'Orléans* (1965) (translated and published in London as *The True Story of the Maid of Orléans*). The theory attempted to explain some of the puzzles and paradoxes of Joan's career: how she happened to offer her services to the king, why they were accepted, what the "secret" was that she told him at Chinon, and how a peasant girl could manage the prodigies she achieved, and also to account for the appearance and brief acceptance of an impostor five years after Joan's death.

According to the hypothesis of David-Darnac and his successors, Joan was an illegitimate daughter of Queen Isabelle of France and Louis of Orleans, and therefore Charles VII's half-sister (one version had it that Charles himself was Louis's son, and he and Joan were full siblings). Born shortly after the assassination of Louis of Orleans in 1407 (five years earlier than the usual date given for Joan's birth), she was smuggled out of Paris as an infant to save her from her father's enemies, in the custody of a lady-in-waiting named Jeanne d'Arc, and raised by the lady's brother-in-law Jacques d'Arc of Domremy—not a peasant but a country gentleman. Summoned by the dauphin's party in 1429, she divulged to the king the secret of their relationship. (Another version of the theory made Joan the tool of the dauphin's mother-in-law, Yolande of Aragon.) Joan was never executed; at Rouen another woman was burned in her place, while she was smuggled out, to reappear five years later.

The bastardy theory, hardly credible enough to be worthy of a novel by Dumas (who in writing about Joan limited himself to sober biography), creates far more problems than it solves, and is firmly contradicted by convincing testimony at the trial and the Rehabilitation, and by other documents.[38]

Joan has recently joined a number of other historical figures in suffering the indignities of "psychohistory." A psychological approach to her voices has potential validity, but terming them hallucinations, attributing them to "wish fulfillment," or stating that they were "conjured up out of her own mind . . . a fantasy realm," as does one recent biographer, leaves the essential mystery untouched.[39] Invoking twentieth-century agnostic, middle-class, male-chauvinist Freud has led to more extravagant interpretations, with Joan's historic role attributed to problems of sexual identity, father fixation, latent homosexual tendencies, penis envy, all by way of explaining her playing what the male writers consider a "man's role."[40]

The most important scholarly authority to emerge in the past two decades is Régine Pernoud, author of several books based on sound scholarship and command of the materials. But Mlle. Pernoud has adopted as the main thrust of her studies the demonstration that Joan's trial at Rouen was a miscarriage of justice, a point amply made by the Rehabilitation proceedings and echoed by nearly every serious writer in the half-millennium since. In Mlle. Pernoud's eyes Joan's tragedy was that she was falsely condemned for "an infamous crime," that of heresy, a sentence which identified her with "agitators" who spread "disquieting doctrines," such as the proto-Protestant Lollards and Hussites (whom it was apparently all right to burn).[41]

Thus five and a half centuries after her death, Joan of Arc still inspires an unending stream of interpretation, explanation, conjecture, and absurdity. Part of the reason lies in the controversial character of her story, especially in respect to religion and the Church. Much, however, is owing to the story's baffling uniqueness.

A Spanish *Historia de la Poncella d'Orleans* published in 1562 furnished a happy ending. Instead of dying at the stake in Rouen, Joan won a series of further victories and settled in Paris laden with honors. Her father was made a count, her brother an archbishop, and she herself was besieged with marriage proposals from all the princes of Europe, while she passed her time in her palace reading the stories of ancient heroes and discussing them with the king's chronicler. To write her history, the author concluded, one should be as eloquent as Joan was valorous; in fact, "God alone, who created such a famous and marvelous woman, could write her chronicle."[42]

Like the author of the *Historia,* every biographer and historian who has written about Joan has in one way or another expressed dissatisfaction with her real story, from the advocates of the "bastardy theory," pretending that she was really a princess and was never burned, to writers like Anatole France, who wished that she had crowned the victory of Patay with the capture of Paris, and Andrew Lang, who found it intolerable that Charles VII negotiated with Philip of Burgundy instead of betting his kingdom on Joan. Almost more to be regretted than her burning, in some eyes, was her failure in her lifetime to complete her announced mission to drive the English out of France. (Had she not been captured, she probably would have lived to participate in its completion, as did Charles, Dunois, Xaintrailles, Alençon, and others.)

Both French and English academic (male) historians have been some-what embarrassed by her role in the French recovery and inclined to belittle it, mainly by asserting that the real turning point in the war was the peace between the French and the Burgundians signed at Arras in 1435. But the way to the treaty of Arras was paved by the relief of Orleans, the Loire campaign, and the battle of Patay. These victories made possible the march to Reims and the liberation of the towns around Paris, which in turn brought about the shift of Anglo-Burgundian power in favor of the Burgundians and the consequent estrangement of the two allies. That Joan's mission was not completed in her lifetime detracts nothing from its success or from her contribution.

Few historical characters, and no women, are more famous than Joan of Arc. Her name and story are known throughout the world. In the Middle Ages there were women who led armies, female mystics who prophesied and gave advice, and men and women alike whose beliefs led them to the stake. Joan's story has a unique quality, a fairy tale with a tragic ending, invested with her own personality—her common sense, her trenchant speech, her indomitable courage, before the judges at Rouen as in the moat at Orleans.

Her appeal bridges the political spectrum from Charles de Gaulle, who in her honor adopted the cross of Lorraine as the emblem of Free France, to the Communist poet Louis Aragon, who in a 1940 poem used her as a symbol of hope in a dark hour:

> *Il est un temps pour la souffrance*
> *Quand Jeanne vint à Vaucouleurs*
> *Ah coupez en morceaux la France*
> *Le jour avait cette paleur. . . .*[43]
> [*It is a time for suffering*
> *When Joan came to Vaucouleurs*
> *Ah cut France to pieces*
> *Daybreak had this paleness.*]

To a heroine's courage, resolution, and purity—knightly virtues much admired in her century—modern writers and especially Shaw have added an appreciation of her superior intelligence.

Beyond these qualities of mind and character, which mark Joan as an extraordinary person, deserving of her fame, there is the political cause she stands for, the elemental force of nationalism, perhaps decadent today in the developed world, but intensely alive in the developing countries. By no accident Joan was a girlhood heroine of Indira Gandhi, as Indira's father Jawaharlal Nehru reminded her in the letters that became *Glimpses of World History*.[44]

Finally, there is the cruelty of her martyrdom, made the more painful by her heroic obstinacy. The martyr's death seems necessary to sanctify even the noblest cause. Without it, patriotism is worthy of admiration, but with it, in Yeats's words, referring to martyrs in another struggle for national liberation, "A terrible beauty is born."

Notes

1. JOAN OF ARC: THE STORY AND ITS SOURCES

1. The trial record was first published in unabridged form by Jules Quicherat in the first volume of his five-volume work, *Procès de condamnation et de réhabilitation de Jeanne d'Arc, dite la Pucelle,* Paris, 1841–1849. Quicherat prints what is believed to be a copy of Manchon's French minutes in the version of the fragmentary d'Urfé manuscript, from the Bibliothèque Nationale, as footnotes to the Latin text. (Quicherat and other scholars believed the Orleans manuscript to be an abridged French translation of the Latin record.) A more recent edition, prepared by Pierre Tisset and Yvonne Lanhers, *Procès de condamnation de Jeanne d'Arc,* 3 vols, Paris, 1960, 1970, includes the Latin text, the French version of the Orleans manuscript, and a modern French translation of the Latin. In 1952 Paul Doncoeur advanced the theory that the Orleans manuscript was a copy of the French minutes, with lacunae, but more complete than the d'Urfé, publishing it as *La Minute française des interrogatoires de Jeanne la Pucelle,* Melun, 1952.

The trial record was translated into English in abridged form by T. Douglas Murray, *Jeanne d'Arc, Maid of Orléans,* London, 1902. Mark Twain wrote an introduction for Murray's edition, but when Murray, a wealthy amateur, took the liberty of making extensive corrections in red ink, Twain protested the Englishman's "schoolgirl attempts at 'editing' " by withdrawing his introduction. Another English translation of the trial record was made by W. P. Barrett in 1931 (*The Trial of Joan of Arc,* published in New York in 1932), but like Murray's, Barrett's version is hard to find today. The best source of the trial record for a non-French, non-Latin reader is probably the translation by W. S. Scott of the Orleans manuscript (French minutes): *The Trial of Joan of Arc,* London, 1956. References in this book for both the trial and the Rehabilitation, as well as some of the less easily available chronicles, are to Quicherat's original publication, which can be found in most university libraries in the United States and in a paperback reprint.

2. The Rehabilitation record constitutes Volumes II and III in Quicherat's work. It is also published in Paul Doncoeur and Yvonne Lanhers, *L'Enquête ordonnée par Charles VII en 1450 et le codicille de Guillaume Bouillé,* Paris, 1956; *L'Enquête du Cardinal Estouteville en 1452,* Paris, 1958; and *La Rédaction épiscopale du procès de 1455–6,* Paris, 1961. No English translation exists, apart from excerpts published in Régine Pernoud's *Retrial of Joan of Arc,* New York, 1955, a translation by J. M. Cohen of her *Vie et mort de Jeanne d'Arc,* Paris, 1953.

3. Perceval de Cagny, *Chronique,* in Quicherat, IV, pp. 1–37.

4. Guillaume Gruel, *Chronique d'Arthur de Richemont,* ed. by Achille le Vavasseur, Paris, 1890.

5. *Journal du Siège d'Orléans,* in Quicherat, IV, pp. 94–202.

6. Le Hérault Berri, in Quicherat, IV, pp. 40–50.

7. Jean Chartier, *Chronique,* in Quicherat, IV, pp. 51–93.

8. Thomas Basin, *Histoire de Charles VII,* ed. and trans. (from Latin into French) by Charles Samarin, 2 vols., Paris, 1933.

9. *Chronique de la Pucelle,* ed. by A. Vallet de Viriville, Paris, 1859.

10. Enguerrand de Monstrelet, *Chronique,* 6 vols., ed. by L. Douet d'Arcq, Paris, 1857–1862.

11. Jean Le Fèvre de St.-Rémi, *Chronique,* ed. by François Morand, Paris, 1881.

12. Jean Wavrin du Forestal, *Anciennes chroniques d'Engleterre,* ed. by M. Dupont, Paris, 1858.

13. *Journal d'un Bourgeois de Paris, 1408–1449,* ed. by A. Tuetey, Paris, 1881, reprinted in Geneva, 1975. A recent English translation is *A Parisian Journal, 1408–1449,* trans. by Janet Shirley, Oxford, 1968.

14. Eberhard de Windecken, in Quicherat, IV, pp. 485–501.

15. Extracts from accounts are published in Quicherat, V, 257–363.

16. Most of the letters pertinent to Joan's story are published in Quicherat, V, pp. 95–169. Joan's letters have also been translated into English by Clare Quintal, in *Letters of Joan of Arc,* Pittsburgh, 1969.

17. Antonio Morosini, *Chronique: Extraits relatifs à l'histoire de France,* ed. and trans. (from Italian into French) by Leon Durez, 4 vols., Paris, 1898–1902.

18. Some of the documents are published in Quicherat, V, pp. 141–205. Excerpts from the register of the Parlement of Paris are given in Quicherat, IV, pp. 451–459, also in the *Journal de Clement de Fauquembergue,* 3 vols., ed. by Alexandre Tuetey, Paris, 1909. Excerpts from the register of La Rochelle in Jules Quicherat's "Relation inédite sur Jeanne d'Arc," in *Revue historique,* Vol. 4, 1877, pp. 327–344.

2. DOMREMY

1. Information from the Maison Natale de Jeanne d'Arc in Domremy.

2. On the agrarian economy of early fifteenth-century France: Harry Miskimin, *The Economy of Early Renaissance Europe, 1300–1460,* Englewood Cliffs, N.J., 1969, pp. 14–57; Marcellin Defourneaux, *La Vie quotidienne au temps de Jeanne d'Arc,* Paris, 1952, "La vie des campagnes," pp. 22–32; Georges Duby, *Rural Economy and Country Life in the Medieval West,* trans. by Cynthia Postan, Columbia, S.C., 1968, pp. 293–357; N. J. G. Pounds, *An Economic History of Medieval Europe,* London, 1974, pp. 217–222, 440–448; Georges Duby, "Medieval Agriculture, 900–1500," in the *Fontana Economic History of Europe,* Vol. I, *The Middle Ages,* ed. by Carlo M. Cippola, New York, 1976; Roger Grand, *L'Agriculture au Moyen Age,* Paris, 1950, pp. 673–696; M. M. Postan, "The Fifteenth Century," in *Economic History Review,* Vol. 9, 1939, pp. 160–167.

3. Simeon Luce, *Jeanne d'Arc à Domremy,* Paris, 1886.

4. Quicherat, I, p. 46.

5. Ibid., p. 191.

6. Ibid., p. 46. On the subject of Joan's family: F. de Bouteiller, "De quelques faits relatifs à Jeanne d'Arc et à sa famille," *Revue des questions historiques,* Vol. 24, 1878, pp. 241–249.

7. Quicherat, V, p. 116; Marius Sepet, "La lettre de Perceval de Boulainvilliers," in *Bibliothèque de l'École des Chartes,* Vol. 77, 1916, pp. 439–447.

8. Luce, *Jeanne d'Arc à Domremy.*

9. On the Hundred Years War: Edouard Perroy, *The Hundred Years War,* trans. by W. B. Wells, London, 1962; K. A. Fowler (ed.), *The Hundred Years War,* New York, 1971; C. T. Allmand (ed.), *War, Literature and Politics in the Late Middle Ages,* Liverpool, 1976; C. T. Allmand (ed.), *Society at War,* New York, 1973; C. W. Oman, *The Art of War in the Middle Ages* (revised edition), Ithaca, N.Y., 1953, pp. 124–144; A. H. Burne, *The Crécy War,* London, 1955, *The Agincourt War,* London, 1956;

Philippe Contamine, *Guerre, État, et Société à la fin du Moyen Age,* Paris, 1972; Defourneaux, *La Vie quotidienne,* "Le Cadre de la vie," pp. 9–21, "La Guerre et l'aventure," pp. 184–230.

10. Gaston Dodu, "La Folie de Charles VI," in *Revue historique,* Vol. 150, 1924, pp. 161–188.

11. On the dukes of Burgundy: Joseph Calmette, *The Golden Age of Burgundy,* trans. by Doris Weightman, New York, 1963; Richard Vaughan, *John the Fearless,* London, 1966, *Philip the Good,* London, 1970, *Valois Burgundy,* London, 1975; William R. Tyler, *Dijon and the Valois Dukes of Burgundy,* Norman, Okla., 1971.

12. *Geste des ducs de Bourgogne,* cited in Calmette, *Golden Age,* p. 197.

13. M. G. A. Vale, *Charles VII,* Berkeley, 1974, p. 31.

14. Henri Pirenne, *Histoire de Belgique,* Brussels, 1972, Vol. I, pp. 374–375.

15. Allmand (ed.), *Society at War,* pp. 34–35.

16. Miskimin, *Economy of Early Renaissance Europe,* pp. 51–54; P. S. Lewis (ed.), *The Recovery of France in the Fifteenth Century,* New York, 1971, pp. 25–51; C. T. Allmand, "The War and the Non-Combatant," in Fowler (ed.), *The Hundred Years War;* Defourneaux, *La Vie quotidienne,* "La guerre et l'aventure," pp. 184–230, "L'occupation étrangère et la résistance nationale," pp. 273–296.

17. Luce, *Jeanne d'Arc à Domremy.*

18. Quicherat, I, p. 46, 67; II, pp. 388–389, 395, 398, 402, 408, 410, 412, 415, 419–420, 422, 426, 429, 433.

19. Testimony of Gobert Thibaut, Quicherat, III, p. 74.

20. Quicherat, I, pp. 46–47.

21. Ibid., pp. 131–132.

22. Ibid., p. 51.

23. Ibid., II, pp. 396, 398, 407, 410, 415, 418, 422, 433.

24. Ibid., pp. 407, 410, 415, 418, 424, 430, 433.

25. Testimony of Hauviette, Quicherat, II, p. 418; I, p. 66.

26. Testimony of Gerardin of Épinal, Quicherat, II, p. 422; p. 390, footnote, Edmond Richer, who saw the tree in 1628, said that it was then at least 300 years old.

27. Testimony of Beatrix Estellin, Quicherat, II, p. 396.

28. Quicherat, I, p. 67; II, p. 404.

29. Ibid., II, pp. 390–391, 394, 398–399, 400–401, 404, 407, 411, 413–414, 416, 418, 420–421, 422–423, 425, 427–428, 430, 434.

30. Testimony of Perrin Drappier, Quicherat, II, p. 413.

31. Testimony of Beatrix Estellin, Quicherat, II, pp. 396–397; for Rogation Days celebration: George C. Homans, *English Villagers of the Thirteenth Century,* New York, 1975, p. 368.

32. Quicherat, I, pp. 65–66.
33. Ibid., p. 66.

3. VOICES

1. Quicherat, I, p. 52.
2. Ibid., pp. 169–170.
3. Ibid., p. 73.
4. Ibid., pp. 170–171.
5. Ibid., p. 130.
6. Ibid., pp. 85, 86.
7. Ibid., p. 128.
8. Quicherat omits the word *"non"* in his text, apparently by accident (Quicherat, I, p. 52). It is present in all three versions of the manuscript of the trial record and is so cited by Tisset and Lanhers, I, 47. Later in the trial the promoter (prosecutor) Jean Estivet gives a somewhat different version, stating that Joan "was fasting then, but she did not fast the preceding day" (Quicherat, I, p. 216).
9. Quicherat, I, p. 186.
10. Ibid., p. 89.
11. Sidney Spencer, author of *Mysticism in World Religion,* in the article "Mysticism," *Encyclopaedia Britannica,* 15th edition.
12. *Patrologia Latina,* Vol. 197, Turnhout (Belgium), n.d., Col. 384. For information on Hildegarde of Bingen: Frances and Joseph Gies, "An Abbess: Hildegarde of Bingen," in *Women in the Middle Ages,* New York, 1978; Lina Eckenstein, *Women under Monasticism,* New York, 1963 (reprint of 1896 edition), pp. 270–277; Charles Singer, "The Scientific Views and Visions of Saint Hildegarde," in *Studies in the History and Method of Science,* Oxford, 1917.
13. Eckenstein, *Women under Monasticism,* pp. 277–285.
14. Sister Mary Jeremy, *Scholars and Mystics,* Chicago, 1962, pp. 19–22; *Revelations of Mechthild of Magdeburg, 1210–1297,* trans. by Lucy Menzies, London, 1953.
15. Walter H. Capps and Wendy M. Wright (eds.), *Silent Fire,* New York, 1978, pp. 142–148.
16. Eckenstein, *Women under Monasticism,* p. 282.
17. Quicherat, III, p. 219.
18. Michelet, *Joan of Arc,* p. 9.
19. John J. Sciarra, *Gynecology and Obstetrics,* New York, 1976, Vol. II, pp. 32–37.
20. Quicherat, III, p. 100.

21. Frederick F. Cartwright and Michael D. Biddiss, *Disease and History,* New York, 1972, pp. 198-200.
22. Lawrence Kolb, *Modern Clinical Psychiatry,* 8th edition, 1973, Philadelphia, pp. 100-102.
23. Testimony of Simonin Musnier, Quicherat, II, p. 424.
24. Testimony of Isabelle, wife of Gerardin of Épinal, Quicherat, II, p. 427.
25. Quicherat, II, pp. 418-419.
26. Ibid., p. 390.
27. Testimony of Étienne de Sionne, Quicherat, II, p. 402; Jean Colin, Quicherat, II, 434.
28. Testimony of Jean Colin, Quicherat, II, p. 433; Michel Lebuin, Quicherat, II, p. 439.
29. Quicherat, II, p. 389.
30. Testimony of Jean Waterin, Quicherat, II, p. 420; Jean Colin, Quicherat, II, p. 433.
31. Testimony of Simonin Musnier, Quicherat, II, p. 424.
32. Quicherat, II, p. 430.
33. Testimony of Perrin Drappier, Quicherat, II, p. 431.
34. Quicherat, I, p. 68.
35. Ibid., p. 52.
36. Ibid., pp. 131-132.
37. Ibid., p. 53.
38. Ibid., pp. 128-129.
39. Ibid., II, p. 423.
40. Testimony of Durand Laxart, Quicherat, II, pp. 443-444.
41. Testimony of Jean Barbin, Quicherat, II, pp. 83-84; Noel Valois, "Jeanne d'Arc et la prophétie de Marie Robine," in *Mélanges Paul Fabre,* Paris, 1902, pp. 453-467.
42. Quicherat, I, p. 53.
43. Ibid., p. 53. On Vaucouleurs: Henri Bataille, *Jeanne d'Arc, Baudricourt, Vaucouleurs,* Nancy, 1973.
44. Quicherat, II, p. 456.
45. Testimony of Durand Laxart, Quicherat, II, p. 444.
46. Quicherat, I, p. 51; testimony of Jean Moreau, Quicherat, II, p. 392; Bertrand Lacloppe, Quicherat, II, p. 411; Perrin Drappier, Quicherat, II, p. 414; Gerard Guillemette, Quicherat, II, p. 416.
47. Scott, *Trial of Joan of Arc,* pp. 66-67 (the Latin record gives this passage incorrectly); testimony of Jacques de St. Amance, Quicherat, II, p. 409; Gerardin of Épinal, Quicherat, II, p. 423.
48. Testimony of Isabelle, wife of Gerardin of Épinal, Quicherat, II, p. 428.
49. Quicherat, I, pp. 127-128.

50. Testimony of Beatrix Estellin, Quicherat, II, p. 396.
51. Quicherat, II, p. 440.
52. Ibid., pp. 431, 416.
53. Testimony of Jean de Metz, Quicherat, II, pp. 436–437.
54. Quicherat, II, pp. 460–461.
55. Testimony of Catherine le Royer, Quicherat, II, pp. 446–447.
56. Quicherat, II, pp. 444–445.
57. Ibid., II, pp. 436–437.
58. Ibid., p. 457.
59. Ibid., I, p. 54.
60. Testimony of Marguerite La Touroulde, Joan's hostess later in Bourges, Quicherat, II, p. 87.
61. Testimony of Jean Moreau, Quicherat, II, p. 391; Louis de Montigny, Quicherat, II, p. 406.
62. Quicherat, II, p. 437.
63. Ibid., I, p. 55.
64. Ibid., II, pp. 448–449.
65. Testimony of Jean de Metz, Quicherat, II, p. 437.
66. Quicherat, I, p. 54.
67. Testimony of Jean de Metz, Quicherat, II, p. 438.
68. Quicherat, II, p. 87.
69. Ibid., pp. 438, 457.
70. Testimony of Marguerite La Touroulde, Quicherat, II, pp. 86–87.
71. Quicherat, II, pp. 437–438.

4. CHINON

1. Bertrand de Girard, Seigneur du Haillan, *De l'Estat et succez des affaires de France,* Paris, 1580, p. 137.
2. Vallet de Viriville, *Histoire de Charles VII,* Vol. I, p. 256.
3. Carl Stephenson, *Medieval History,* New York, 1935, p. 624.
4. Albert Guerard, *France, a Modern History,* Ann Arbor, Mich., 1959, pp. 108–109.
5. J. F. C. Fuller, *A Military History of the Western World,* London, 1954–1956, Vol. I, p. 477.
6. Yvonne Lanhers, "Charles VII," in *Encyclopaedia Britannica,* 15th edition.
7. Shaw, *Saint Joan,* p. 25.
8. Georges Chastellain, *Oeuvres,* 8 vols., ed. by Kervyn de Lettenhove, Brussels, 1863–1868, Vol. II, p. 178.
9. Pierre de Fènin, *Mémoires,* Paris, 1837, p. 195.

10. Jean Rogier, in Quicherat, IV, p. 298.
11. Chastellain, *Oeuvres*, II, p. 178.
12. Fénin, *Mémoires*, p. 195.
13. Chastellain, *Oeuvres*, II, ii, pp. 181–185.
14. Pierre de Bourdeille, Seigneur de Brantome, cited in Gaston Dodu, "Le roi de Bourges, ou dix-neuf ans de la vie de Charles VII," in *Revue historique*, Vol. 159, 1928, p. 71.
15. The basic source of the story about Isabelle's liaison with Louis of Orleans was a Burgundian chronicler known as the Religieux of St. Denis, who is also responsible for blackening Isabelle's reputation in other ways—notably a story repeated by other chroniclers, mostly Burgundian, that her licentious behavior at the castle of Vincennes in 1417 caused the dauphin Charles to break with her (though by this time Isabelle was so fat that she was hardly able to walk, and moved about in a wheelchair). The idea that Charles was disowned by his father as a bastard at the time of the treaty of Troyes comes from Burgundian chronicler Georges Chastellain, but has no basis in fact. See Pierre Champion and Paul de Thoisy, *Bourgogne-France-Angleterre au Traité de Troyes*, Paris, 1943; Colonel de Liocourt, *La Mission de Jeanne d'Arc*, Paris, 1874, Vol. I; Marcel Thibault, *Isabelle de Bavière, reine de France*, Paris, 1970; Francis Darwin, *Louis d'Orléans (1372–1407)*, London, 1936.
16. For Charles's life as "king of Bourges," Dodu, "Le roi de Bourges," pp. 38–78.
17. Gilles Le Bouvier, *Chronique*, cited in Dodu, "Le roi de Bourges," p. 69.
18. Fenin, *Mémoires*, p. 195.
19. Chastellain, *Oeuvres*, II, p. 181.
20. Ibid., pp. 184–185.
21. *The Religious of Dumferlane*, cited in Vale, *Charles VII*, p. 54.
22. Basin, *Histoire de Charles VII*, Vol. I, p. 34.
23. Quicherat, IV, p. 280.
24. Matthieu Thomassin, *Registre Delphinal*, Quicherat, IV, pp. 308–309.
25. Testimony of Dunois, Quicherat, II, p. 3; Guillaume de Ricarville, Quicherat, III, p. 21.
26. Quicherat, I, pp. 75–76.
27. Ibid., p. 56.
28. Testimony of Jean Pasquerel, Quicherat, II, p. 102.
29. Quicherat, II, p. 219.
30. Jules Quicherat, "Relation inédite sur Jeanne d'Arc," in *Revue historique*, Vol. IV, 1877, p. 336.
31. Quicherat, V, p. 120.

32. *Chronique des quatre premiers Valois (1327–1393),* ed. by Simeon Luce, Paris, 1862, pp. 46–49.
33. Quicherat, II, p. 115; for Joan's first interview with the king: Claude Desama, "La première entrevue de Jeanne d'Arc et de Charles VII à Chinon (Mars 1429)," in *Analecta Bollandiana,* Vol. 84, fasc. 1–2, 1966, pp. 113–126.
34. Testimony of Simon Charles, Quicherat, II, p. 115.
35. Quicherat, I, pp. 75–76.
36. Ibid., p. 56.
37. Ibid., II, pp. 115–116; III, p. 190.
38. Ibid., IV, pp. 52–53.
39. Ibid., II, pp. 16–17.
40. Ibid., p. 116.
41. Ibid., V, p. 133.
42. Testimony of Dunois, Quicherat, III, pp. 3–4.
43. Quicherat, III, pp. 102–103.
44. Ibid., p. 209.
45. Basin, *Histoire de Charles VII,* Vol. II, p. 133.
46. Quicherat, "Relation inédite," p. 337.
47. Seigneur de Rotselaer, Quicherat, IV, p. 426.
48. Quicherat, IV, p. 280.
49. Quicherat, I, pp. 139–145.
50. Jules Michelet, *Histoire de France,* Paris, 1876, Vol. VI, p. 195, Note 1 (omitted from later editions).
51. Testimony of Alençon, Quicherat, III, p. 91.
52. Testimony of Louis de Coutes, Quicherat, III, pp. 65–66.
53. For a discussion of the examination at Poitiers: Paul Boissonade, "Une étape capitale de la mission de Jeanne d'Arc," in *Revue des questions historiques,* July 1930, pp. 12–67.
54. Testimony of Gobert Thibaut, Quicherat, III, p. 74.
55. Testimony of Seguin Seguin, Quicherat, III, p. 204.
56. Ibid., pp. 204–205.
57. Testimony of Marguerite La Touroulde, Quicherat, III, p. 86.
58. Quicherat, III, p. 20.
59. Ibid., p. 209.
60. Ibid., p. 102.
61. Ibid., p. 210.
62. Ibid., pp. 83–84.
63 Testimony of Jean Barbin, Quicherat, III, p. 82.
64. Quicherat, III, p. 205.
65. Morosini, *Chronique,* pp. 51–53.

66. Quicherat, III, p. 74.
67. Ibid., pp. 391–392.
68. Ibid., pp. 393–410.
69. Dorothy G. Wayman, "The Chancellor and Jeanne d'Arc," in *Franciscan Studies,* Vol. 17, Nos. 2–3, 1957, pp. 273–305.
70. Quicherat, III, p. 116.
71. Quicherat, I, pp. 240–241 (although Joan protested three of the phrases in the letter as entered into the trial record, Quicherat points out that all the copies that exist from other sources are identical with that of the record).
72. Testimony of Alençon, Quicherat, III, p. 93.
73. Boucher de Molandon and Adalbert de Beaucorps, *L'Armée anglaise vaincue par Jeanne d'Arc,* Orleans/Paris, 1892, p. 193.
74. Boucher de Molandon, *L'Armée anglaise,* pp. 178, 193, 175.
75. Quicherat, III, p. 85.
76. Quicherat, V, pp. 257–258.
77. For Joan's standard: "L'Étandard de Jeanne d'Arc," in *Bulletin de la Société Archéologique et Historique de l'Orléanais,* Vol. 15, 1908–1910, pp. 245–265; Joan's own description, Quicherat, I, pp. 76, 78.
78. Quicherat, I, p. 78.
79. A. Vallet de Viriville, "Un episode de la vie de Jeanne d'Arc," in *Bibliothèque de l'École des Chartes,* Vol. 4, pp. 486–491; also Quicherat, V, p. 271.
80. Quicherat, I, p. 76.
81. Ibid., III, p. 101.
82. Ibid., p. 93.
83. Ibid., pp. 104–105.

5. ORLEANS

1. Boucher de Molandon, *L'armée anglaise,* p. 59.
2. Ibid., pp. 51–52.
3. Jacques Debal, "Nouvelles observations sur les ponts anciens d'Orléans," in *Bulletin de la Société Archéologique et Historique de l'Orléanais,* Nouvelle Serie, Vol. 7, No. 48, 1978.
4. *Journal du Siège,* Quicherat, IV, pp. 96–100.
5. Boucher de Molandon, *L'armée anglaise,* p. 76.
6. Ibid., pp. 81–84.
7. Quicherat, IV, pp. 103–104.
8. Ibid., p. 105.
9. *Journal du Siège,* Quicherat, IV, pp. 106–107.
10. Ibid., pp. 120–125.
11. Ibid., p. 130.

12. Ibid., p. 131.
13. Ibid., p. 146; Morosini, *Chronique,* pp. 19–23; *Chronique de la Pucelle,* pp. 269–270.
14. Boucher de Molandon, *L'armée anglaise,* p. 134; *Chronique de la Pucelle,* p. 270.
15. Boucher de Molandon, *L'armée anglaise,* pp. 134–143.
16. *Journal du Siège,* Quicherat, IV, p. 150.
17. Testimony of Jean d'Aulon, Quicherat, III, p. 210; Theobald des Termes, Quicherat, III, p. 119.
18. Quicherat, IV, pp. 150–151.
19. Ibid., III, pp. 5–7.
20. Ibid., p. 105.
21. Ibid., pp. 7, 18.
22. Testimony of Dunois, Quicherat, III, pp. 8–9.
23. *Journal du Siège,* Quicherat, IV, pp. 152–153.
24. Quicherat, III, p. 68.
25. Ibid., p. 7.
26. *Journal du Siège,* Quicherat, IV, pp. 154–155.
27. Contamine, *Guerre, État, et Société,* p. 451, note 4.
28. St. Bernard, *Sermones in Cantica,* in *Patrologia Latina,* Turnhout (Belgium), n.d., Vol. 183, col. 1091.
29. Testimony of Louis de Coutes, Quicherat, III, p. 68.
30. Receipt in archives of Orleans, printed in *Le Siège d'Orléans,* pamphlet published by the Centre Jeanne d'Arc, Orléans.
31. Testimony of Jean d'Aulon, Quicherat, III, p. 211.
32. *Journal du Siège,* Quicherat, IV, pp. 155–156.
33. Ibid., p. 156.
34. Ibid., p. 156.
35. Quicherat, III, p. 211.
36. Fuller, *Military History,* p. 484.
37. M. G. A. Vale, "New Techniques and Old Ideals: The Impact of Artillery and Chivalry at the End of the Hundred Years War," in Allmand (ed.), *War, Literature and Politics,* p. 69.
38. Testimony of Jean d'Aulon, Quicherat, III, p. 212.
39. Ibid., p. 212.
40. Testimony of Louis de Coutes, Quicherat, III, p. 68.
41. Testimony of Jean d'Aulon, Quicherat, III, p. 212.
42. Testimony of Louis de Coutes, Quicherat, III, p. 68.
43. Testimony of Colette, wife of Pierre Milet, Quicherat, III, p. 124.
44. Quicherat, III, p. 213; *Journal du Siège,* Quicherat, IV, p. 157 (St. Pouair was just south of the fort "Paris").

45. *Journal du Siège,* Quicherat, IV, p. 157.
46. Quicherat, III, p. 107.
47. *Journal du Siège,* Quicherat, IV, p. 158.
48. Quicherat, IV, pp. 62–63.
49. Testimony of Pasquerel, Quicherat, III, pp. 107–108.
50. Testimony of Jean d'Aulon, Quicherat, III, pp. 213–214; Simon Beaucroix, Quicherat, III, p. 79; Louis de Coutes, Quicherat, III, pp. 69–70.
51. Testimony of Jean d'Aulon, Quicherat, III, p. 214.
52. Ibid., p. 94.
53. Ibid., p. 214.
54. Ibid., p. 79.
55. Ibid., pp. 214–215.
56. *Chronique de la Pucelle,* p. 291.
57. Quicherat, III, p. 79.
58. *Le Siège d'Orléans,* p. 19.
59. Testimony of Pasquerel, Quicherat, III, pp. 108–109.
60. Testimony of Colette, wife of Pierre Milet, Quicherat, III, pp. 124–125.
61. Quicherat, III, pp. 116–117.
62. Ibid., pp. 215–216.
63. *Journal du Siège,* Quicherat, IV, p. 160.
64. Quicherat, III, pp. 109–110.
65. Testimony of Dunois, Quicherat, III, p. 8; *Journal du Siège,* Quicherat, IV, pp. 160–161.
66. Quicherat, IV, p. 160.
67. Ibid., III, p. 8.
68. Ibid., pp. 70–71.
69. Ibid., pp. 216–217.
70. *Journal du Siège,* Quicherat, IV, p. 161.
71. Ibid., pp. 161–162.
72. Ibid., p. 162.
73. Quicherat, III, p. 110.
74. *Journal du Siège,* Quicherat, IV, p. 162.
75. *Journal d'un Bourgeois de Paris,* p. 234.
76. *Journal du Siège,* Quicherat, IV, p. 163.
77. Quicherat, III, p. 9.
78. Testimony of Dunois, Quicherat, III, p. 9.
79. *Journal du Siège,* Quicherat, IV, p. 164.
80. *Chronique de la Pucelle,* p. 296.
81. Quicherat, III, p. 217.
82. *Journal du Siège,* Quicherat, IV, pp. 164–165.

6. THE LOIRE CAMPAIGN AND THE BATTLE OF PATAY

1. France, *Vie de Jeanne d'Arc, in Oeuvres,* Vol. XV, p. 371.
2. Perroy, *The Hundred Years War,* p. 283.
3. Quicherat, III, p. 13.
4. Ibid., p. 100.
5. Ibid., p. 120.
6. France, *Vie de Jeanne d'Arc, in Oeuvres,* Vol. XV, p. 41.
7. Perroy, *The Hundred Years War,* p. 283.
8. For the role of artillery: Contamine, *Guerre, État, et Société,* pp. 228–230; Vale, "New Techniques and Old Ideals," in Allmand (ed.), *War, Literature and Politics;* A. R. Hall, "Military Technology in the Medieval Period," in Charles Singer, E. J. Holmyard, A. R. Hall, and Trevor Williams (eds.), *History of Technology,* Vol. II, New York, 1956, pp. 79–86.
9. Quicherat, III, p. 100.
10. Ibid., pp. 7–8.
11. Ibid., V, pp. 136–137 (spelling here modernized).
12. Monstrelet, *Chronique,* p. 388.
13. Quicherat, III, p. 94.
14. Ibid., p. 218.
15. Testimony of Marguerite La Touroulde, Quicherat, III, p. 86.
16. Contamine, *Guerre, État, et Société,* pp. 260–261.
17. *Journal du Siège,* Quicherat, IV, pp. 165–166.
18. Eberhard Windecken, Quicherat, IV, pp. 496–497.
19. Testimony of Dunois, Quicherat, III, p. 9.
20. *Journal du Siège,* Quicherat, IV, p. 169.
21. Testimony of Alençon, Quicherat, III, p. 96.
22. Testimony of Jean Barbin, Quicherat, III, p. 84.
23. Quicherat, V, pp. 106–111.
24. *Journal du Siège,* Quicherat, IV, pp. 169–170.
25. Contamine, *Guerre, État, et Société,* p. 226.
26. Testimony of Alençon, Quicherat, III, p. 94.
27. *Journal du Siège,* Quicherat, IV, p. 170.
28. Testimony of Alençon, Quicherat, III, p. 95.
29. Quicherat, I, p. 80.
30. Testimony of Alençon, Quicherat, III, pp. 95–97.
31. *Journal du Siège,* Quicherat, IV, p. 172.
32. Testimony of Alençon, Quicherat, III, p. 97.
33. Le Hérault Berri, Quicherat, IV, p. 45.
34. Quicherat, "Relation inédite," p. 340.

35. Quicherat, III, p. 97.
36. *Journal du Siège,* Quicherat, IV, p. 173.
37. Ibid., p. 174.
38. Cagny, *Chronique,* Quicherat, IV, p. 13.
39. Testimony of Alençon, Quicherat, III, p. 97.
40. Ibid., p. 98.
41. Gruel, *Chronique,* pp. 70–72.
42. Cagny, *Chronique,* Quicherat, IV, pp. 14–15.
43. Testimony of Alençon, Quicherat, III, pp. 98–99.
44. Wavrin, *Chroniques,* p. 286.
45. Ibid., pp. 283–287.
46. Ibid., pp. 287–291.
47. Testimony of Dunois, Quicherat, III, pp. 10–11.
48. Quicherat, III, p. 71.
49. Wavrin, *Chroniques,* pp. 291–293.
50. Quicherat, III, p. 71.
51. Monstrelet, *Chronique,* p. 330.
52. Wavrin, *Chroniques,* p. 295.
53. Quicherat, III, pp. 71–72.
54. Wavrin, *Chroniques,* p. 293.
55. Ibid., pp. 293–295.
56. Ibid., p. 288.
57. Testimony of Alençon, Quicherat, III, p. 99.

7. THE CORONATION JOURNEY

1. *Journal d'un Bourgeois de Paris,* pp. 239–240.
2. Testimony of Dunois, Quicherat, III, pp. 12–13.
3. Ibid., p. 13.
4. Gruel, *Chronique,* p. 74.
5. *Journal du Siège,* Quicherat, IV, p. 179.
6. Quicherat, V, pp. 112–113.
7. Ibid., III, p. 116.
8. Cagny, *Chronique,* Quicherat, IV, pp. 16–17.
9. Quicherat, V, p. 125.
10. Testimony of Pierre Vaillant, Quicherat, III, p. 31.
11. Quicherat, I, pp. 183–184.
12. Cagny, *Chronique,* Quicherat, IV, pp. 17–18.
13. Testimony of Gobert Thibaut, Quicherat, III, p. 76.
14. Cagny, *Chronique,* Quicherat, IV, p. 18.
15. *Chronique de la Pucelle,* pp. 312–313.

16. *Journal du Siège,* Quicherat, IV, p. 180.
17. Cagny, *Chronique,* Quicherat, IV, p. 18.
18. *Journal du Siège,* Quicherat, IV, p. 181; Jean Chartier, *Chronique,* Quicherat, IV, p. 72; *Chronique de la Pucelle,* p. 313.
19. Monstrelet, *Chronique,* p. 336.
20. *Journal du Siège,* Quicherat, IV, p. 181.
21. Much of the information about Charles's dealings with the inhabitants of Troyes comes from an early seventeenth-century account by Jean Rogier of Reims, included in Quicherat, which reproduces or summarizes fifteenth-century letters and documents which have since disappeared but were then in the archives of Reims. Quicherat, IV, p. 285.
22. *Journal du Siège,* Quicherat, IV, p. 165.
23. *Journal d'un Bourgeois de Paris,* pp. 233–237.
24. Quicherat, I, pp. 99–100.
25. Jean Rogier, Quicherat, IV, pp. 287–288.
26. Ibid., pp. 289–290.
27. Ibid., pp. 286–287, 288–290.
28. Testimony of Dunois, Quicherat, III, pp. 13–14.
29. Quicherat, I, p. 102.
30. Jean Rogier, Quicherat, IV, p. 297.
31. Quicherat, I, p. 103.
32. Jean Rogier, Quicherat, IV, p. 298.
33. Quicherat, II, p. 391.
34. Ibid., p. 423.
35. Jean Rogier, Quicherat, IV, pp. 292–294.
36. Ibid., pp. 298–299.
37. *Journal du Siège,* Quicherat, IV, p. 185; Cagny, *Chronique,* Quicherat, IV, p. 19.
38. *Journal du Siège,* Quicherat, IV, p. 185.
39. Quicherat, V, p. 266.
40. *Journal du Siège,* Quicherat, IV, pp. 185–186.
41. Ibid., p. 186. For the coronation ceremony: J. du Pange, *Le roi très chrétien,* Paris, 1949, pp. 368–377, 432–438.
42. Letter of three Angevin gentlemen to Charles VII's wife and mother-in-law, Quicherat, V, pp. 128–129.
43. Ibid., p. 129.
44. *Journal du Siège,* Quicherat, IV, p. 186.

8. THE ROAD TO PARIS

1. Quicherat, V, pp. 126–127.
2. Ibid., I, p. 233.
3. Ibid., pp. 233–234.
4. *Memoirs of a Renaissance Pope, The Commentaries of Pius II, an Abridgement,* trans. by Florence A. Gragg, New York, 1950, p. 206.
5. Joseph Stevenson (ed.), *Letters and Papers Illustrative of the Wars of the English in France,* London, 1864, Vol. II, pp. 101, 104.
6. *Journal d'un Bourgeois de Paris,* pp. 236, 242–243.
7. *Memoirs of a Renaissance Pope,* Book VI, p. 206. For the "king's touch" Marc Bloch, *Les rois thaumaturges,* Strasbourg, 1924.
8. Monstrelet, *Chronique,* p. 340, gives a figure of 4,000 men-at-arms, but Quicherat's version of Monstrelet (IV, p. 381) gives a more credible figure of 400.
9. Quicherat, V, pp. 137–138.
10. Ibid., pp. 139–140.
11. *Journal du Siège,* Quicherat, IV, pp. 187–188.
12. Testimony of Dunois, Quicherat, III, pp. 14–15.
13. Testimony of Alençon, Quicherat, III, p. 99.
14. Monstrelet, *Chronique,* pp. 340–345.
15. *Journal du Siège,* Quicherat, IV, pp. 189–190.
16. For the battle of Montépilloy: Cagny, *Chronique,* Quicherat, IV, pp. 21–24; Monstrelet, *Chronique,* pp. 345–347; Le Hérault Berri, Quicherat, IV, pp. 46–47; Le Fèvre de St.-Rémi, *Chronique,* pp. 147–149; *Journal du Siège,* Quicherat, IV, pp. 195–197; Jean Chartier, *Chronique,* Quicherat, IV, pp. 81–84.
17. *Journal du Siège,* Quicherat, IV, p. 193.
18. Monstrelet, *Chronique,* p. 347.
19. Cagny, *Chronique,* Quicherat, IV, pp. 23–24.
20. Ibid., p. 24.
21. Quicherat, I, pp. 245–246.
22. Monstrelet, *Chronique,* pp. 348–349.
23. Ibid., p. 354.
24. *Journal de Clement de Fauquembergue,* Vol. II, pp. 318–320.
25. *Journal d'un Bourgeois de Paris,* pp. 243–244.
26. Morosini, *Chronique,* Vol. IV, Annexes, "Armistice de Compiègne," pp. 340–347; G. du Fresne de Beaucourt, "Jeanne d'Arc trahie par Charles VII," in *Revue des questions historiques,* Vol. 2, 1867, pp. 286–291.
27. Cagny, *Chronique,* Quicherat, IV, pp. 25–26; *Journal du Siège,* Quicherat,

IV, p. 197; Jean Chartier, *Chronique,* Quicherat, IV, p. 85; Monstrelet, *Chronique,* p. 355.

28. Cagny, *Chronique,* Quicherat, IV, p. 26.
29. *Journal de Clement de Fauquembergue,* Vol. II, pp. 322-323.
30. *Journal d'un Bourgeois de Paris,* pp. 243-244.
31. *Journal de Clement de Fauquembergue,* Vol. II, pp. 323-324.
32. Quicherat, I, pp. 146-147.
33. *Journal d'un Bourgeois de Paris,* pp. 244-245.
34. Ibid., p. 245.
35. Cagny, *Chronique,* Quicherat, IV, pp. 26-27; *Journal du Siège,* Quicherat, IV, pp. 198-199; Monstrelet, *Chronique,* pp. 354-356.
36. *Journal d'un Bourgeois de Paris,* pp. 244, 246.
37. Monstrelet, *Chronique,* p. 356.
38. Cagny, *Chronique,* Quicherat, IV, pp. 28-29.
39. Quicherat, I, p. 179.
40. *Journal d'un Bourgeois de Paris,* pp. 246-247.
41. Cagny, *Chronique,* Quicherat, IV, p. 29.
42. Monstrelet, *Chronique,* pp. 358-359.

9. WINTER: THE LAST CAMPAIGN

1. Cagny, *Chronique,* Quicherat, IV, pp. 29-30.
2. *Mémoire sur Guillaume de Flavy,* Quicherat, V, pp. 175-176; Pierre Champion, *Guillaume de Flavy,* Paris, 1906, pp. 31-35.
3. *Journal d'un Bourgeois de Paris,* pp. 247-248.
4. Ibid., p. 248.
5. Testimony of Marguerite La Touroulde, Quicherat, III, pp. 87-88.
6. Quicherat, I, pp. 106-109.
7. Ibid., p. 108.
8. Ibid., p. 109.
9. Testimony of Jean d'Aulon, Quicherat, III, pp. 217-218.
10. Quicherat, V, pp. 147-148.
11. Ibid., p. 146.
12. Ibid. pp. 268-269.
13. Cagny, *Chronique,* Quicherat, IV, p. 31.
14. Quicherat, I, p. 109.
15. Chartier, *Chronique,* Quicherat, IV, p. 91.
16. Quicherat, V, pp. 150-153.
17. Ibid., I, pp. 118-119.
18. Ibid., V, p. 270.
19. John T. Ferguson, *English Diplomacy, 1422-1461,* Oxford, 1972, p. 13.

20. Quicherat, V, pp. 159–160.
21. Ibid., pp. 161–162.
22. Theodore de Sichel, "Lettre de Jeanne d'Arc aux Hussites," in *Bibliothèque de l'École des Chartes*, 3rd Ser., Vol. 2, p. 81; Quicherat, V, pp. 156–159.
23. *Journal d'un Bourgeois de Paris*, pp. 248, 250.
24. Ibid., p. 251.
25. Ibid., pp. 251–253.
26. Cagny, *Chronique*, Quicherat, IV, p. 32.
27. Quicherat, I, pp. 118–119.
28. Le Hérault Berri, Quicherat, IV, p. 49; Quicherat, I, p. 97.
29. Quicherat, I, p. 115.
30. Monstrelet, *Chronique*, pp. 384–385.
31. Quicherat, I, p. 158.
32. Monstrelet, *Chronique*, p. 385.
33. Quicherat, I, p. 105.
34. Le Fèvre de St.-Rémi, *Chronique*, pp. 177–178.
35. Le Hérault Berri, Quicherat, IV, pp. 49–50; Champion, *Guillaume de Flavy*, p. 168.
36. Quicherat, I, p. 111.
37. Cagny, *Chronique*, Quicherat, IV, p. 33.
38. Quicherat, I, p. 114.
39. Monstrelet, *Chronique*, pp. 386–387; Flavy, Quicherat, V, 176.
40. Monstrelet, *Chronique*, p. 386.
41. Flavy, Quicherat, V, p. 176.
42. Quicherat, I, p. 114.
43. Ibid., 115–117; Monstrelet, *Chronique*, pp. 385–388; Flavy, Quicherat, V, pp. 176–177; Le Hérault Berri, Quicherat, IV, p. 50. Joan's cloth of gold *hucque*, mentioned by Georges Chastellain (who was not present), is confirmed by the trial record, Quicherat, I, p. 224.
44. Monstrelet, *Chronique*, p. 388.
45. Chastellain, *Chronique*, Quicherat, IV, p. 447.
46. Cagny, *Chronique*, Quicherat, IV, p. 34.
47. Quicherat, I, p. 47.
48. Monstrelet, *Chronique*, p. 388.
49. Quicherat, V, pp. 166–167.

10. CAPTIVITY

1. Quicherat, I, p. 9.
2. Ibid., pp. 10–11.

3. Jean-Baptiste Ayrolles, *La Vraie Jeanne d'Arc,* 5 vols., Paris, 1890–92, Vol. I, p. 79.

4. Morosini, *Chronique,* III, pp. 336–339.

5. Quicherat, V, p. 168.

6. *Journal d'un Bourgeois de Paris,* p. 266.

7. Quicherat, V, pp. 253–254.

8. Testimony of Pierre Cusquel, Quicherat, II. pp. 305–306; on the question of the legality of Joan's being sold to the English: Pierre Tisset, "Capture et rançon de Jeanne d'Arc," in *Revue historique de droit français et étranger,* 1968, pp. 63–69.

9. Testimony of Thomas Marie, Quicherat, II, p. 370.

10. For the role of the University of Paris in politics: Hastings Rashdall, *The Universities of Europe in the Middle Ages,* Oxford, 1936, Vol. I, pp. 540–584; Jacques Verger, "The University of Paris at the End of the Hundred Years War," in *Universities in Politics,* ed. by John W. Baldwin and Richard A. Goldthwaite.

11. Verger, "University of Paris," pp. 64–69.

12. Albert Sarrazin, *Pierre Cauchon, juge de Jeanne d'Arc,* Paris, 1901.

13. Shaw, *Saint Joan,* 1, lxiii.

14. Quicherat, I, pp. 8–10.

15. Cagny, *Chronique,* Quicherat, IV, pp. 34–35.

16. Quicherat, I, p. 163.

17. Ibid., pp. 109–110.

18. Henri Debout, *Jeanne d'Arc, prisonnière à Arras,* Arras, 1894, pp. 14–18.

19. Charles Gomart, "Jeanne d'Arc au château de Beaurevoir," in *Mémoires de la Société d'émulation de Cambrai,* Vol. 28, part 2, 1865, pp. 305–331.

20. Quicherat, I, p. 231.

21. Ibid., pp. 95–96.

22. Testimony of Haimond de Macy, Quicherat, III, p. 121.

23. Eugene Lomier, *Les prisons de Jeanne d'Arc,* Paris, 1938, p. 61.

24. Quicherat, I, pp. 109–111.

25. *Journal d'un Bourgeois de Paris,* pp. 259–260.

26. Quicherat, I, p. 326.

27. Ibid., V, pp. 194–195.

28. Ibid., pp. 178–190.

29. Ibid., I, pp. 17–18.

30. Ibid., pp. 15–16.

11. THE TRIAL: PRELIMINARIES, PREPARATORY INTERROGATION

1. Testimony of Pierre Cusquel, Quicherat, III, p. 345; Nicolas Taquel, Quicherat, II, p. 317.
2. Testimony of Jean Massieu, Quicherat, III, p. 154; Isambart de la Pierre, II, 302.
3. Elizabeth Chirol, *Joan of Arc and the Keep of Rouen Castle,* trans. by Anne Curry, Rouen, 1964.
4. Testimony of Pierre Bouchier, Quicherat, II, pp. 322–323.
5. Testimony of Jean Massieu, Quicherat, III, p. 154; Pierre Daron, Quicherat, III, p. 200.
6. Testimony of Jean Massieu, Quicherat, III, pp. 154–155.
7. Testimony of Pierre Cusquel, Quicherat, II, pp. 306, 345; III, p. 180.
8. Testimony of Jean Massieu, Quicherat, III, p. 154.
9. Testimony of Nicolas Taquel, Quicherat, II, p. 318.
10. Testimony of Guillaume Manchon, Quicherat, II, pp. 148–149.
11. Testimony of Jean Massieu, Quicherat, III, p. 155.
12. Testimony of Jean Lefèvre, Quicherat, III, p. 175.
13. Testimony of Boisguillaume, Quicherat, III, p. 163.
14. Testimony of Jean Monnet, Quicherat, III, p. 63.
15. Testimony of Jean Massieu, Quicherat, III, p. 155.
16. Testimony of Guillaume Manchon, Quicherat, III, pp. 147–148.
17. Testimony of Jean Marcel, Quicherat, III, p. 89.
18. Quicherat, I, pp. 20–23, pp. 18–19.
19. On the Inquisition: a recent book by a Catholic scholar, John O'Brien, *The Inquisition,* New York, 1973, presents a less prejudiced view than the old Protestant classic by Henry Charles Lea, *The Inquisition of the Middle Ages,* London, 1887 (paperback edition, New York, 1963); also Fernand Hayward, *The Inquisition* (trans. of *Que faut-il penser de l'Inquisition?*), New York, 1966 (published by the Pauline Fathers); Pierre Dominique, *L'Inquisition,* Paris, 1969; Franciscus Willett, *Understanding the Inquisition,* North Easton, Mass., 1968 (Holy Cross Press).
20. Quicherat, I, pp. 33–35.
21. Ibid., pp. 35–37.
22. Testimony of Jean Massieu, Quicherat, III, p. 153.
23. Testimony of Nicolas de Houppeville, Quicherat, II, pp. 325–326, II, pp. 171–172.
24. Testimony of Jean Lefèvre, Quicherat, III, p. 175.
25. Testimony of Thomas de Courcelles, Quicherat, III, p. 59.
26. Testimony of Guillaume Manchon, Quicherat, III, p. 137.
27. Testimony of Dominique Jacob, Quicherat, II, p. 394.

28. Testimony of Nicolas Bailly, Quicherat, II, pp. 451–453.
29. Testimony of Jean Moreau, Quicherat, III, pp. 192–193.
30. Quicherat, I, pp. 27–29.
31. On witches and witchcraft trials: Richard Kieckhefer, *European Witch Trials, Their Foundations in Popular and Learned Culture, 1300–1500,* Berkeley, 1976; Jeffrey Burton Russell, *Witchcraft in the Middle Ages,* Ithaca, N.Y., 1972; Keith Thomas, *Religion and the Decline of Magic,* London, 1971; Hugh Trevor-Roper, *The European Witch Craze of the Sixteenth and Seventeenth Centuries,* New York, 1969; E. William Munter, *Witchcraft in France and Switzerland,* Ithaca, N.Y., 1976; Mary Douglas (ed.), *Witchcraft Confessions and Accusations,* London, 1970.
32. Testimony of Boisguillaume, Quicherat, III, p. 162.
33. Testimony of Guillaume Manchon, Quicherat, III, p. 141.
34. Ibid., pp. 161–162; Pierre Miget, Quicherat, III, p. 133.
35. Testimony of Guillaume Manchon, Quicherat, II, pp. 10–11; III, p. 141.
36. Testimony of Jean Lefèvre, Quicherat, II, p. 368.
37. Testimony of Richard Grouchet, Quicherat, II, p. 358.
38. Testimony of Jean Tiphaine, Quicherat, III, p. 48.
39. Testimony of Jean Marcel, Quicherat, III, p. 89.
40. Testimony of Guillaume Manchon, Quicherat, III, pp. 141–142; Pierre Daron, Quicherat, III, p. 201.
41. Testimony of Pierre Daron, Quicherat, III, p. 201.
42. Testimony of Nicolas Taquel, Quicherat, II, p. 318.
43. Testimony of Richard Grouchet, Quicherat, II, p. 358.
44. Testimony of Jean Beaupère, Quicherat, II, p. 21.
45. Testimony of Guillaume Manchon, Quicherat, III, p. 135.
46. Ibid., Quicherat, II, pp. 340–341; III, p. 135.
47. Ibid., Quicherat, II, p. 12.
48. Ibid., Quicherat, III, pp. 135–136.
49. Testimony of Jean Monnet, Quicherat, III, pp. 62–63.
50. Testimony of Guillaume Manchon, Quicherat, III, p. 146.
51. Ibid., Quicherat, II, pp. 340–341; III, pp. 145–146; Pierre Miget, Quicherat, III, p. 132.
52. Quicherat, I, pp. 44–45.
53. Ibid., pp. 45–46; Doncoeur, *La minute française,* p. 60.
54. Jacques Charpentier, "À propos du procès de Jeanne d'Arc," in *Revue de Paris,* Nov. 1963, pp. 48–52.
55. Lang, *Maid of France,* p. 100.
56. Quicherat, I, pp. 46–47.
57. Testimony of Jean Massieu, Quicherat, II, p. 332; III, p. 155; Guillaume Manchon, Quicherat, III, p. 135.
58. Quicherat, I, pp. 47–48.

59. Testimony of Jean Massieu, Quicherat, II, p. 16.
60. Quicherat, I, pp. 49–50.
61. Ibid., pp. 50–51.
62. Ibid., pp. 51–57.
63. Ibid., pp. 60–61.
64. Ibid., pp. 61–62.
65. Ibid., pp. 63–64.
66. Ibid., pp. 64–65.
67. Ibid., p. 65.
68. Louis Carolus-Barbé, "Jeanne, êtes-vous en état de grace?" in *Bulletin de la société des antiquaires de France,* 1958, pp. 204–208; Quicherat, III, p. 163.
69. Quicherat, I, pp. 65–66.
70. Ibid., pp. 66–68.
71. Ibid., p. 68.
72. Ibid., pp. 70–74.
73. Ibid., p. 74.
74. Ibid., p. 75.
75. Ibid., pp. 75–76.
76. Ibid., p. 78; for Brother Richard's unorthodoxy: J. de la Martinière, "Frère Richard et Jeanne d'Arc à Orléans, Mars–juillet 1430," in *Moyen Age,* XLIV (1934), pp. 189–198.
77. Quicherat, I, pp. 79–80.
78. Ibid., II, p. 48.
79. Ibid., I, pp. 81–82.
80. Ibid., pp. 82–83.
81. Ibid., pp. 83–84.
82. Ibid., pp. 84–85.
83. Ibid., pp. 85–86.
84. Ibid., pp. 85–86.
85. Ibid., pp. 86–88.
86. Ibid., p. 88.
87. Ibid., pp. 88–90.
88. Ibid., pp. 90–91.
89. Ibid., p. 93.
90. Ibid., p. 94.
91. Ibid., pp. 94–95.
92. Ibid., pp. 96–98.
93. Ibid., pp. 99–102.
94. Ibid., pp. 102–104.
95. Ibid., pp. 104–105.

96. Ibid., p. 105.
97. Ibid., pp. 106–107.
98. Ibid., p. 109.
99. Ibid., pp. 1⁰⁰–111.
100. Ibid., pp 11–113.
101. Testimony of Guillaume Manchon, Quicherat, II, pp. 11–12; III, p. 138; Thomas de Courcelles, Quicherat, III, p. 58.
102. Quicherat, I, pp. 114–117.
103. Ibid., pp. 117–118.
104. Ibid., pp. 118–122.
105. Ibid., pp. 126–127.
106. Ibid., p. 127.
107. Ibid., pp. 127–128.
108. Ibid., pp. 128–129.
109. Ibid., p. 130.
110. Ibid., pp. 130–131.
111. Ibid., pp. 131–132.
112. Ibid., pp. 132–133.
113. Ibid., p. 133.
114. Ibid., pp. 134–138.
115. Ibid., pp. 139–146.
116. Ibid., pp. 146–148.
117. Ibid., pp. 150–153.
118. Ibid., pp. 153–154.
119. Ibid., pp. 154–156.
120. Ibid., p. 156.
121. Ibid., p. 156.
122. Ibid., pp. 158–159.
123. Ibid., pp. 159–161.
124. Ibid., pp. 162–163.
125. Ibid., pp. 163–164.
126. Ibid., pp. 164–166.
127. Ibid., p. 166.
128. Ibid., pp. 166–172.
129. Ibid., pp. 173–174.
130. Ibid., pp. 174–176.
131. Ibid., pp. 176–177.
132. Ibid., p. 178.
133. Ibid., pp. 179–180.
134. Ibid., pp. 182–183.
135. Ibid., p. 183.

136. Ibid., p. 183.
137. Ibid., pp. 183–184.
138. Ibid., pp. 184–185.
139. Ibid., pp. 185–187.
140. Ibid., p. 187.

12. THE TRIAL: CHARGES AND JUDGMENT

1. Quicherat, I, pp. 188–190.
2. Ibid., pp. 190–193.
3. Ibid., pp. 194–195.
4. Ibid., pp. 200–201.
5. Testimony of Guillaume Duval, Quicherat, II, p. 9.
6. Quicherat, I, pp. 205–213.
7. Ibid., pp. 214–216.
8. Ibid., pp. 200–229.
9. Ibid., pp. 231–233.
10. Ibid., pp. 233–234.
11. Ibid., pp. 234–243.
12. Ibid., pp. 243–247.
13. Testimony of Guillaume Duval, Quicherat, II, pp. 9–10.
14. Quicherat, I, pp. 247–248.
15. Ibid., pp. 249–250.
16. Ibid., pp. 255–257.
17. Ibid, pp. 259–261.
18. Ibid., pp. 261–271.
19. Ibid., pp. 271–276.
20. Ibid., pp. 276–282.
21. Ibid., pp. 282–294.
22. Ibid., pp. 294–295.
23. Ibid., pp. 295–298.
24. Ibid., pp. 298–299.
25. Ibid., pp. 304–305.
26. Ibid., pp. 305–313.
27. Ibid., pp. 313–317.
28. Ibid., pp. 317–320.
29. Ibid., pp. 320–321.
30. Ibid., pp. 321–323.
31. Ibid., pp. 323–326.
32. Ibid., pp. 326–328; Testimony of Jean Monnet, Quicherat, III, p. 64; Guil-

laume Manchon, Quicherat, III, pp. 142–145; Thomas de Courcelles, Quicherat, III, p. 60.
33. Quicherat, I, pp. 328–337.
34. Ibid., pp. 337–374.
35. Ibid., pp. 369–370.
36. Ibid., II, p. 359.
37. Ibid., p. 325.
38. Ibid., I, pp. 367–369.
39. Ibid., pp. 370–374.
40. Ibid., II, pp. 5–6.
41. Testimony of Jean Tiphaine, Guillaume de Chambre, Quicherat, III, pp. 48–49, 50–52.
42. Quicherat, I, pp. 374–381.
43. Testimony of Guillaume Manchon, Quicherat, II, pp. 13–14.
44. Quicherat, I, pp. 381–394.
45. Ibid., II, pp. 4–5, 304, 349–350.
46. Ibid., I, pp. 394–399.
47. Ibid., pp. 399–401.
48. Testimony of Maugier le Parmentier, Quicherat, III, p. 185.
49. Quicherat, I, pp. 401–402.
50. Ibid., III, p. 58.
51. Ibid., I, pp. 402–404.
52. Régine Pernoud, "Un document nouveau sur Jeanne d'Arc," in *Revue de Paris,* June 1960, pp. 101–106; also in her *Jeanne devant les Cauchons,* Paris, 1970, pp. 82–83.
53. Testimony of Haimond de Macy, Quicherat, III, pp. 121–122.
54. Quicherat, I, pp. 414–419.
55. Ibid., pp. 422–429.
56. Ibid., pp. 437–441.
57. Ibid., p. 441.
58. Ibid., pp. 441–442.

13. ABJURATION, RELAPSE, DEATH

1. Testimony of Jean Beaupère, Quicherat, II, pp. 20–21.
2. Testimony of Guillaume Manchon, Quicherat, III, p. 146.
3. Quicherat, I, pp. 443–444; Testimony of Jean de Mailly, Quicherat, III, p. 54.
4. Testimony of Jean de Lenozolles, Quicherat, III, p. 113.
5. Quicherat, I, p. 444.
6. Testimony of Guillaume Manchon, Quicherat, II, pp. 15, 344–345; Isam-

bart de la Pierre, Quicherat, II, p. 303; Jean Massieu, Quicherat, II, p. 335; Jean Riquier, Quicherat, III, p. 190.

7. Quicherat, I, pp. 444–446.
8. Testimony of Jean de Mailly, Quicherat, III, pp. 54–55.
9. Testimony of Pierre Bouchier, Quicherat, II, p. 322; Jean de Mailly, Quicherat, III, p. 55.
10. Testimony of Guillaume Manchon, Quicherat, III, pp. 146–147; Jean Massieu, Quicherat, III, pp. 156–157.
11. Testimony of Jean Massieu, Quicherat, III, p. 157.
12. Testimony of Haimond de Macy, Quicherat, III, p. 123.
13. Testimony of Jean Massieu, Quicherat, III, p. 157.
14. Testimony of Pierre Bouchier, Quicherat, II, p. 323.
15. Testimony of Thomas de Courcelles, Quicherat, III, p. 61.
16. Testimony of Haimond de Macy, Quicherat, III, p. 123; Jean Massieu, Quicherat, II, p. 17.
17. Testimony of Thomas de Courcelles, Quicherat, III, p. 65; Guillaume de Chambre, Quicherat, II, p. 52.
18. Testimony of Jean Massieu, Quicherat, III, p. 156.
19. Scott, *The Trial of Joan of Arc,* p. 164.
20. Quicherat, I, pp. 447–450.
21. Testimony of Jean de Mailly, Quicherat, III, p. 55.
22. Testimony of Jean Massieu, Quicherat, III, p. 157; Guillaume Manchon, Quicherat, III, p. 174; Jean Moreau, Quicherat, III, p. 194.
23. Quicherat, III, p. 123.
24. Testimony of Guillaume Manchon, Quicherat, III, p. 147; Guillaume du Desert, Quicherat, II, p. 338.
25. Testimony of Haimond de Macy, Quicherat, III, p. 123; Jean Massieu, Quicherat, II, p. 17; Comte C. de Maleissye, *Les Lettres de Jeanne d'Arc et la prétendue abjuration de Saint Ouen,* Paris, 1908.
26. Testimony of Pierre Miget, Quicherat, II, p. 361; Jean de Mailly, Quicherat, III, p. 55; Jean Marcel, Quicherat, III, p. 90; André Marguerie, Quicherat, III, p. 184.
27. Testimony of Jean Massieu, Quicherat, III, p. 157; Nicolas Taquel, Quicherat, III, p. 197.
28. Quicherat, I, pp. 450–452.
29. Testimony of Guillaume Manchon, Quicherat, II, p. 14.
30. Testimony of Jean Massieu, Quicherat, II, pp. 17–18, III, p. 157.
31. Testimony of Jean Fave, Quicherat, II, p. 376.
32. Quicherat, I, p. 453.
33. Testimony of Jean Beaupère, Quicherat, II, p. 21.
34. Quicherat, II, pp. 18, 333–334; III, pp. 157–158.

35. Ibid., pp. 8, 365; III, p. 168.
36. Ibid., III, p. 55.
37. Ibid., II, p. 300.
38. Ibid., p. 5.
39. Testimony of Guillaume Manchon, Quicherat, II, p. 14; III, p. 148.
40. Testimony of André Marguerie, Quicherat, III, p. 184.
41. Quicherat, I, pp. 454–456.
42. Ibid., pp. 456–459.
43. Testimony of Martin Ladvenu, Quicherat, II, p. 8; Isambart de la Pierre, Quicherat, II, p. 5.
44. Testimony of Boisguillaume, Quicherat, II, p. 164.
45. Quicherat, I, pp. 459–476.
46. Ibid., II, pp. 3–4.
47. Ibid., III, p. 168.
48. Ibid., p. 149.
49. Testimony of Jean Massieu, Quicherat, II, pp. 19, 334, III, pp. 158–159.
50. Testimony of Jean Toutmouillé, Quicherat, II, p. 4; Martin Ladvenu, Quicherat, II, p. 8; III, p. 169.
51. Quicherat, I, pp. 477–485.
52. Testimony of Jean Riquier, Quicherat, III, p. 191.
53. Quicherat, III, p. 170.
54. Testimony of Jean Massieu, Quicherat, III, p. 159.
55. Testimony of Nicolas Taquel, Quicherat, II, pp. 320–321.
56. Testimony of Jean de Mailly, Quicherat, III, p. 55.
57. *Journal de Clement de Fauquembergue,* Vol. III, pp. 13–14.
58. Testimony of Jean de Lenozolles, Quicherat, III, p. 114; Quicherat, I, p. 470.
59. Quicherat, I, pp. 470–475.
60. Testimony of Jean Massieu, Quicherat, III, p. 159.
61. Ibid., Quicherat, II, p. 19; III, p. 159; Guillaume Manchon, Quicherat, III, p. 159.
62. Testimony of Jean Massieu, Quicherat, II, pp. 19–20; Jean Lefèvre, Quicherat, III, p. 177; Isambart de la Pierre, Quicherat, II, p. 352; Guillaume de Chambre, Quicherat, III, p. 53.
63. Testimony of Martin Ladvenu, Quicherat, II, pp. 8–9; III, p. 169; Laurent Guesdon, Quicherat, III, p. 188.
64. Testimony of Guillaume Manchon, Quicherat, II, p. 344; III, p. 150; Isambart de la Pierre, Quicherat, II, p. 6.
65. Testimony of Jean Massieu, Quicherat, II, p. 20; III, p. 159.
66. Ibid., Quicherat, II, p. 20; Isambart de la Pierre, Quicherat, II, p. 6.
67. Testimony of Jean Massieu, Quicherat, II, p. 20.

68. Testimony of Isambart de la Pierre, Quicherat, II, p. 6.
69. Testimony of Pierre Daron, Quicherat, III, p. 202; André Marguerie, Quicherat, II, p. 355; III, p. 184; Guillaume de Chambre, Quicherat, III, p. 53.
70. Quicherat, II, p. 9.
71. Testimony of Maugier le Parmentier, Quicherat, III, p. 186; Jean Riquier, Quicherat, III, p. 191.
72. Testimony of Jean Riquier, Quicherat, III, p. 191; Pierre Daron, Quicherat, III, p. 202.
73. Testimony of André Marguerie, Quicherat, III, p. 185; Laurent Guesdon, Quicherat, III, p. 188; Pierre Daron, Quicherat, III, p. 202.

14. AFTERWARD

1. Quicherat, II, p. 7; also repeated by Jean Massieu, Quicherat, III, pp. 159–160.
2. Quicherat, II, p. 352.
3. Ibid., pp. 306, 347; III, p. 182; also told by Isambart de la Pierre, Quicherat, II, p. 352.
4. Quicherat, II, p. 375; III, p. 191.
5. Ibid., p. 15; III, p. 150.
6. Testimony of Jean de Mailly, Quicherat, III, p. 56.
7. Monstrelet, *Chronique,* Vol. IV. p. 442.
8. *Journal d'un Bourgeois de Paris,* pp. 275–276.
9. Ibid., pp. 274–278, 279.
10. Ferguson, *English Diplomacy,* p. 18.
11. *Journal d'un Bourgeois de Paris,* pp. 281–282.
12. Perroy, *The Hundred Years War,* p. 294.
13. Ibid., pp. 294–295.
14. Ferguson, *English Diplomacy,* p. 21.
15. *Journal d'un Bourgeois de Paris,* pp. 317–318.
16. "Documents sur la fausse Jeanne d'Arc," Quicherat, V, pp. 321–335.
17. A. Lecoy de la Marche, "Une fausse Jeanne d'Arc," in *Revue des questions historiques,"* October 1871, pp. 576–579.
18. Perroy, *The Hundred Years War,* pp. 297–304.
19. Perroy, *The Hundred Years War,* pp. 309–322.
20. For an account of the Rehabilitation process: Pernoud, *The Retrial of Joan of Arc;* the introductions to the three volumes of the Rehabilitation record edited by Doncoeur and Lanhers (see notes to Chapter 1); also Vale, *Charles VII,* pp. 59–69.
21. Morosini, *Chronique,* III, p. 352–355.
22. *Memoirs of a Renaissance Pope,* Book VI, p. 209.

23. Quicherat, IV, p. 281.
24. *L'Enquête ordonnée par Charles VII*, p. 7.
25. Quicherat, II, pp. 1–2.
26. Ibid., pp. 3–20.
27. Ibid., pp. 20–21.
28. Ibid., III, pp. 322–326.
29. Ibid., II, pp. 293–295.
30. Ibid., pp. 311–316.
31. Ibid., pp. 83–85.
32. Ibid., pp. 385–386.
33. Ibid., p. 361.
34. François Villon, *Oeuvres,* Paris, 1918, p. 37.
35. Jean Leclercq, François Vandenbroucke, and Louis Bouyer, *The Spirituality of the Middle Ages,* London, 1961, p. 505.

15. FIVE AND A HALF CENTURIES OF JOAN OF ARC

1. Christine de Pisan, in Quicherat, V, pp. 4–21.
2. Monstrelet, *Chronique,* Vol. IV, p. 442.
3. Le Fèvre de St.-Rémi, *Chronique,* II, pp. 143–144.
4. *Journal d'un Bourgeois de Paris,* pp. 266–272.
5. Thomas Rymer (ed.), *Foedera, conventiones, literae et cujuscunque generis acta publica,* Vol. X, London, 1816, p. 459.
6. Ibid., pp. 408–409.
7. *Chronicles of London,* ed. by Charles L. Kingsford, London, 1977, pp. 98, 133: N. H. Nicholas and E. Tyrrell (eds.), *Chronicle of London*, London, 1827. On the subject of Joan in English fifteenth-century chronicles, see Charles L. Kingsford, *English Historical Literature in the Fifteenth Century,* New York, 1962; also W. T. Waugh, "Joan of Arc in English Sources of the Fifteenth Century," in *Historical Essays in Honor of James Tait,* Manchester, 1933.
8. *The Brut or the Chronicles of England,* ed. by Friedrich W. D. Brie, New York, 1971 (reprint of 1908 edition), Part II, pp. 500–501.
9. *Hall's Chronicle,* New York, 1965 (reprint of 1809 edition), pp. 148–159.
10. *Shakespeare's Holinshed,* ed. by Richard Hosley, New York, 1968, pp. 154–158.
11. *The First Part of King Henry VI,* ed. by John Dover Wilson, Cambridge (England), 1968, pp. xxxii–xli; *The First Part of King Henry the Sixth,* ed. by Tucker Brooke (the Yale Shakespeare), New Haven, 1949, pp. 128–132; Kenneth Muir, *The Sources of Shakespeare's Plays,* New Haven, 1978, pp.

24–31; Geoffrey Bullough, *Narrative and Dramatic Sources of Shakespeare,* 8 vols., Vol. III, London and New York, 1960.

12. *Memoirs of a Renaissance Pope,* trans. by Florence A. Gragg, pp. 201–209.
13. Du Haillan, *De l'Estat de France,* pp. 137–139.
14. On the subject of Joan in seventeenth-century literature: Nathan Edelman, *Attitudes of Seventeenth-Century France toward the Middle Ages,* New York, 1946, pp. 245–276.
15. Dorothy McDougall, *Madeleine de Scudéry,* London, 1938, pp. 61–63.
16. Jean Chapelain, *Les Douze dernier chants du poème de la Pucelle,* ed. by René Kerviler, Orleans, 1882.
17. On the subject of eighteenth-century attitudes toward the Middle Ages: Lionel Gossman, *Medievalism and the Ideologies of the Enlightenment, the World and Work of La Curne de Sainte-Palaye,* Baltimore, 1968.
18. Voltaire, *Essai sur les moeurs,* Ch. 94, in *Oeuvres complètes,* Vol. XXVIII, Paris, 1785.
19. Charles Louis Secondat, baron de Montesquieu, *Mes Pensées,* in *Oeuvres complètes,* Paris, 1827, p. 1022.
20. Voltaire, *Essai sur les moeurs,* Ch. 80, in *Oeuvres complètes,* pp. 252–263.
21. *La Pucelle d'Orléans,* in *The Complete Works of Voltaire,* ed. by Theodore Besterman, Vol. VII, Geneva, 1970.
22. *La Petite République Française,* May 30, 1878.
23. Robert Southey, *Poetical Works in Ten Volumes,* Vol. I, Boston, 1860.
24. Friedrich Schiller, *Die Jungfrau von Orleans,* Berlin, 1801.
25. Jules Michelet, *Joan of Arc,* trans. by Albert Guerard, Ann Arbor, 1974.
26. Alexandre Dumas père, *Jehanne la Pucelle,* Paris, 1842.
27. Henri-Alexandre Wallon, *Jeanne d'Arc,* Paris, 1867, 2 vols.
28. Marius Sepet, *Jeanne d'Arc,* Tours, 1885.
29. A. Vallet de Viriville, *Histoire de Charles VII,* Paris, 1862–1865, 3 vols.
30. Charles Péguy, *Oeuvres poétiques complètes,* Vol. I, Paris, 1957.
31. Dixon Wecter, *Sam Clemens of Hannibal,* Boston, 1952, pp. 211–212.
32. *Susy and Mark Twain: Family Dialogues,* arranged and edited by Edith Colgate Salisbury, New York, 1965, p. 318.
33. George Bernard Shaw, *Saint Joan,* New York, 1933, p. xl.
34. Francis Cabot Lowell, *Joan of Arc,* Boston, 1896.
35. Anatole France, *Vie de Jeanne d'Arc,* in *Oeuvres complètes d'Anatole France,* Vol. XV and XVI, Paris, 1929.
36. Andrew Lang, *Maid of France,* London, 1909.
37. Margaret Murray, *The Witch Cult in Western Europe,* Oxford, 1921, pp. 238–239, 270–276.
38. Some of the books espousing the "bastardy theory" in addition to David-Darnac's: Jean Grimod, *Jeanne d'Arc a-t-elle été brulée?,* Paris, 1952;

Eugene Schneider, *Jeanne d'Arc et ses lys, la légende et l'histoire,* Paris, 1952; André Guérin and Jack Palmer White, *Operation Shepherdess,* London, 1961; G. Pesme, *Jeanne d'Arc n'a pas été brulée,* Paris, 1960; Pierre de Sermoise, *Missions secrètes de Jehanne la Pucelle,* Paris, 1970; Jean Bancal, *Jeanne d'Arc, princesse royale,* Paris, 1971; Étienne Weill-Reynal, *Le Double secrète de Jeanne la Pucelle,* Paris, 1972; Jacques Guerillon, *Mais qui es-tu, Jeanne d'Arc?,* Paris, 1972; Jean-François Xerri, *Jeanne d'Arc n'a pas existé,* Paris, 1973. On the subject of the theory: Charles Samaran, "Pour la défense de Jeanne d'Arc," in *Annuaire-Bulletin de la Société de l'histoire de France,* 1952–1953, pp. 50–63.

39. John Holland Smith, *Joan of Arc,* London, 1973, p. 39.

40. An article in the *British Journal of Medical Psychology,* Vol. 13, 1933, by Roger Money-Kyrle, "A Psychoanalytic Study of the Voices of Joan of Arc," was used extensively by Edward Lucie-Smith in his *Joan of Arc,* London, 1976.

41. Among Régine Pernoud's books: *Vie et Mort de Jeanne d'Arc,* Paris, 1953 (trans. by J. M. Cohen as *The Retrial of Joan of Arc*); *Jeanne d'Arc par elle-même et par ses témoins,* Paris, 1962 (trans. by Edward Hymans as *Joan of Arc, by Herself and Her Witnesses,* New York, 1966). Quotation is from *Retrial,* pp. 4–5.

42. Comte de Puymaigre, "La Chronique espagnole de la Pucelle d'Orléans," in *Revue des questions historiques,* Vol. 29, 1881, pp. 553–566.

43. Louis Aragon, "Richard II Quarante," in *Le Crève-coeur,* New York, n.d.

44. Jawaharlal Nehru, *Glimpses of World History,* New York, 1942, p. 235.

Bibliography

All significant sources are included in the notes. The following is a list of selected books on Joan of Arc, and a bibliography on related subjects not cited in the notes. The important categories of sources found in the notes are as follows:

Original sources: Chapter 1, notes 1–18
On fifteenth-century agricultural economy: Chapter 2, note 2
On the Hundred Years War: Chapter 2, note 9
On the dukes of Burgundy: Chapter 2, note 11
On destruction in the war: Chapter 2, note 15
On woman mystics: Chapter 3, notes 12–16
On the role of artillery in the war: Chapter 5, note 37, and Chapter 6, note 8
On the University of Paris: Chapter 10, note 12
On witchcraft trials: Chapter 11, note 31

BOOKS ABOUT JOAN OF ARC

Ayroles, Jean-Baptiste. *La Vraie Jeanne d'Arc,* 5 vols. Paris, 1890–1902.
Bossuat, André. *Jeanne d'Arc.* Paris, 1968.
Buchan, Alice. *Joan of Arc and the Recovery of France.* London, 1948.
Calmette, Joseph. *Jeanne d'Arc.* Paris, 1953.
Champion, Pierre. *Jeanne d'Arc.* Paris, 1933.
Duby, Georges, and Duby, Andrée. *Les Procès de Jeanne d'Arc.* Paris, 1973.
Fabre, Joseph. *Jeanne, libératrice de la France.* Paris, 1883.
France, Anatole. *Vie de Jeanne d'Arc,* in *Oeuvres complètes.* Paris, 1929, Vols. XV and XVI.
Guillemin, Henri. *Joan, Maid of Orleans.* Translated by Harold J. Salemson. New York, 1970.
Guitton, Jean. *Problème et mystère de Jeanne d'Arc.* Paris, 1961.
Holland Smith, John. *Joan of Arc.* London, 1973.
Jewkes, Wilfred T., and Landfield, Jerome B. *Joan of Arc: Fact, Legend, and Literature.* New York, 1964.
Lang, Andrew. *The Maid of France.* London, 1909.
Lightbody, Charles Wayland. *The Judgements of Joan: A Study in Cultural History.* London, 1961.
Lowell, Francis C. *Joan of Arc.* Boston, 1896.
Lucie-Smith, Edward A. *Joan of Arc.* New York, 1976.
Michelet, Jules. *Joan of Arc.* Translated by Albert Guerard. Ann Arbor, 1974.
Pernoud, Régine. *Joan of Arc, by Herself and Her Witnesses.* Translated by Edward Hyams. New York, 1966.
———. *The Retrial of Joan of Arc.* Translated by J. M. Cohen. New York, 1955.
Richer, Edmond. *Histoire de la Pucelle d'Orléans.* 2 vols. Edited by R. H. Dunand. Paris, 1912.
Sackville-West, Vita. *Saint Joan of Arc.* London, 1936.
Scott, Walter Sidney. *Jeanne d'Arc.* London, 1974.
Sepet, Marius. *Jeanne d'Arc.* Tours, 1869.
Shaw, George Bernard. *Saint Joan.* London, 1920.
Thomas, Édith. *Jeanne d'Arc.* Paris, 1947.
Twain, Mark. *Personal Recollections of Joan of Arc,* 2 vols. New York, 1896.
Wallon, Henri. *Jeanne d'Arc,* 2 vols. Paris, 1876.

BOOKS ON RELATED SUBJECTS

Bataille, Michel. *Gilles de Rais.* Paris, 1967.
———. *Le Procès de Gilles de Rais.* Paris, 1965.
Billard, André. *Jeanne d'Arc et ses juges.* Paris, 1933.
Bossuat, André. *Perrinet Gressart et François de Surienne.* Paris, 1936.

Boucher de Molandon. *La Famille de Jeanne d'Arc.* Orleans, 1878.
———.*La Première expedition de Jeanne d'Arc.* Orléans, 1874.
Brousillon, Bertrand de. *La Maison de Laval.* Paris, 1900.
Champion, Pierre. *Guillaume de Flavy.* Paris, 1906.
Chapoy, Henri. *Les Compagnons de la pucelle.* Paris, 1898.
Contamine, Philippe. *La Vie quotidienne pendant la guerre de cent ans, France et Angleterre.* Paris, 1976.
Favier, Jean. *Paris au XV siècle.* Paris, 1974.
Hale, J. R.; Highfield, R. L. L.; and Smalley, B. (eds.). *Europe in the Late Middle Ages.* New York, 1965.
Jacob, E. F. *The Fifteenth Century.* London, 1961.
Lanery d'Arc, Pierre. *Le Culte de Jeanne d'Arc au XVᵉ siècle.* Orléans, 1887.
LeCacheux, Paul. *Rouen au temps de Jeanne d'Arc.* Rouen/Paris, 1931.
Lewis, P. S. *Later Mediaeval France: The Polity.* New York, 1968.
Lognon, Auguste. *Paris pendant le domination anglaise.* Paris, 1878.
Orliac, Jehanne d'. *Yolande d'Aragon.* Paris, 1933.
Pernoud, Régine. *La Libération d'Orléans.* Paris, 1969.
Rolland, Monique. *Dunois, compagnon de Jeanne d'Arc.* Châteaudun, 1968.
Rousseau, François. *La Hire de Gascogne.* Paris, 1969.
Samaran, Charles. *La Maison d'Armagnac au XVᵉ siècle.* Paris, 1907.
Villaret, A. de. *Louis de Coutes, Page de Jeanne d'Arc.* Orleans, 1890.

Index

Italic numbers refer to captions of illustrations and maps.

ABOUT THE AUTHOR

Frances Carney Gies is the co-author (with Joseph Gies) of a number of books on medieval history. Research for *Women in the Middle Ages* (Thomas Y. Crowell, 1978; Barnes & Noble, 1980) revived a lifelong interest in Joan of Arc. An alumna (B.A., M.A.) of the University of Michigan, Mrs. Gies has three grown children and lives in a Virginia suburb of Washington, D.C.